Best Hikes Near
Sacramento

TRACY SALCEDO-CHOURRÉ

FALCONGUIDES

GUILFORD, CONNECTICUT
HELENA, MONTANA

AN IMPRINT OF GLOBE PEQUOT PRESS

For Karen, Kelly, Sara, Kerin, and Julie

To buy books in quantity for corporate use
or incentives, call **(800) 962-0973**
or e-mail **premiums@GlobePequot.com**.

FALCONGUIDES®

Copyright © 2012 Morris Book Publishing, LLC

FalconGuides is an imprint of Globe Pequot Press.
Falcon, FalconGuides, and Outfit Your Mind are registered trademarks of Morris Book Publishing, LLC.

Interior photos by Tracy Salcedo-Chourré
Compass on p. i licensed by Shutterstock.com
Maps by Trailhead Graphics, Inc. © Morris Book Publishing, LLC.

Text design: Sheryl P. Kober
Project editor: Julie Marsh
Layout: Maggie Peterson

Library of Congress Cataloging-in-Publication Data

Salcedo-Chourré, Tracy.
  Best hikes near Sacramento / Tracy Salcedo-Chourre.
    p. cm.
  Summary: "Featuring 41 of the best hikes in the greater Sacramento area, this exciting new guide-book points locals and visitors alike to trailheads within an hour's drive of the city" — Provided by publisher.
  ISBN 978-0-7627-8090-7 (pbk.)
  1. Hiking—California—Sacramento Region—Guidebooks. 2. Sacramento Region (Calif.)—Guide-books. I. Title.
  GV199.42.C22S237 2012
  917.94'54—dc23
                                                                                            2012017911

Printed in the United States of America

10 9 8 7 6 5 4 3 2 1

Contents

Overview

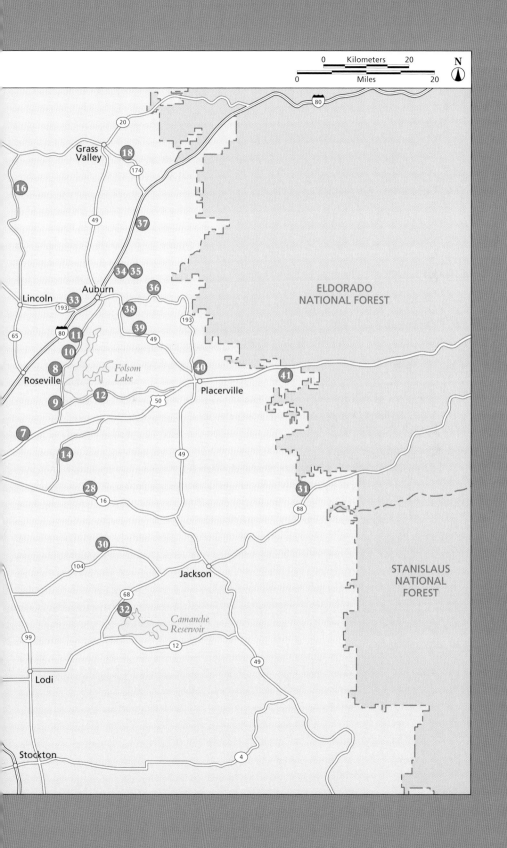

Acknowledgments

I am indebted to the lovers of parks and open spaces that have worked over the years to preserve pockets of wildland throughout the Sacramento area. A guidebook like this wouldn't be possible without their efforts.

Thanks to the land managers who have taken the time to review the hikes described in this guide, and to other writers who have shared their impressions of and experiences on Sacramento-area trails both in books and online.

Thanks to all the kind folks I met on the trails who pointed me in the direction of their favorite regional hikes. I hope I've done justice to the recommendations, and that this guide helps them find new favorites.

Thanks to the expert team of editors and production staff at Globe Pequot Press for helping make this guide the best it can be.

Thanks also to family and friends who support my work as a guidebook writer. Family is my backbone, whether they are jealous of my weekly escapes on new adventures or merely tolerate them. My cousin, Meg Blakiston, gave me nice tips about where to eat in the Sacramento region. For general support, my gratitude always to my parents Jesse and Judy Salcedo, my second mom Sarah Chourré, Martin Chourré, my brothers Nick and Chris Salcedo, and especially my sons Jesse, Cruz, and Penn. Whether on the trail or not, I'm very lucky to be able to share my journey with them.

HELP US KEEP THIS GUIDE UP TO DATE

Every effort has been made by the author and editors to make this guide as accurate and useful as possible. However, many things can change after a guide is published—trails are rerouted, regulations change, techniques evolve, facilities come under new management, and so on.

We would appreciate hearing from you concerning your experiences with this guide and how you feel it could be improved and kept up to date. While we may not be able to respond to all comments and suggestions, we'll take them to heart, and we'll also make certain to share them with the author. Please send your comments and suggestions to the following address:

GPP
Reader Response/Editorial Department
PO Box 480
Guilford, CT 06437

Or you may e-mail us at: editorial@globepequot.com

Thanks for your input, and happy trails!

Introduction

When I set about researching my first guide to the Sacramento area, *Best Easy Day Hikes Sacramento,* the trails and parks of the region were an unknown. Sacramento and the smaller satellite cities within an hour's drive of the state capital, including Fairfield, Davis, Auburn, and Placerville, were hiccups along the highway between my home in the San Francisco Bay Area and the Sierra Nevada. I'd done a bit of exploring, mostly along the American River and in the foothills, but the Central Valley was essentially a flat wasteland that had to be traversed—preferably as quickly as possible—to get to Lake Tahoe.

Discovering the best short hikes was a revelation—I found myself immersed in a surprisingly varied landscape with an unexpectedly large number of trail options to explore. Expanding that small guide into this larger one meant discovering an even greater number of the southern Sacramento Valley's hiking gems.

The sprawling Sacramento metropolitan area has built into its cityscape and suburbs a number of urban trails. Paved, flat, and often following riverbanks, levee roads, or abandoned railroad grades, these routes satisfy a number of needs for area residents. They accommodate after-work escapes, lunchtime power walks, needed perambulation for the cooped-up canine, the walk-and-

Sporting leaves bigger than a hiker's head, an exotic fig grows to giant proportions along the trail in Delta Meadows River Park (Hike 27).

talks of parents pushing buggies, the marathoner's workout, and Sunday sunset walking meditations.

Often straddling the borders of suburbia and the agricultural landscapes that most Californians associate with the Central Valley—and many along the creeks and streams of the Sacramento and San Joaquin River watersheds—an increasing number of regional parks and preserves have been established. Not all of them allow public access or have developed trail systems but some do, and hiking in these open spaces offers a glimpse into what the landscape was like when its only inhabitants were tribal hunters and gatherers.

Sacramento's great rivers and their tributaries inform nearly every park and trail in this guide. The Sacramento, the three forks of the American, the Feather, and the Cosumnes: They are wonders that evolve as they flow out of the mountains and merge on the flatlands, growing from clear, fast-moving streams into navigable waterways that look lazy until the sun highlights the complicated currents that churn below the surface. Trails around the rivers and their levees and sloughs—especially where the Sacramento and San Joaquin Rivers splinter into a complex delta as they empty into San Francisco Bay—support complex riparian habitats and saturate wetlands that support a wealth of bird, plant, and animal life. You'll be hard-pressed to find a trail in the delta, or in any riverside park, that doesn't ring with birdsong.

History also informs the region's trails. Bedrock mortars used by California's native peoples may be all that survived the passage of time, but remnants of the state's fabled gold rush and the endeavors of its argonauts can be found throughout the area, especially in the foothills. Urban hikes through Old Sacramento and down the Capitol Mall to Capitol Park recall the evolution of the city from its origins as a stopping point for gold seekers to its present-day role as California's political epicenter.

Each hike in this guide is unique for its ecology, history, topography, or natural beauty. Lying within an hour's drive of Sacramento's city center, they represent a sampling of the best of what can be found in the region. I hope that you will find these treks as satisfying as I have and that they will inspire you to explore further.

Weather

The climate of the Central Valley is essentially Mediterranean, with rainy and dry seasons. Hiking is both possible and pleasant year-round, but hikers should remember that each season poses unique challenges.

The rainy season generally runs from November through March and includes storms that can drop anywhere from a trace to several inches of precipitation. The valley lies in the rain shadow of California's Coast Ranges, so average monthly rainfall totals in winter are relatively modest, ranging from 2 to 4 inches. Average daytime high temperatures are in the 50s and 60s; average lows are in the 40s, with occasional dips into the 30s.

Winter rains may not be intimidating, but the fog can be. Inversions occasionally trap moisture on the valley floor, creating dense banks of "tule" fog that can reduce visibility, in the extreme, to less than 50 feet. The fog is primarily a hazard for drivers on area freeways, but it also significantly limits the vistas that can be enjoyed from any trail.

Conditions on some trails can degenerate into boot-sucking mud after a winter rain. A day or two of dry weather quickly hardens most surfaces so they are passable. The occasional cold front may deposit snow on the peaks of the coastal mountains and in the foothills: Usually this does not render the trails impassable, but hikers should be prepared for slick conditions.

In the dry season, from April through October, rainy days are sparse to non-existent. With hot temperatures and warm winds blowing in from the delta to the west, vegetation crisps to a crackly crunch, and hikers will crisp up too if they don't carry enough drinking water. Average daytime high temperatures range from the high 80s to the 90s, with heat waves raising the mercury into the 100s. Lows average in the 50s.

The greatest danger a hiker faces on hot summer days is dehydration. No matter the trail's length or the amount of shade along the route, carry plenty of water. When the temperatures soar, avoid hiking in the heat of the day. Morning and evening

In a thrilling display, cranes, ducks, and geese take flight from ponds in the Gray Lodge Wildlife Area (Hike 17).

hours offer lovely light and a greater opportunity to see wildlife, as well as mitigate the risks of heat-related illness.

Flora and Fauna

Landscapes traversed by trails within an hour's drive of Sacramento include oak woodlands, grasslands (or savanna), wetlands (both freshwater and saltwater), and lower montane forests.

The most recognizable is the grassland, as that is the setting for the city and its suburbs. Covered in annual grasses that green up in winter and dry golden in summer, the terrain is flat and springtime wildflower displays are typically spectacular. Vernal pools may also appear in spring, supporting a variety of ephemeral wildflowers and rare fauna, including fairy shrimp.

On the west end of the Great Valley, several trails venture into saltwater wetland, characterized by stands of pickleweed and frequented by shorebirds and waterbirds such as herons, egrets, and many species of ducks.

Freshwater marshes are scattered throughout the region, recharging in winter and spring with rain and meltwater from the Sierra Nevada. The marshes attract numerous birds, including migrating species like the sandhill crane, and are thick with tules, reeds, and cattails, which provide cover for songbirds and other marsh inhabitants such as muskrats and frogs.

Oak woodlands blanket the slopes of the Coast Ranges and the lower slopes of the foothills. California is home to a variety of oaks, some evergreen and some deciduous, including the blue oak, the live oak, and the tanoak. The trees require an expert eye to differentiate, especially since they hybridize. Other trees found with oaks include bay laurel, buckeye, and, in the foothills, digger pine. Nut-loving critters, such as acorn woodpeckers and gray squirrels, thrive in this habitat.

Venture a little higher into the foothills, and you'll encounter the mixed evergreen forest of the lower montane ecosystem. Fragrant incense cedar, a variety of pines, Douglas fir, and black oak provide shade, with manzanita and ceanothus in the understory. This can be bear country, but it also harbors deer and squawking jays.

Etiquette for Animals

You'll encounter mostly benign, sweet creatures on these trails—deer, rabbits, chirping chickadees. More rarely seen (during the daylight hours especially) are coyotes, raccoons, and opossums. Deer in some of the parks are remarkably tame and may linger on or close to the trails. Make noise and do not approach any wildlife—and never offer food to a wild creature. It's safer for you, and for the wildlife, if the animal walks or runs away.

Among the common domestic creatures you are likely to encounter on the trail are cows. They are passive and will usually move away as you approach. If you are uncertain of a cow's intentions, extend your arms and make noise.

Sacramento's parklands, especially in remoter regions of the foothills and coastal mountains, are habitat for mountain lions, bears, and rattlesnakes. Encounters are infrequent, but you should be prepared to react properly if you meet a snake, cat, or bear while hiking.

Rattlesnakes generally only strike if they are threatened. You are too big to be dinner, so they typically don't want to waste venom on you. Keep your distance and they will keep theirs. If a snake doesn't retreat or assumes a threatening posture—coiling up and shaking its rattle in warning—back slowly away and pick another route.

If you come across a mountain lion, make yourself as big as possible. If you are hiking with a child, pick him or her up: This will not only make you appear bigger, but also protect your kid. Maintain eye contact and do not run. If you don't act or look like prey, you stand a good chance of not being attacked. Make noise and back away slowly, and hopefully the animal will retreat. If you are attacked, fight back.

Black bears are generally not a threat, but you don't want to take any chances. If you see a bear, make lots of noise, and usually the animal will run away. If the bear appears aggressive or charges, make yourself as big as possible. Bears sometimes charge as a bluff, then veer away, so stand your ground and do not run. You don't want to resemble prey. Retreat slowly. In the event of an attack, again, fight back.

Buckeyes, one of the hallmark trees of California's coastal woodlands, bear fruits that resemble holiday ornaments in fall, and fragrant flowerheads in spring.

Plants to Avoid

Poison oak is a California native plant that, if touched or handled, deposits an oil that can cause a nasty skin rash. When the leaves turn red in autumn, the plant is easy to spot and stay away from. In spring when it's green, the adage "Leaves of three, let it be" will help you steer clear. In winter the plant loses its leaves entirely and becomes indistinguishable from other leafless vines, shrubs, and ground cover. That's when you'll want to employ the best tactic for avoiding poison oak—and one that works year-round: Stay on the trail.

Stinging nettle is another irritating plant that may be encountered along Sacramento-area trails. This produces a stinging sensation that's quite uncomfortable and long-lasting. Common in grasslands and along waterways, the best way to avoid contact is, again, to stay on the trail.

Wilderness Restrictions/Regulations

All of the trails described in this guide are on public lands. While day-use fees, parking fees, and registration may be required to access certain trails, specialized permits are not required.

A few of the trails cross properties managed by the California Department of Fish and Game. Charged with managing their properties for the benefit of wildlife, not necessarily humankind, land managers occasionally restrict hiking access. This can be to accommodate a particular species' breeding season, or to allow seasonal hunts (which help keep wildlife populations at healthy numbers). Go to the department web page for the area you wish to visit (for example, Grizzly Island Wildlife Area) to check on restrictions before you visit. The specific pages also contain notifications of closures for other reasons, such as flooding.

A number of California's state parks and recreation areas were targeted for closure in 2012. While those anticipated closures were not expected to affect trails listed in this guide, be sure to check the official web page (supplied as part of the hike descriptions) of the park you would like to hike in before visiting, just to make sure it hasn't been added to the hit list. Some parks, like Delta Meadows River Park, are "closed" but foot access is permitted.

Support the park system by paying required fees; you can also become active in any of the nonprofit volunteer organizations that support many of California's parks.

Green Tips

Given the great beauty of the parks, trails, and wildlands in and around Sacramento, and especially given the heavy use all receive, it's important that we do all we can to keep them clean, lovely, and healthy. The Green Tips scattered throughout this guide will help you do just that.

Getting Around

This guide targets the local Sacramento-area hiker and describes trails within his or her extended "backyard." All hikes are within a one-hour drive of downtown Sacramento, which excludes some wonderful hikes in the high country of the Sierra Nevada and in popular Coast Range destinations. Seek out other Falcon-Guides for further information about these regions.

Hikes are located in Sacramento, Yolo, Sutter, Placer, and El Dorado Counties. The guide includes hikes in or near Fairfield, Davis, Winters, Marysville/Yuba City, Grass Valley, Auburn, Placerville, Galt, and Jackson.

A number of major highways and interstates converge in Sacramento. Directions to trailheads are given from these arteries, which include I-5 (north–south), I-80 (east–west), US 50 (east–west), CA 99 (north–south), and CA 49 (north–south in the foothills, linking Grass Valley, Auburn, and Placerville).

Public Transportation

The Sacramento Regional Transit District offers bus and light rail service throughout the greater Sacramento metropolitan area, with service to suburban cities including North Highlands, Roseville, Folsom, Rancho Cordova, and Elk Grove. Contact information is PO Box 2110, Sacramento 95812-2110; (916) 321-BUSS (2877); www.sacrt.com.

Lush foliage, some native and some invasive, crowds the edges of the mown treadway of the Marsh Trail at Rush Ranch (Hike 22).

How to Use This Guide

This guide is designed to be simple and easy to use. Each hike is described with a map and summary information that delivers the trail's vital statistics, including length, difficulty, fees and permits, park hours, canine compatibility, and trail contacts. Directions to the trailhead are also provided, along with a general description of what you'll see along the way. A detailed route finder (Miles and Directions) sets forth mileages between significant landmarks along the trail.

Hike Selection

The trails in this guide are accessible to every hiker. The hikes range from short educational excursions perfect for families with small children to challenging all-day adventures. While these trails are among the best, keep in mind that nearby trails, sometimes in the same park or preserve, may offer options better suited to your needs. Hikes are categorized by region, with sections covering hikes within the metro area, the north valley (up to the Marysville/Yuba City area), the west valley (including hikes near Davis and Fairfield), the south valley (including hikes near Galt), and the foothills (including hikes near Auburn and Placerville).

Difficulty Ratings

To aid in the selection of a hike that suits particular needs and abilities, each is rated easy, moderate, or challenging. Ratings are based primarily on elevation gain and loss, challenges on the treadway (uneven footing, exposure to steep dropoffs), and trail length. Bear in mind that even the most challenging routes can be made easy by hiking within your limits and taking rests when you need them.

Easy hikes are generally short and flat, taking no longer than an hour to complete.

Moderate hikes involve increased distance and relatively mild changes in elevation, and will take one to three hours to complete.

Challenging hikes feature steep stretches, greater distances, and generally take four or more hours to complete.

These are completely subjective ratings. A hike's relative difficulty is entirely dependent upon an individual hiker's level of fitness and the adequacy of his or her gear (primarily shoes). Take both fitness and gear into consideration when selecting a hike. If you are hiking with a group, select a hike with a rating that's appropriate for the least fit and prepared in the party.

Hiking times are based on the assumption that on flat ground, most walkers average 2 miles per hour. Adjust that rate by the steepness of the terrain and your level of fitness (subtract time if you're an aerobic animal and add time if you're hiking with kids), and you have a ballpark hiking duration. Be sure to add more time if you plan to picnic or take part in other activities like bird watching or photography.

Towering above the route to Lake Clementine (Hike 35), the Foresthill Bridge was intended to skim the surface of the reservoir that would have filled the American River canyon behind the proposed (now essentially defunct) Auburn Dam.

Trail Finder

Hike No.	Hike Name	Best Hikes for Bird Lovers	Best Hikes for Children	Best Hikes for Dogs	Best Hikes for Great Views	Best Hikes for History Buffs	Best Hikes for Lake Lovers	Best Hikes for Nature Lovers	Best Hikes for River Lovers	Best Urban Trails	Best Hikes for Waterfalls
1	Old Sacramento and Waterfront Promenade		●		●	●				●	
2	Capitol Mall and Capitol Park					●				●	
3	William Land Park Tour		●							●	
4	Jedediah Smith Memorial Trail / Discovery Park									●	
5	Sacramento Northern Rail-Trail									●	
6	Gibson Ranch Loop Trail							●			
7	Effie Yeaw Nature Loop		●								
8	Miners Ravine Nature Reserve		●								
9	Lake Natoma Loop						●				
10	Beeks Bight Nature Trail at Dotons Point		●								
11	Sterling Pointe to Rattlesnake Bar						●				
12	Sweetwater Trail			●			●				
13	Yolo Bypass Wildlife Area Loop	●									
14	Mather Nature Loops							●			

Trail Finder

Hike No.	Hike Name	Best Hikes for Bird Lovers	Best Hikes for Children	Best Hikes for Dogs	Best Hikes for Great Views	Best Hikes for History Buffs	Best Hikes for Lake Lovers	Best Hikes for Nature Lovers	Best Hikes for River Lovers	Best Urban Trails	Best Hikes for Waterfalls
15	Bobelaine Audubon Sanctuary	●									
16	Shingle Falls										●
17	Gray Lodge Wildlife Area	●									
18	Empire Mine State Historic Park					●					
19	Putah Creek Loop Trail							●			
20	UC Davis Arboretum Trail									●	
21	Covell Greenbelt									●	
22	Rush Ranch					●					
23	Howard Slough at Grizzly Island Wildlife Area							●			
24	Rockville Hills Regional Park			●							
25	Homestead and Blue Ridge Loop (Stebbins Cold Canyon Reserve)				●						
26	Stone Lakes National Wildlife Refuge										
27	Delta Meadows River Park								●		

Trail Finder

Hike No.	Hike Name	Best Hikes for Bird Lovers	Best Hikes for Children	Best Hikes for Dogs	Best Hikes for Great Views	Best Hikes for History Buffs	Best Hikes for Lake Lovers	Best Hikes for Nature Lovers	Best Hikes for River Lovers	Best Urban Trails	Best Hikes for Waterfalls
28	Deer Creek Hills Preserve							•			
29	Cosumnes River Walk								•		
30	Howard Ranch Trail							•			
31	Indian Grinding Rock State Historic Park					•					
32	China Gulch Trail						•				
33	Hidden Falls Regional Park			•							•
34	Mountain Quarry Railroad Trail								•		
35	Lake Clementine Trail								•		
36	Olmstead Loop							•			
37	Codfish Falls			•							•
38	Cronan Ranch Regional Trails Park Loop			•	•						
39	Dave Moore Nature Trail								•		
40	Monroe Ridge / Marshall Monument Trail Loop				•	•					
41	Jenkinson Lake Loop						•				

Map Legend

Freeway/Interstate Highway	Boat Ramp
U.S. Highway	Bridge
State Highway	Building / Point of Interest
Paved/Improved Road	Campground
Unpaved Road	Cave
Gravel Road	Dam
Railroad	Gate
Featured Trail	Mountain / Peak
Trail	Park Headquarters
Paved Trail	Parking
Levee	Picnic Area
Boardwalk	Radio Tower
National Forest	Restroom
State / Local Park	Scenic View / Overlook
Body of Water	Towns and Cities
Swamp / Marsh	Trailhead
River or Creek	Visitor / Information Center
Intermittent Stream	Waterfall

Sacramento Metro Area

The Delta King is just one of the historic attractions you can visit as you walk along the waterfront in Old Sacramento (Hike 1).

Sacramento's metropolitan area includes satellite cities such as North Highlands, Rio Linda, West Sacramento, Folsom, and Rancho Cordova. Parks and trails are integral to the metro area, which includes nationally recognized urban routes. The American River Parkway, a paved path nestled in a greenbelt along its namesake river, stretches for more than 30 miles from the confluence of the American and Sacramento Rivers to Folsom Lake State Recreation Area. Other trails in the metro area have an urban setting, and several are paved, which makes them accessible to parents pushing strollers and folks who employ wheelchairs and scooters in their outdoor endeavors. Others are short explorations of urban parks that are perfect for family outings.

Trails through urban parks and along rivers

Though the rich lands along the rivers were long inhabited by native peoples, and John Sutter established his famed fort on the banks of the American when Mexico still governed what was then known as Alta California, Sacramento's urban identity originated in the days of California's gold rush. The city at the base of the Sierra Nevada's foothills burgeoned with the wealth of the argonauts. Once the rush was over, Sacramento thrived as California's capital. The bounty of its environment, its history, and its political relevance continue to draw both new residents and visitors to the region.

Growth has been a constant, with urban development stretching in all directions. But like many of the state's metropolitan areas, the Great Valley's greatest city has preserved what all Californians cherish—green spaces and wildlands, and trails upon which to enjoy them.

The walk down Capitol Mall is bookended by the capitol building on the east and the historic Tower Bridge, shown here, on the west (Hike 2).

Old Sacramento and Waterfront Promenade

A boardwalk and promenade follow the waterfront of the Sacramento River, beginning among the bustling shops and restaurants of historic Old Sacramento, heading down past the eastern foot of the Tower Bridge, and following a scenic promenade to the edge of downtown.

Start: Behind the California State Railroad Museum in Old Sacramento, adjacent to the Sacramento River

Distance: 1.1 miles lollipop

Hiking time: 30 minutes to 1 hour (longer if you stop to enjoy the sights)

Difficulty: Easy

Trail surface: Pavement, boardwalk

Best season: Year-round

Other trail users: Cyclists

Trailhead amenities: While there are no specific amenities at the trailhead proper, you'll find restrooms, water (and other libations), food, and other resources galore in Old Sacramento.

Canine compatibility: Leashed dogs permitted

Fees and permits: None

Schedule: 24 hours a day, 7 days a week, year-round

Maps: USGS Sacramento West CA. The trail is straightforward enough that no map is needed.

Trail contact: Ed Cox, Bicycle Coordinator, City of Sacramento, 915 I St., Room 2000, Sacramento 95814; (916) 808-8434

Other: Have your wallet handy—and an appetite wouldn't hurt either. Old Sacramento encompasses a mother lode of restaurants, shops, parlors, and museums. Clothing, cotton candy, champagne, caviar . . . you can find it here.

Finding the trailhead: The trailhead is located in downtown Sacramento. Take the J Street exit from I-5 and follow the signs to Old Sacramento. Both on-street parking and parking garages are available in the area; fees are charged. The closest garage is at the end of J Street across the street from the railroad museum, which is at 111 I St. GPS: N38 35.058'/W121 30.256'

THE HIKE

Culture and history are the focal points of this short urban route, with great views of fishing and pleasure boats on the Sacramento River adding to the appeal. Sandwiched between the river and a working rail line in the heart of the capital city, the trail serves up restaurants, riverboat rides, tattoo parlors, candy shops, a history lesson, and the chance to see an old-time locomotive cruising on a historic set of tracks.

The trail begins where the rail line begins, in front of the historic Central Pacific Railroad Depot in Old Sacramento. It traces the tracks of the working Sacramento Southern Railroad, upon which the California State Railroad Museum runs excursion trains from April through September. The railroad dates back to the turn of the twentieth century, when the Southern Pacific built the line to facilitate transportation of the bounty of the Central Valley's fields and orchards to port cities in the San Francisco Bay Area.

The Sacramento River, flowing broad and deep alongside the route, also connects Sacramento to San Francisco. The trail offers views down onto boats plying the quick waters, which look deceptively smooth but harbor powerful currents. This is no place for a swim.

The paved promenade offers views of the historic Tower Bridge.

A rustic boardwalk leads south past touristy restaurants and the *Delta King* paddleboat, ending at the intersection with the Capitol Mall. The yellow pylons of the Tower Bridge rise on the right (west), and the capitol building graces the end of the mall on the left (east). Carefully cross the road and continue south along the wide, lighted promenade, lined with lampposts and flower-filled planters bearing plaques that describe Sacramento's colorful history. River travel and locomotives, wharves and warehouses, food-packing plants and laundry houses: You can read all about it. Benches overlook the river, making this the perfect place to rest and digest after a meal in one of the old town restaurants. The glass-faced high rises of downtown rise behind you, and the glassy river flows in front of you, making the whole scene glow in a sunset.

A bike trail continues from the end of the promenade, leading south along the river and the tracks to Marina Park. You can explore farther, but the end of the promenade is the turnaround point for this short excursion. Another option is to pair this route with an amble on Capitol Mall to Capitol Park, described as a separate hike but a nice addition if you have the time and energy.

Regardless of your choice, retrace your steps back down the promenade and boardwalk to the trailhead.

MILES AND DIRECTIONS

0.0   Start on the riverfront levee, heading south on the top of the levee between the railroad tracks and the river. You'll pass a few interpretive signs as you ramble beneath the sycamores.

0.1   The wide boardwalk begins. Pass the *Delta King* paddleboat and the railroad depot, with the Tower Bridge looming ahead.

0.4   Arrive at the junction with Capitol Mall. Cross the street and continue on the promenade.

0.5   The promenade ends at Front and O Streets. Retrace your steps to Old Sacramento, looping back through the historic district. The historic area stretches several blocks parallel to the trail's end.

1.1   Arrive back at the trailhead near the railroad museum.

Option: Whether outward bound or returning on the trail, you have the opportunity to venture a block or two away from the riverside and into Old Sacramento. Historic buildings housing restaurants and shops line the cobbled streets. This won't add significantly to the mileage, so you really can't justify that caramel apple by saying you took a longer hike . . .

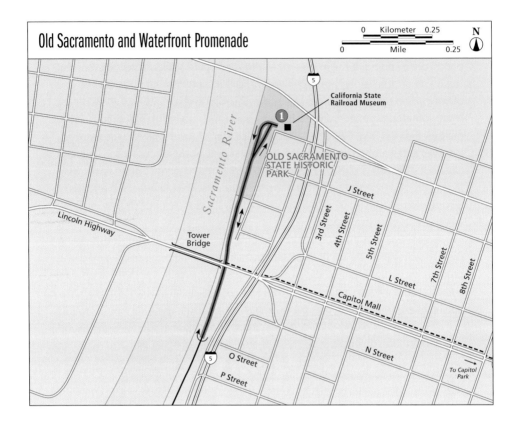

Old Sacramento and Waterfront Promenade

0   Kilometer   0.25
0   Mile   0.25

N

California State
Railroad Museum

Sacramento River

OLD SACRAMENTO
STATE HISTORIC
PARK

Lincoln Highway

Tower
Bridge

J Street

3rd Street
4th Street
5th Street
7th Street
8th Street

L Street

Capitol Mall

N Street

O Street

To Capitol
Park

P Street

HIKE INFORMATION

Local information: Old Sacramento merchants have teamed up with city and state officials to promote the historic district. The website, with listings of events, businesses, and activities, as well as historical information, is at http://old sacramento.com. You can also call (916) 442-8575 for more information.

Local events/attractions: Sutter's Fort State Historic Park, 2701 L St., Sacramento; (916) 445-4422; www.parks.ca.gov/?page_id. Located not far from the riverfront, this re-creation of Sutter's Fort contains a museum and hosts living-history days, as well as other special events.

Restaurants: Indulge in a gourmet taste of Old Sacramento at the Cafe Americain Champagne and Caviar House, 1023 Front St., Sacramento; (916) 498-9098; www.cafeamericain.info. Be sure to check out the speakeasy saloon downstairs.

The Origins of the City of Sacramento

The land at the confluence of the American and Sacramento Rivers had long been occupied by the Nisenan, a tribal people who established villages in the bottomlands. But it wasn't until settlers from the United States drifted west into what was, at the time, Mexico's Alta California, that a "city" was born.

The transformation began with the arrival of John Sutter in 1839. Sutter was awarded a land grant by the Mexican governor and established his fabled Sutter's Fort not far from the riverfront. The fort was more than a frontier outpost: It was the centerpiece of what was essentially a small town. Sutter's Fort accommodated trappers, emigrants, and explorers, but wouldn't gain historical prominence until miners swarmed into California during the gold rush.

The area that is now Old Sacramento was, in those pre-gold-rush days, known as Sutter's Embarcadero. Recognizing the prime location of the embarcadero, enterprising businessman Sam Brannan opened a store on the site. Once gold was discovered, Brannan profited mightily by outfitting the thousands of miners who poured down out of the mountains for provisions. A city grid, with numbered streets running north–south and lettered streets running east–west, was imposed on the riverfront, and other businesses catering to the forty-niners were established. Within a couple of years, "Sacramento City" was burgeoning.

In its early days the fledgling city was repeatedly inundated by floodwaters (the American and Sacramento having not yet been corralled by levees) and was also devastated by fires, but it endured. The muddy miners camp would one day be California's capital city.

William Tecumseh Sherman, who would gain fame during the Civil War by leading a fabled triumphant march through the Confederacy, helped survey and lay out Sacramento's street grid.

Capitol Mall and Capitol Park

California's stately capitol building, with its high dome and classic columned facade, is the centerpiece of this urban exploration. Begin at the historic Tower Bridge, travel through the heart of downtown, and complete your tour amid the roses and statuary of Capitol Park.

Start: At the foot of the Capitol Mall at the Tower Bridge
Distance: 2.3-mile lollipop
Hiking time: 1 to 2 hours
Difficulty: Easy
Trail surface: Pavement
Best season: Year-round
Other trail users: None
Trailhead amenities: None. Restrooms, water, and information are available at the state capitol and in various businesses along the route.
Canine compatibility: Leashed dogs permitted

Fees and permits: None
Schedule: 24 hours a day, 7 days a week, year-round
Maps: USGS Sacramento West CA; a map of Capitol Park in front of the capitol building. The trail is straightforward enough that no map is needed.
Trail contact: Capital District Office, California State Parks, 111 I St., Sacramento 95814; (916) 445-7373; www.parks.ca.gov

Finding the trailhead: The trailhead is the corner of Front Street and Capitol Mall, at the east end of the Tower Bridge. Parking, for a fee, is available on city streets and in parking garages near the trailhead. The length of the hike will vary depending on where you park (not a bad thing, considering the variety of sights and amenities available in downtown Sacramento). GPS: N38 34.809'/W121 30.418'

THE HIKE

Starting at the evocative Tower Bridge, and culminating in a tour of the varied gardens surrounding California's state capitol building, this classic urban walk immerses you in the culture and evolution of Sacramento's historic downtown.

Sacramento is the last in a long list of cities that have been designated the state's capital. Reaching back into the era of Spanish exploration and conquest, San Diego and Monterey both could claim the seat. After Mexico won its independence from Spain, and Mexican governors took control of Alta California, cities such as Vallejo (named for General Mariano Vallejo, a powerful Mexican landowner) and Benicia (named for General Vallejo's wife) were proclaimed capitals. Sacramento got the nod in 1860, and construction on the capitol building commenced. The main building, capped with a dome and grandly styled, was completed in 1874. The East Wing, which contains the governor's suite, was added as part of a remodel and restoration performed between 1949 and 1951.

California's historic capitol building is a highlight of the urban hike down the Capitol Mall and through Capitol Park.

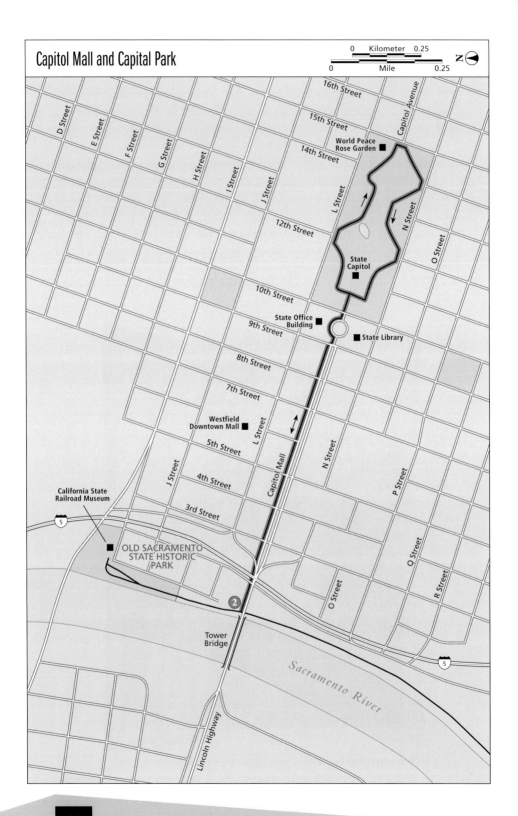

Capitol Mall and Capital Park

0   Kilometer   0.25

0   Mile   0.25

N

16th Street

15th Street

Capitol Avenue

D Street

E Street

F Street

G Street

H Street

I Street

J Street

14th Street

World Peace
Rose Garden

L Street

N Street

O Street

12th Street

State
Capitol

10th Street

State Office
Building

9th Street

State Library

8th Street

7th Street

Westfield
Downtown Mall

L Street

5th Street

N Street

Capitol Mall

P Street

J Street

4th Street

California State
Railroad Museum

3rd Street

5

O Street

O Street

R Street

OLD SACRAMENTO
STATE HISTORIC
PARK

2

Tower
Bridge

Sacramento River

5

Lincoln Highway

The walk begins at the Tower Bridge's easternmost endpoint, at the western end of the Capitol Mall. You can walk up either side of the mall; the street is divided by a green grass median. National banks and investment firms have offices in the glass-walled high rises along the mall, with restaurants and pubs occupying some of the first-floor spaces, many featuring outdoor patios fronting on the street. Closer to the capitol building itself, government offices occupy buildings with stodgy, uninspired architecture that is reminiscent of Communist block apartment complexes.

Cross 9th Street and the business of the mall gives way to formal gardens and the halls of government. The distinctly classical architecture of the State Office Building and the State Library are bookends to a plaza containing a circular drive and are buffered by spreading shade trees and flower-bordered lawns. "Bring Me Men to Match My Mountains" is carved into the stone facade over the entrance to the office building—hardly the language of bankers or communists, but rather that of frontiersmen inspired by the formidable Sierra Nevada, which they'd crossed to reach their Golden State and which was reluctantly yielding riches to their enterprise.

Cross 10th Street and you are at the foot of the stairs leading up to the capitol building itself. A map shows the intertwining paths of the park that stretches several blocks east of the edifice, with plantings of both native and foreign flora identified. You can pick your own route through the park, but a rough counterclockwise loop is described.

Themed gardens and honorary statuary highlight the route. On the north side of the capitol, in a glade shaded by redwoods, you'll find a monument to the Sisters of Mercy, who cared for the children of miners, the sick, and the homeless during the state's early days. The building itself was built on land that once was the site of the sisters' school.

Heading east along the palm-lined sidewalk, take the first asphalt path toward the park's central promenade, passing benches, fruiting Valencia orange trees, and more statuary. The California Firefighters Memorial is at the center of the park on the wide promenade.

Continue east up the promenade to the Vietnam Memorial, inscribed with the names of lost warriors and decorated with provocative sculptures and bas-reliefs. The rose garden is at the eastern border of the park, the blooms accented by poetry composed by California schoolchildren.

Capitol Park contains more than 800 trees and shrubs, with more than 200 varieties represented. Look for the labels that identify each of the unique plantings, including natives like the redwood and exotics like the Japanese persimmon.

Heading back west toward the capitol building, take time to check out the cactus garden (the century plant, or agave, was blooming in 2011), then continue to the stark obelisk of the Veterans Memorial. Continue along the garden paths to the palm-lined sidewalk that leads back to the front of the capitol building. From here, with the Tower Bridge in your sights, retrace your steps to the trailhead.

MILES AND DIRECTIONS

0.0   Start at the Tower Bridge on Front Street, heading up the Capitol Mall toward the capitol building.

0.3   At 5th Street you can hitch left a block and visit the Westfield Downtown Plaza mall. Unless you have a hankering to break up your walk with some shopping, stay straight on the Capitol Mall.

0.6   At 9th Street the business district gives way to greenery and the more classical architecture of the State Office Building and the State Library. Cross 10th Street and head left around the capitol building to access the paths of Capitol Park.

1.1   Reach the International World Peace Rose Garden and the eastern boundary of Capitol Park at 15th Street. Head left to explore the paths and plantings in the other half of the park as you head back toward the capitol.

1.7   Return to the front of the capitol building at 10th Street. From here, retrace your steps to the Tower Bridge.

2.3   Arrive back at the Tower Bridge.

HIKE INFORMATION

Local information: Sacramento Metro Chamber, One Capitol Mall, Ste. 300, Sacramento 95814; (916) 552-6800; http://metrochamber.org.

Local events/attractions: California State Capitol Museum, 10th and L Streets (State Capitol), Room B-27, Sacramento; (916) 324-0333; www.capitolmuseum .ca.gov. Housed in the same historic structure as California's legislature, the museum contains portraits of governors, historic artifacts, and collections of artwork. Open daily, year-round, from 9 a.m. to 5 p.m.

Hike tours: Tours of the capitol building and the capitol museum are conducted daily on the hour, beginning at 10 a.m. and ending at 4 p.m. Call (916) 324-0333 for more information.

To take part in the Take A Hike—City Walks program offered by the state parks department, visit www.parks.ca.gov.

William Land Park Tour

Flat, easy paths wind through one of Sacramento's premier city parks, circling ponds, skirting a golf course, and permitting access to family attractions including the Sacramento Zoo and Fairytale Town.

Start: On the sidewalk in front of Fairytale Town
Distance: 1.9-mile lollipop
Hiking time: About 1 hour
Difficulty: Easy
Trail surface: Pavement, a bit of grass and gravel
Best season: Year-round
Other trail users: Cyclists, joggers, golfers
Trailhead amenities: Restrooms, water, picnic facilities, ball fields, golf course, zoo, amusement park
Canine compatibility: Leashed dogs permitted

Fees and permits: None
Schedule: Open daily, sunrise to sunset, year-round
Maps: USGS Sacramento West CA and Sacramento East CA; online at www.cityofsacramento.org/parks andrecreation/parks/sites/pdf/ aerial_land_park.pdf
Trail contact: City of Sacramento Department of Parks and Recreation, 915 I St., Fifth Floor, Sacramento 95814; (916) 808-5200; www.cityofsacramento.org/parks andrecreation

Finding the trailhead: From downtown Sacramento head south on I-5 for about 2.5 miles to the Sutterville Road exit (also signed for the Sacramento Zoo and William Land Park). Head left (east) on Sutterville Road for 0.4 mile to Land Park Drive. Turn left (north) on Land Park Drive and go about 0.1 mile to the entrances of Fairytale Town and the zoo. Park alongside the road; the suggested route begins in front of Fairytale Town. GPS: N38 32.322′/W121 30.123′

H iking purists will no doubt scoff at this easy tour of William Land Park, but hikers with children—or a love of fairy tales and zoo animals that hasn't faded with age—will appreciate being able to stretch their legs before indulging in the park's other delights.

William Land Park is one of Sacramento's first urban sanctuaries. The park was conceived in 1911, when former mayor William Land gifted the city a generous sum of money earmarked for a city park. The parcel, called a "swamp" by Land's heirs, according to writer Steven Avella, was purchased in 1918, though controversy about its suitability landed the acquisition in court. The dust settled in 1922, the wetlands were drained, a levee was built, and amenities were installed, including fountains, sculptures, plantings of trees and shrubs, a golf course, and eventually a zoo and children's amusement park.

This hike describes a lollipop loop through the eastern portion of the park. But many variations exist, and getting lost is virtually impossible. The park encompasses a bit more than 166 acres, roughly divided by Land Park Drive, and is sur-

A stretch of paved trail skims one of a pair of small lakes in William Land Park, which also features a golf course, a zoo, a fairytale park, and other amenities, making this an ideal family excursion.

rounded by city blocks. It is crisscrossed by paved drives, so taking a shortcut or stretching the route is easily accomplished.

Begin by taking the dirt track that heads north, past the entrance to Fairytale Town and parallel to Land Park Drive. Cross 15th Street, skirt a parking lot, and head around the gazebo, then the amphitheater. Cross the grass to the paved path around the shore of the first lake, where geese and ducks float peacefully while youngsters and their parents try their luck fishing.

A quick walk up the gravel track along Land Park Drive leads to 13th Avenue, where you'll turn right and enjoy a long stretch of trail shaded by sycamores and enlivened by the varied architecture of the homes across the street to the left. Updated brick ranch-style homes with green lawns and borders planted with colorful annuals frame the occasional brick facade of a Tudor, which in turn may be nestled against a home with an art deco flair, and something colonial may be a couple of doors down. The bulk of Land Park, shady and green, is on the right.

The pavement ends at busy Freeport Boulevard, and you'll follow grass and dirt tracks back into the park. If you're pushing a stroller, you may want to return as you came.

The latter part of the loop brings you back along 14th Avenue, walking on the close-clipped grass of the verge. The route is shaded by redwoods, eucalyptuses, and different varieties of oaks; looking beneath the canopies you can watch the golfers play. The kids (or the dog) can scour the grass between the roadway and the fairway for errant golf balls.

Cross the park road at the triangle junction of 14th Avenue and 18th Street, then drop across the grass to a second lake, enjoyed by picnickers and geese alike. Leave the lakeside path for the grass again, returning to the corner of 14th Avenue and Land Park Drive. From there, retrace your steps to the trailhead.

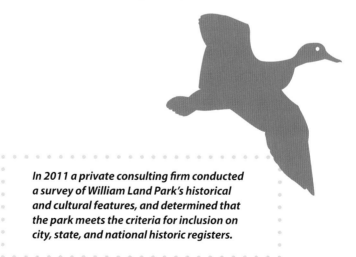

In 2011 a private consulting firm conducted a survey of William Land Park's historical and cultural features, and determined that the park meets the criteria for inclusion on city, state, and national historic registers.

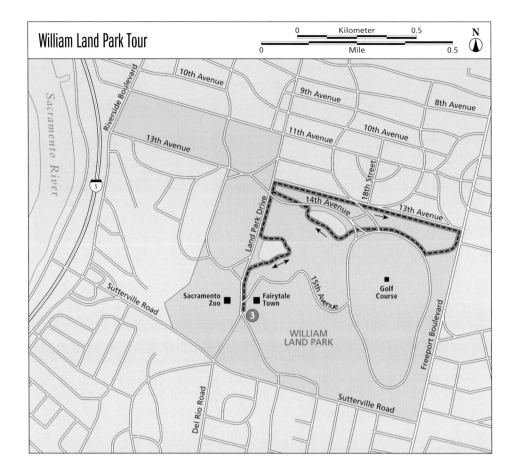

0   Kilometer   0.5

0   Mile   0.5

N

MILES AND DIRECTIONS

0.0   Start in front of Fairytale Town, heading north to cross 15th Street.

0.2   Pass the gazebo and amphitheater, cross the grass, and pick up the paved path at the small lake. Turn right to follow the path around the lake.

0.3   Cross the lawn to the gravel walking/jogging trail alongside Land Park Drive. Turn right and follow the path north to 14th Avenue.

0.4   Turn right onto the path alongside 13th Avenue.

0.7   Cross a park road and continue on the street-side path.

1.0   Reach Freeport Boulevard and turn right on the gravel path. Go 1 block and turn right again, walking on the grass along the left side of 14th Avenue.

1.2 At the junction of 14th Avenue and 18th Street, cross the triangle and drop down across the grass to the side of the small lake. Go left on the lakeside path.

1.6 Cross the grass to the junction of Land Park Drive and 14th Avenue. Turn right and retrace your steps to the trailhead.

1.9 Arrive back at the trailhead.

HIKE INFORMATION

Local information: Sacramento Metro Chamber, One Capitol Mall, Ste. 300, Sacramento 95814; (916) 552-6800; http://metrochamber.org

Local events/attractions: Sacramento Zoo, 3930 West Land Park Dr., Sacramento; (916) 808-5885; www.saczoo.org. Creatures on exhibit include lemurs, big cats, Masai giraffe, and a variety of exotic birds and reptiles. The zoo is open from 9 a.m. to 4 p.m. daily. Admission is charged.

Fairytale Town, 3901 Land Park Dr., Sacramento; (916) 808-5233 (24-hour information line) or (916) 808-7462 (main office); www.fairytaletown.org. Bring the wee ones to play amid a variety of exhibits that allow children to act out their favorite fairy tales. Open year-round, weather permitting, Mar through Oct from 9 a.m. to 4 p.m., and Nov through Feb from 10 a.m. to 4 p.m. Closed Thanksgiving, Christmas Day, and New Year's Day. Admission is charged.

A fine urban stroll explores one of Sacramento's premier, and oldest, city parks.

4

Jedediah Smith Memorial Trail / Discovery Park

This sampling of Sacramento's premier trail begins at the confluence of the American and Sacramento Rivers, and stretches east through manicured parklands and strips of tangled riparian woodland.

Start: At the boat ramp parking area near the confluence of the American and Sacramento Rivers

Distance: 4.4 miles out and back

Hiking time: 2.5 hours

Difficulty: Moderate due only to length

Trail surface: Pavement with shoulder of decomposed granite for pedestrian use

Best season: Year-round, though the trailhead area at the confluence may flood in winter or with spring runoff

Other trail users: Cyclists (lots of them), trail runners, in-line skaters, equestrians

Trailhead amenities: Large parking lot, restrooms, informational boards, water, picnic facilities, boat launch. There are no amenities at the Northgate Boulevard turnaround. Call boxes are located along the route.

Canine compatibility: Leashed dogs permitted

Fees and permits: A day-use fee is levied at Discovery Park. Fees are charged at other American River Parkway access points, though generally neighborhood access is free.

Schedule: Park is open daily, sunrise to sunset, year-round. Trail may be accessed 24 hours a day, 7 days a week, year-round.

Maps: USGS Sacramento East CA and Sacramento West CA; Jedediah Smith Memorial Bicycle Trail map produced by the Sacramento County Regional Parks Department, available for purchase at various locations along the trail including the Effie Yeaw Interpretive Center in Ancil Hoffman County Park. The map is also available at www.msa2.saccounty.net/parks/Documents/ParkwayMap.pdf.

Trail contact: Sacramento County Regional Parks Department, 4040 Bradshaw Rd., Sacramento 95827; (916) 875-6961; www.msa2.saccounty.net/parks.

Other: The trail is wheelchair accessible.

Special considerations: This trail is extremely popular with cyclists. The speed limit is 15 mph but it is not always obeyed. Stay on the parallel gravel path so that cyclists have room to pass. Most cyclists warn of their approach.

Summertime temperatures can reach into the 100s. If you hit the trail in the heat of a summer's day, bring plenty of drinking water and wear a hat.

Finding the trailhead: Discovery Park is at the confluence of the American and Sacramento Rivers just north of the state capitol. Take the Garden Highway exit from I-5 and follow the Garden Highway east for 0.4 mile to the Discovery Park entrance. The boat ramp and trailhead are in the west end of the park. GPS: N38 36.024'/W121 30.455'

THE HIKE

The American River Parkway, a 31-mile-long linear greenbelt that stretches from downtown Sacramento to Folsom Lake, is without question the most loved open space in the Sacramento metropolitan area. It's also the most well used, with an estimated eight million people visiting the park each year.

If the American River is the parkway's lifeblood, then the paved Jedediah Smith Memorial Trail is the artery that connects the river to the hearts of the people. Starting at Discovery Park, the national recreation trail links to local neighborhoods via access paths and staging areas, some with facilities including picnic areas, restrooms, and boat launches. The paved path roughly parallels the route of US 50, and access to the trail and parkway is identified on freeway signs.

The parkway concept dates back to 1915, when mention of an American River Parkway was made in a city plan, according to a Sacramento County Regional Parks fact sheet. Legendary landscape architect Fredrick Law Olmsted, perhaps best known as a designer of New York's Central Park, included a parkway along the American River when he surveyed California for potential park sites in the late 1940s. Land acquisitions started in 1960 and weren't completed until 2008, but by then the Jedediah Smith Memorial Trail, and many of the other 82 miles of trail in the parkway, were completed.

To explore the length of the memorial trail on foot would require days, a feat worthy of the route's mountaineering namesake, Jedediah Smith, who hiked across the Sierra in the early 1800s and camped along the river. Taken in segments, however, the trail easily accommodates six to eight fun day hikes. You could explore the confluence of the Sacramento and American Rivers at Discovery Park one day, move upstream to check out the protected area at Cal Expo the next, then spend another day on the riverfront in Pond and River Bend (formerly Goethe) Parks. Farther upstream the trail passes through the Lower and Upper Sunrise areas and rambles through oak woodlands with wonderful river views to the Nimbus Dam and fish hatchery. A circuit of Lake Natoma, also described in this guide, makes a nice daylong outing. And then there's a link along the shoreline of Folsom Lake . . .

The trail through Discovery Park, easy to access and remarkable because of its location at the dynamic confluence of the Sacramento and American Rivers, makes for a pleasant out-and-back hike. The park is busy in spring, summer, and fall, with boats launching, families throwing parties in the picnic grounds, anglers casting lines from the riverbanks, hikers and cyclists heading out on the trail, and archers practicing at the nearby archery range. It's a hustle and bustle start, but the trail enters a mellower environment by the 0.5-mile mark.

Interpretive signs are sprinkled along the path as it meanders through a relatively quiet stretch in the river's floodplain, in the shade of oaks and sycamores. The signs offer insights into the nature of the riparian habitat and the creatures that live there. Call boxes line the route as well, just in case you have an emergency.

The trail breaks away from the river, separated by a wetland that is flooded in winter and spring, and dries by late summer. The marshland is populated by a variety of birds, and kites may perch on the power lines overhead, scanning the reeds for prey. The trail is not shaded along this stretch, though the Natomas East Main Drainage, a water-filled channel that parallels the trail on the north side, supports a thick riparian ribbon that includes blackberry brambles and wild grape.

The turnaround point is Northgate Boulevard, but you can continue on . . . and on . . .

A jogger passes through a bower of shade trees along the Jedediah Smith National Recreation Trail in Discovery Park.

Additional options along the trail include a 4-mile out-and-back hike between Watt Avenue (where you'll find parking) and the Guy West pedestrian suspension bridge (a scaled-down Golden Gate Bridge). This segment of path is bordered by quiet residential neighborhoods on one side and the river on the other. A dirt track runs parallel to the paved path at the foot of a levee; you can also walk on the levee-top path. Or . . .

Pick up the trail in the William B. Pond Recreation Area and head east, across the scenic Jedediah Smith pedestrian bridge, into River Bend Park. Both parks offer all kinds of amenities, including picnic areas, playing greens, and river frontage. This is a little more than 2 miles out and back. If you want to add something a bit more wild to this outing, continue east into the more undeveloped areas of River Bend Park, where the route traverses oak woodlands and savanna. The grasses support a nice wildflower bloom, but this area can be hot and exposed in summer. Or . . .

Take in the scenic gorge, the Fair Oaks pedestrian bridge, great river views, riverside beaches—all from beneath the shade of overhanging oaks—on the 4-mile out-and-back trail segment between the Upper Sunrise access point and the Nimbus Fish Hatchery at Hazel Avenue.

Jedediah Smith

Born in New York State in 1799, Jedediah Smith would become one of the premier mountain men of the early 1800s. His expeditions in the American West included first-time explorations of some of the most forbidding landscapes in the region, including the Salt Lake basin, the Great Basin, and the forging of a new route through the Rocky Mountains.

Smith's explorations were financed by the fur trade, the pelts of beavers being a source of wealth for him and his partners. Two of his journeys led into California, where he and his party were detained by Spanish authorities who suspected Smith was up to no good. The Spanish governor later allowed Smith to carry on, permitting him to survey and hunt in the territory. He spent some time during his second trip hunting in the Sacramento Valley.

Though Smith, reportedly a deeply religious man, survived serious challenges on his expeditions, including a mauling by a grizzly bear that left him with distinctive scars, he was destined to die young. His last adventure was to lead a supply party along the Santa Fe Trail to Santa Fe in 1831. The story goes that while scouting alone for water, Smith disappeared. It's assumed he was killed by Comanche Indians, but his body was never found.

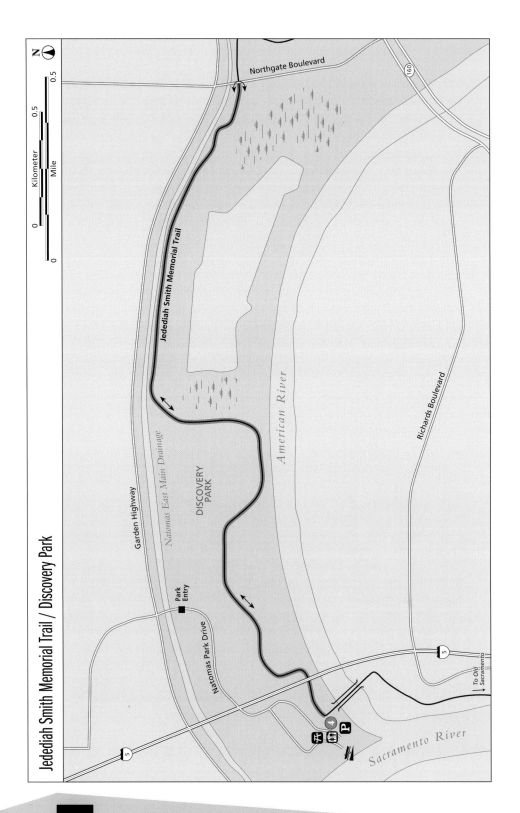

Jedediah Smith Memorial Trail / Discovery Park

Northgate Boulevard

160

Jedediah Smith Memorial Trail

Garden Highway

Natomas East Main Drainage

DISCOVERY PARK

American River

Richards Boulevard

Park Entry

Natomas Park Drive

5

5

To Old Sacramento

Sacramento River

N

Kilometer
0   0.5
Mile
0   0.5

0.0 Start near the boat launch and the I-5 overpass, where yellow posts mark the trailhead. Pass under the freeway and head east along the American River past lawns and picnic areas.

0.4 Noise from the freeway fades as fields and parking lots open on the left (north).

0.6 Pass the archery range on the left (north). As you enter the riparian woodland, an interpretive sign describes the trail and the cottonwood forest that surrounds you.

0.8 Pass an interpretive sign about habitat restoration.

1.3 Reach a stop sign where the Jedediah Smith Memorial Trail meets a paved access trail. Continue straight (east) on the Jedediah Smith trail. The river is out of sight to the right (south), separated from the route by the grassy floodplain.

1.9 Pass a call box. A hedge of blackberry shields a utility yard on the right (south), then the floodplain opens again. The paved route is shadowed by a gravel track.

2.2 Reach the Northgate Boulevard trail junction and the turnaround point. Retrace your steps toward the confluence.

4.4 Arrive back at the trailhead.

HIKE INFORMATION

Local information: Sacramento Metro Chamber, One Capitol Mall, Ste. 300, Sacramento 95814; (916) 552-6800; http://metrochamber.org
Restaurants: Sushi King, 2550 W. El Camino Real Ave., Ste. 13, Sacramento; (916) 921-6299; www.sushikingsac.com. Delicious Japanese fare, served in a clean setting just off I-5 north of downtown, includes grilled eel steaks over rice and colorful, exotic custom sushi rolls.

Sacramento Northern Rail-Trail

This rail-trail, mostly flat and nicely paved, cuts north from downtown Sacramento into the suburbs of Rio Linda and Elverta. A short section is described here, illustrating the provocative dilemmas that urban trails strive to bridge. The route begins amid industry and runs through the strip of riparian parkland along the American River at the border of Discovery Park.

Start: At the archway between 19th and 20th Streets next to the almond-packing plant

Distance: 3.4-mile lollipop

Hiking time: About 2 hours

Difficulty: Easy

Trail surface: Asphalt

Best season: Year-round

Other trail users: Cyclists, in-line skaters, dog walkers, joggers

Trailhead amenities: On-street parking. Public facilities are at the Rio Linda–Elverta Community Center.

Canine compatibility: Leashed dogs permitted

Fees and permits: None

Schedule: 24 hours a day, 7 days a week, year-round

Maps: USGS Sacramento East CA; online at www.msa2.saccounty .net/parks/Documents/Parkway Map.pdf

Trail contact: Ed Cox, Bicycle Coordinator, City of Sacramento, 927 10th St., Sacramento 95814; (916) 264-5011

Other: The paved portion of the trail is wheelchair accessible.

Special considerations: When the American River runs high in spring, the trail section between CA 160 and the intersection with the Jedediah Smith Memorial Trail may be flooded.

Finding the trailhead: The trailhead is located in downtown Sacramento. From the westbound lanes of the Capitol City Freeway, take the 15h Street (CA 160) exit (the 16th Street exit if you are headed eastbound). Go north on 16th Street, which is a one-way road, to D Street. Go right (east) on D Street to 20th Street. Turn left (north) on 20th Street to reach C Street. The trail, denoted with an archway, is located between 19th and 20th Streets, on the north side of the road. There is plentiful street-side parking. GPS: N38 35.052'/W121 28.575'

THE HIKE

The complexities of downtown Sacramento are in evidence along this section of the long Sacramento Northern rail-trail. The paved path links the graceful Victorian homes of a tree-shaded neighborhood, the industrial yards that line the adjacent railroad lines, and the greenbelt that has been nurtured along the American River, offering a snapshot of the heartland city's diverse urban landscape.

The trail follows the former Sacramento Northern Interurban Electric Rail line, which carried passengers between the bustling agricultural communities of Sacramento and Chico. Trains stopped running in the mid-1940s, and the rail line was eventually abandoned. Construction on the trail, which has been upgraded through the years, began in 1980.

The trail begins on C Street between 19th and 20th Streets, at the edge of a charming old neighborhood of classic homes and sycamore-lined streets. To borrow a word most often applied to the edges of natural habitats, the trail straddles the "ecotone" between industry and residential community, with the Blue Diamond Almond factory complex on one side and the neighborhood on the other. An archway marks the entry point.

An old railroad bridge spans the American River along the Sacramento Northern rail-trail near downtown.

The trail runs north, passing first through a tunnel under the bridge of the active Union Pacific Railroad tracks. Narrow strips of greenery line the path on either side, but they are not nearly dense enough to hide the rail yards and shipping containers to the east.

But industry is history by the 0.5-mile mark, where the trail reaches a junction with a path leading into a neighborhood. Go right, and climb gently to the star attraction: the trestle bridge spanning the American River. Take a break mid-span, as all your fellow hikers and cyclists will do, and gaze down on the seemingly passive waters of the American, wide and green and deepening before the confluence with the even mightier Sacramento River just a few miles downstream.

From the trestle the trail drops into the riparian greenery along the riverbank. You are briefly enveloped in a pocket of nearly pristine open space, but this is not wildland: The cottonwoods and willows, blackberries, and wildflowers that flourish along the river's edge have also found a way to thrive between the columns supporting CA 160, which soars overhead. The clash of concrete and thicket is paradoxical enough, but there's another juxtaposition that becomes apparent as you travel toward the junction with the American River Parkway and Jedediah Smith Memorial Trail. Modern-day hobos have beaten tracks into the greenery under the freeway and along the river, and have set up camps in the thickets. Some tents are visible; others are out of sight. Some of the inhabitants are also visible: Sometimes they are fellow travelers on the route, and sometimes they are spectators, watching you pass by.

The Sac Northern merges briefly with the Jedediah Smith trail at the next trail intersection, at an old raised wooden trestle. Head left (north) on the merged trails, across Del Paso Boulevard and into Discovery Park.

The bottomlands of the American River, which cradle the trails at this juncture, may be flooded in spring when the river runs full with Sierra snowmelt. Ponds form amid the thickets, ringing with birdsong. In summer the ponds may dry up, but the wetland atmosphere, thick with foliage and the flutter and chatter of hidden wildlife, remains. The paved paths split, with the Sacramento Northern trail taking the high road, climbing right onto its raised bed, from which you can look down upon the ponds.

At the 1.7-mile mark the rail-trail drops across the railroad tracks, then continues north. Just before the tracks a gravel road switchbacks sharply to the left. Take this gravel track, dropping onto a wide dirt pathway that parallels the rail-trail, but along the base of its raised bed. On the right, the wetlands and ponds of the bottomlands press close (indeed, if the water is high, you may be forced to retrace your steps on the elevated path). Side paths lead into the tangled undergrowth of wild grape, scrub oak, and blackberry. The walking is easy along the pathway, which leads back to the Sac Northern/Jed Smith trail junction near Del Paso Boulevard.

From the junction, retrace your steps to the trailhead.

The Magic of a Rail-Trail

Rail-trails are an urban ideal. The Sac Northern rail-trail is a perfect example of what they do best, linking neighborhoods with other neighborhoods, businesses, parks, schools, and public transportation.

Beyond the greenery of Discovery Park, the Sac Northern takes on a distinctly urban demeanor. Industry hitches up to neighborhoods as you pass under arches that mark the borders of different towns and neighborhoods: Noralto, Robla, Del Paso Heights. Paths break from the trail to both the right and left, giving access to quiet neighborhood streets. At times the trail is strictly urban; at other times it has a more suburban feel, broadening and featuring gazebos that offer shade and benches that offer respite.

Busy Rio Linda Boulevard and the I-80 overpass mark where the Sac Northern abandons an urban setting for a rural one. The trail enters country proper as it continues north, stretching between green pastures that bleach blonde after the long, hot summer. The canopies of broad-leafed trees shade the route and insulate it from the few signs of the metro area that it passes, including the Rio Linda Airport. The community park at Rio Linda, which the trail passes through, offers a tot lot, broad lawns, and the Rio Linda Depot, an open, gazebo-like structure housing picnic tables.

The route ends on Elverta Road, providing still more access to neighborhoods and green space. In the span of little more than 10 miles, the trail has linked central city with industry with parkland with suburbia with farmland. It's a remarkable passage. If there's something about a train that's magic, the same can be said for the rail-trail that follows in its tracks.

More than 40 tons of garbage were removed from illegal camps along the American River Parkway in 2008.

Sacramento Northern Rail-Trail **41**

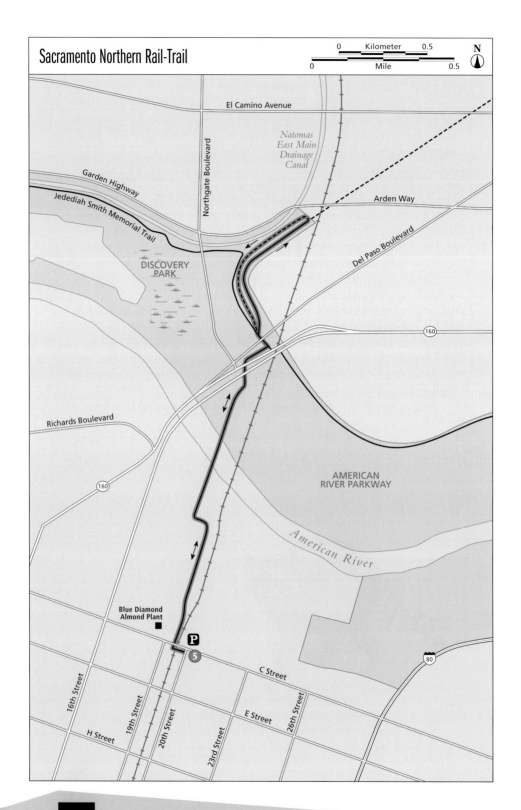

Sacramento Northern Rail-Trail

0 Kilometer 0.5
0 Mile 0.5

N

El Camino Avenue

Natomas
East Main
Drainage
Canal

Northgate Boulevard

Garden Highway

Jedediah Smith Memorial Trail

Arden Way

Del Paso Boulevard

DISCOVERY
PARK

160

Richards Boulevard

AMERICAN
RIVER PARKWAY

160

American River

Blue Diamond
Almond Plant

P

5

C Street

80

16th Street

19th Street

20th Street

23rd Street

E Street

26th Street

H Street

0.0 Start at the archway on C Street, adjacent to the almond-packing plant.

0.5 At the trail junction with a paved path leading into a neighborhood, go right on the Sacramento Northern trail (no sign).

0.7 Cross the trestle bridge over the American River.

1.0 Pass under CA 160.

1.1 Reach the junction with the Jedediah Smith Memorial Trail. Go left on the merged trails. Cross Del Paso Boulevard and enter Discovery Park.

1.2 At the junction just inside Discovery Park, go right on the Sac Northern trail (again, no sign), climbing onto the raised bed.

1.7 Turn left onto the gravel road just before the Sac Northern rail-trail leaves the raised bed and crosses the railroad tracks. Pick up the wide dirt track that runs parallel to the rail-trail at the base of the levee.

2.2 The dirt path ends at the junction with the Jedediah Smith trail on the north side of Del Paso Boulevard. Retrace your steps toward the trailhead.

3.4 Arrive back at the trailhead.

HIKE INFORMATION

Local information: Sacramento Metro Chamber, One Capitol Mall, Ste. 300, Sacramento 95814; (916) 552-6800; http://metrochamber.org

🍂 Green Tip:
If you see someone littering, whether on an urban trail or in the backcountry, muster up the courage to ask him or her not to.

6

Gibson Ranch Loop Trail

The riparian corridor along Dry Creek serves as a semi-wild start to a hiking tour through Gibson Ranch County Park. The route also passes through a wetland area. Between the creek and the wetland lie the park's picnic areas and playing greens, as well as the paddocks and pastures of boarded horses.

Start: In the northeast corner of the park on the banks of Dry Creek
Distance: 3-mile loop
Hiking time: 1.5 hours
Difficulty: Moderate
Trail surface: Dirt singletrack, dirt ranch road, a short stretch along the park road
Best season: Year-round
Other trail users: Equestrians, trail runners
Trailhead amenities: Parking lot. Nearby parking areas have restrooms and water.
Canine compatibility: Leashed dogs permitted
Fees and permits: Day-use fee
Schedule: Open daily, 7 a.m. to sunset, year-round

Maps: USGS Rio Linda CA; park map available at the entry kiosk
Trail contact: Sacramento County Regional Parks Department, 4040 Bradshaw Rd., Sacramento 95827; (916) 875-6961; www.msa2.saccounty.net/parks. Information on equestrian activities at the working ranch is at www.gibson-ranch.com.
Other: The park is a working ranch and accommodates a number of activities including picnicking, trail rides, animal husbandry, and fishing. While you are welcome to explore all facets of the ranch, please do not feed the animals.

Finding the trailhead: From I-80, the Capitol City Freeway, or US 50, take the Watt Avenue exit. Head north on Watt Avenue to Elverta Road (about 5 miles from the I-80 exit). Turn left (west) on Elverta Road and follow it for 0.7 mile to the park entrance on the right (north). The park road leads 1.3 miles, past pastures, paddocks, the park store, and residential facilities, to the parking lot in the northeast corner of the property. The trailhead is marked by a couple of yellow posts at the base of the creek levee. GPS: N38 43.644'/W121 23.912'

A circumnavigation of Gibson Ranch distills, in a few miles, the complex interface of Sacramento's natural, agricultural, and suburban worlds. The richness of the riparian zone along Dry Creek backs up to the pastures of Gibson's working ranch; the pastures back up to the fenced-off backyards of neighboring homes; a birdsong-filled marsh backs up to farm roads and a radio tower. The park's perimeter trail travels through this diversity.

The route begins in Dry Creek's riparian corridor, a 6-mile-long greenbelt in northern Sacramento County that is undergoing restoration, with plans to extend a multiuse path along its length and hook it into a 70-mile regional greenway loop (a paved 1.8-mile segment has been completed, linking Cherry Island Soccer Complex to Dry Creek Road). Contrary to its name, Dry Creek runs year-round. Preserving its floodplain, which includes wetland and riparian habitats, is an objective of parkway planners.

In Gibson Ranch the creek is an inviting waterway bordered by oaks, cottonwoods, buckeyes, and tangled figs. Side trails drop to sandy beaches where you can wade or skip stones. On the park side of the path, fenced pastures and lowing cows can be seen through breaks in the trees and thick brush.

The loop through Gibson Ranch begins with a quiet ramble along Dry Creek, which even in summer may not be dry . . .

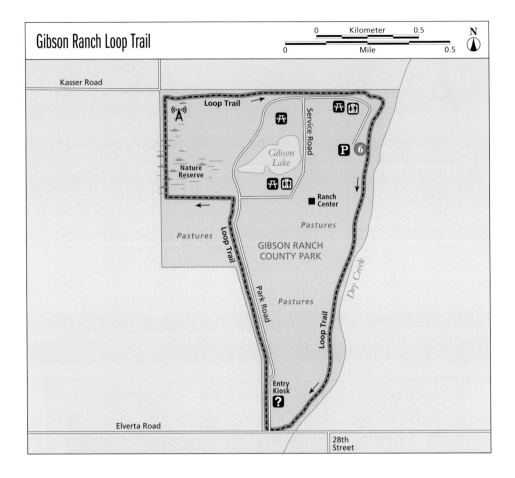

Gibson Ranch Loop Trail

Kasser Road

Loop Trail

Gibson Lake

Nature Reserve

Service Road

Ranch Center

Pastures

GIBSON RANCH COUNTY PARK

Pastures

Loop Trail

Park Road

Dry Creek

Loop Trail

Entry Kiosk

Elverta Road

28th Street

0   Kilometer   0.5

0   Mile   0.5

N

Reach the front of the park, and the suburban interface takes center stage. The trail bumps against a golf course and Elverta Road, then traces the park access road along the fences of a neighboring subdivision. Suburbia ends at the pastures and paddocks where the ranch's horses are boarded. The horses have consumed anything living within their fenced enclosures, leaving only dirt, and some hug the fences, leveling big-eyed gazes on passersby. They, and the cattle that run elsewhere in the park, are part of a long legacy of ranching in the Sacramento Valley and in California as a whole.

Spanish colonizers, and later Mexican dons, ran cattle on vast ranchos throughout what was then known as Alta California. Fattened on the abundant grasses that grow on the slopes of the coastal mountains and on the inland valley floors, the animals provided hides, tallow, and meat for their owners. Though the gold rush and California's eventual inclusion in the United States resulted in huge cultural changes, ranching stayed constant, with European immigrants from Italy, Switzerland, and other nations securing holdings that stayed in families for generations.

The gold came and went, the railroads came and went, but through it all, the ranchers remained. At Gibson Ranch horses reign, but the ranch also supports goats, llamas, and smaller farm animals like chickens and rabbits.

The trail loops through the paddocks, then arcs northward again, into the wetland. The marsh, an expanse of reeds, cattails, willows, and cottonwoods that resounds with birdcall, hugs the park's western boundary, extending north toward the radio tower in the park's northwest corner. Oaks shade the route, providing respite from what can be an unrelenting sun, and algae-covered pools give way gradually to meadows that bloom with wildflowers in season.

Following the trail back east toward the trailhead, the final stretch skirts Gibson Lake, which is surrounded by playing greens, picnic sites, and barbecues.

The park also hosts school groups, horse camps, trail rides, and Civil War reenactments, as well as birthday parties and group picnics. It can be a busy place, but early mornings and weekdays offer the possibility for some solitude along the loop trail.

MILES AND DIRECTIONS

0.0 Start by heading right (south) on the shady elevated trail along Dry Creek. Social trails drop to the creek, and park amenities such as soccer fields and parking lots are visible through riparian thicket on the right (west) side of the path.

0.2 At the trail junction stay straight (south) on the obvious creekside route.

0.5 At the intersection continue straight (south) on the creek trail, passing a shelter at the edge of a fenced pasture. The trees thin, offering views downstream from sandbar to sandbar.

0.8 The trail curves west to another trail junction. You can see the neighboring golf links and hear cars passing on nearby Elverta Road. Continue straight on the loop trail.

1.0 The trail meets Elverta Road. Head west alongside the pavement to Gibson Ranch Road (the main park road), then turn north, following the edge of the park road past the entry kiosk. Hook up with a dirt track that runs parallel to the pavement. Neighborhood homes border the trail on the left (west).

1.5 Pastures border both sides of the road and trail. Continue north.

1.7 Arrive at the stop sign at the junction of Gibson Ranch Road and the paved drive to the park store. Go left (west) on the dirt road that passes between pastures 16 and 10. Horse paddocks border the track.

2.0 Reach the park boundary and turn right (north) on the ranch road that skims the edge of the marsh.

2.2 The radio tower and a fence mark the park's northwest boundary. Go right (east) on the dirt road toward the ranch buildings and pastures.

2.6 The trail reaches the park road, then parallels it past the picnic grounds and tot lots bordering the lake.

2.7 Pass an intersection of park roads at picnic area 3.

2.9 Pass a gate and climb onto the Dry Creek trail at the park's northeastern boundary. Go right (south) on the trail.

3.0 Arrive back at the trailhead and parking lot.

HIKE INFORMATION

Local information: The Rio Linda–Elverta Chamber of Commerce and Civic League, 6730 Front St., PO Box 75, Rio Linda 95673; (916) 991-9344; www.rle chamber.org. Information about community businesses and events are listed on the website.

Local events/attractions: Gibson Ranch hosts an annual Civil War reenactment, complete with mock battles (and authentic cannon fire), food, dancing, crafts, and other Civil War–era attractions. Visit the Gibson Ranch website at www.gibson -ranch.com/civil_war.htm or call (916) 991-7592 for more information.

Green Tip:
Carry a reusable water container that you fill at the tap. Bottled water is expensive, lots of petroleum is used to make the plastic bottles, and they are a disposal nightmare.

Effie Yeaw Nature Loop

Interpretive trails wind through oak woodlands along a scenic stretch of the American River. The area supports an abundance of wildlife, including deer, wild turkeys, and a chattering collection of songbirds.

Start: At the Effie Yeaw Nature Center in Ancil Hoffman County Park
Distance: 1.7-mile lollipop
Hiking time: About 1 hour
Difficulty: Easy
Trail surface: Dirt singletrack
Best season: Year-round, though summertime heat and winter storms may preclude pleasant hiking
Other trail users: None
Trailhead amenities: Information board and plenty of parking. Restrooms are in the Effie Yeaw Nature Center. No water is available along the trail but a drinking fountain is at the trailhead.
Canine compatibility: Dogs not permitted
Fees and permits: Parking fee; donations gratefully accepted
Schedule: Open daily, sunrise to sunset, year-round
Maps: USGS Carmichael CA; online at www.sacnaturecenter .net/images/Nature_trail_map_ Effie_Yeaw.pdf; free trail maps available at Effie Yeaw Nature Center
Trail contact: Sacramento County Regional Parks Department, 4040 Bradshaw Rd., Sacramento 95827; (916) 875-6961; www.msa2.sac county.net/parks. To contact the Effie Yeaw Nature Center, call (916) 489-4918.
Special considerations: Avoid contact with poison oak, rattlesnakes, and ticks by staying on trails.

Finding the trailhead: From US 50 take the Watt Avenue exit. Go north for 1.8 miles on Watt Avenue to Fair Oaks Boulevard. Turn right (east) on Fair Oaks and go 4 miles to Van Alstine Avenue. Go right (east) on Van Alstine for 0.4 mile to California Avenue and turn left (north). Follow California Avenue for 0.1 mile to Tarshes Drive and the entrance to Ancil Hoffman County Park. Follow Tarshes Drive for 1 mile, through the golf course, to San Lorenzo Way. Go left (north) on San Lorenzo Way for 0.2 mile to the interpretive center parking area and trailhead. GPS: N38 37.015'/W121 18.758'

Walk this trail with the web of life in mind. Everything is connected: the river to the shore, the shore to the trees, the trees to the wind, the wind to the wings of the hawk that flies overhead. A quote from Chief Seattle, posted in the Effie Yeaw Interpretive Center, helps set the tone:

Man did not weave the web of life;
He is merely a strand in it.
Whatever he does to the web, he does to himself.

Any hike on these trails should begin with the visit to the interpretive center, which houses a bonanza of information about the natural and human history of the American River basin. The main hall of the center is full of interactive stations that describe the ecology and natural history of the area, including hands-on displays. Resident animals, which cannot be released into the wild, include a great horned owl, a saw-whet owl, a kestrel, and other raptors, as well as snakes and turtles. You can also pick up guidebooks that will help you identify these creatures and more wherever you travel.

Tules, used by the native Nisenan people to weave baskets and build houses, grow in the native garden fronting the Effie Yeaw Nature Center.

The center and trails are named for teacher and environmentalist Effie Yeaw, who, among other endeavors, made it her mission to show local schoolchildren the wonders of nature by leading them on guided walks through what was then known as Deterding Woods. She also spearheaded efforts to preserve the American River Parkway, recognizing its potential as both a natural and cultural landmark. Her legacy shines along these trails, which interpret the human and ecological history of the river. The inspirational educator died in 1970; her namesake interpretive center was completed in 1976.

Paths intertwine on the nature center property, enabling hikers to vary the route to suit their whims. A clockwise loop around the nature study area is described, beginning with a tour of the re-created Nisenan village, where tule huts, a granary, and other native California artifacts have been replicated and a garden of native plantings has been nurtured. The route then heads north along the Riverview History Trail to the banks of the American River, with interpretive signs along the path documenting the human history of the area. Follow the river south on the Observation Trail, skimming the interface between its cobbled banks and the oak woodlands that thrive on its shores, and feasting on river views. The Discovery Trail, with interpretive signs describing inhabitants of the preserve's wildlands, leads back north toward the interpretive center, passing the nature study pond that offers hikers the opportunity to sit and watch the ducks ply the still waters. Interpretive signs along all of the trails offer insights into the history and natural diversity within the 77-acre parcel.

Though interpretive signs delineate the formal routes, informal trails frequently intersect. If you get confused, stay on the well-marked interpretive trails. Informal trails are generally blocked, and hikers are not encouraged to wander at will.

The interconnectedness of the place, even to surrounding suburbia, is not subtle. But if a question lingers, consider that the deer in the park are absolutely fearless, foraging the annual grasses with little or no regard for hikers passing on the trails. Standing close to these wild creatures, with the boundaries of predator and prey broken by familiarity, is a perfect demonstration of how changes on one strand in the web of life affect those on another strand.

Naturalist John Muir echoed the thoughts of Chief Seattle with regard to the web of life when he wrote: "When we try to pick out anything by itself, we find it hitched to everything else in the universe."

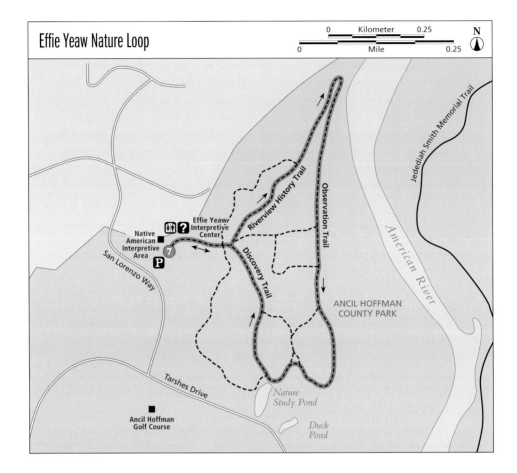

Effie Yeaw Nature Loop

Kilometer

Mile

ANCIL HOFFMAN COUNTY PARK

Jedediah Smith Memorial Trail

American River

Observation Trail

Riverview History Trail

Effie Yeaw Interpretive Center

Native American Interpretive Area

San Lorenzo Way

Discovery Trail

Tarshes Drive

Ancil Hoffman Golf Course

Nature Study Pond

Duck Pond

MILES AND DIRECTIONS

0.0   Start by exploring the Nisenan village cultural demonstration area. Native plantings, identified with signs, line the gravel path.

0.1   The Discovery and Riverview History Trails begin together adjacent to the interpretive center. Head east on the broad dirt path, which is lined with interpretive signs.

0.3   The Riverview History and Discovery Trails split amid a cluster of trail inter-sections. Stay left (northeast) on the broad Riverview History Trail.

0.4   Stay straight at the next unsigned trail intersection, heading northwest toward the river.

0.5   Turn right (east) on the narrow track that leads down to the unsigned sin-gletrack Observation Trail; there is a bench at the intersection. Turn right (south), heading downstream along the riverside in the shade of the riparian zone. Social trails lead down onto the cobbled floodplain; stay high on the well-trod trail lined with interpretive signs.

0.7 Pass interpretive marker 7, which describes how hydraulic mining in the river devastated the ecosystem. The mining technique was eventually outlawed.

0.8 At the trail junction stay straight (south and parallel to the river), heading into the woodland.

1.0 Pass a bench dedicated to Col. Bill Dula and stay left (south; along the river). The trail enters an open grassland.

1.1 At the signed junction for trails to the nature center and the nature study pond, go right (north) on the pond route (the Discovery Trail).

1.2 Turn left (west) to the reed-rimmed pond, where you'll find a couple of benches and an interpretive sign that describes the pond's purpose. When you've finished watching the ducks, head north on the signed trail to the nature center.

1.3 Pass a bench and trail sign.

1.4 Stay left (north) at the trail junction, passing interpretive signs that describe the ecosystem at the woodland's edge, then wild grapes.

1.5 Arrive back at the junction with the Riverview History Trail, at an interpretive sign about redbud. Go left (west) to return to the nature center and trailhead.

1.7 Arrive back at the trailhead.

HIKE INFORMATION

Local information: Carmichael Chamber of Commerce, 6825 Fair Oaks Blvd., Suite 100, Carmichael 95608; (916) 481-1002; www.enutshells.net/profiles/Clusters/Carmichael/Chamber/index.htm

Local events/attractions: The Effie Yeaw Nature Center houses informative displays that are both adult and kid friendly, and is well worth a visit. The center is operated by the American River Natural History Association, a nonprofit organization. The center is open Wed through Sun from 9 a.m. to 5 p.m. Feb through Oct, and from 9:30 a.m. to 4 p.m. Nov though Jan. It is closed Thanksgiving, Christmas Day, and New Year's Day.

8

Miners Ravine Nature Reserve

Two short loops link historic sites, including a grinding stone once used by local Native Americans, with soothing natural features such as a stream, riparian woodlands, and large, smooth granite boulders.

Start: Southern trailhead on Discovery Trail
Distance: 0.8-mile double loop
Hiking time: 30 minutes to 1 hour
Difficulty: Easy
Trail surface: Dirt singletrack
Best season: Spring and late fall
Other trail users: None
Trailhead amenities: Parking, trash cans, information signboard
Canine compatibility: Leashed dogs permitted
Fees and permits: None
Schedule: Open daily, sunrise to sunset, year-round

Maps: USGS Rocklin CA; map on information signboard in parking lot
Trail contact: Placer County Facility Services, Parks and Grounds, 11476 C Ave., Auburn 95603; (530) 886-4900; (530) 889-4901 (parks and grounds); www.placer.ca.gov/Departments/Facility.aspx
Special considerations: Please stay on trails to preserve natural and historic artifacts.

Finding the trailhead: From I-80 in Roseville take the East Douglas Boulevard exit. Go 5.3 miles east on Douglas Boulevard to Auburn-Folsom Road. Turn left (north) on Auburn-Folsom Road and go 4.2 miles to the Miners Ravine parking area, which is on the left. The park address is 7530 Auburn-Folsom Rd. in Granite Bay. GPS: N38 45.300'/W121 10.020'

Poison oak, which thrives in woodlands throughout California, causes a sometimes debilitating rash. Folktales tell that soaproot, which often grows near the irritating plant, can be used as a salve for the rash. Soaproot makes a good shampoo, too.

THE HIKE

Once the site of Hiram and Elizabeth Allen's ranch house, as well as a food preparation site for the native Valley Nisenan and Southern Maidu people, tiny Miners Ravine Reserve is packed with both historical and natural values.

The Allens ranched and farmed more than 400 acres in the Miners Ravine area, including the 24 acres now part of the reserve, beginning in the 1860s. By then the native tribes that had used granite boulders along the creek as bedrock mortars were long displaced, though they left behind permanent reminders of their industry—nearly perfectly circular grinding holes where they had prepared acorns, a staple of their diet.

The Allens prospered on the site, providing food and goods for miners and other workers traveling between Sierran gold fields and Sacramento. In 1909, according to the interpretive sign on-site, a railroad station was planned for the area, and in anticipation of the business this would bring to their ranch, the Allens essentially incorporated their enterprise into Allentown. In the end the station never was built, and Allentown faded from history.

Wedged between Auburn-Folsom Road and perennial Miners Ravine, the reserve boasts two trails. Both are advertised on websites as interpretive, but interpretive placards were only present on the Discovery Trail loop in 2011. This exploration of the reserve begins on the Discovery Trail, a nice, wide path that moves through scrub oak past the unsigned site of the Allen farmhouse (and a sign that provides information about the rattlesnakes that inhabit the area) to a split at

The tiniest of toddlers likely won't be taxed by these short trails, but they can't be topped as an easy introduction to hiking's unexpected treasures, such as bedrock mortars.

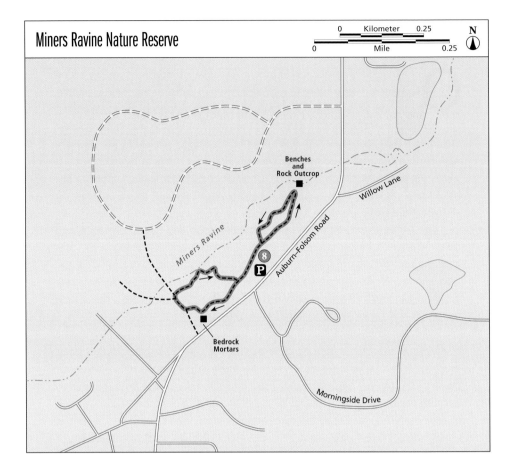

0   Kilometer   0.25   **N**

0   Mile   0.25

Benches and Rock Outcrop

Willow Lane

Miners Ravine

Auburn–Folsom Road

Bedrock Mortars

Morningside Drive

the start of the loop. Travel the loop in a clockwise direction, starting to the left. Road noise from busy Auburn-Folsom Road is constant, but the roadway is mostly screened by the understory.

Cross a little bridge over a seasonal streamlet, and then reach the bedrock mortar site, marked by an Archeological Resource Area sign. For one of the prettiest little outdoor food-prep counters you'll ever see, look carefully along the top of the low, moss-covered rock for the grinding holes. Remain on the trail and don't disturb the site.

There are no trail signs marking the route where it intersects a dirt roadway, but turn right on the broad path to continue on the loop. At the white post about 50 yards beyond, go right again on the narrower path.

Now in dense foliage, the path is littered with leaves and noise from the roadway is muffled. The trail leads past a bench and over another little bridge spanning a seasonal streamlet. Squirrels and jays chatter and yell, warning their neighbors of your presence. A side path to the left leads down to the creek, where you can rest on large sunny rocks. Another side path leads to a capped underground utility riser.

Stay right to close the loop, passing blackberries that ripen in August and poison oak that'll give you a nasty rash year-round if you touch it.

The signed North Loop begins across the parking lot from the Discovery Trail. Take the right fork, again launching into an oak woodland peppered with blackberries and humming with road noise. Snake through an open area and climb up and over a berm, then pass a smooth granite outcrop and drop into a clearing. Another wonderful place for a family to picnic at or explore, the sprawling limbs of an oak tree (as well as the rock itself) are perfect for young climbers (or climbers who are young at heart). Memorial benches dedicated to Michelle Short and Tom Thompson, "Placer County's Tree Guy," provide ideal opportunities to sit and relax. Trails collide in the clearing, but stay left, curling around the benches and the rock outcrop, to stay on the loop. Pass through a cool bower of oaks and brambles before emerging at the trailhead and parking lot.

MILES AND DIRECTIONS

0.0 Start on the signed Discovery Trail. Where the trail splits after 500 feet stay left, traveling the loop clockwise.

0.1 A small bridge spans a seasonal stream. Reach the bedrock mortars.

0.2 At the junction with a wider path/roadway, go right. A white post marks the next junction, about 50 yards beyond. Go right on the path.

0.3 A side trail leads down to the Miners Ravine creek. Continue on the loop by staying right.

0.4 Close the loop and retrace your steps to the parking lot.

0.5 Cross the parking lot to the start of the North Loop. Begin by going right, traveling counterclockwise.

0.6 Reach a clearing with benches, a rock outcrop, and an oak with sprawling limbs. Several trails lead right to utility sites and dirt roads. Stay left on the unsigned path.

0.8 Arrive back at the parking lot and trailhead.

HIKE INFORMATION

Local information: Granite Bay Community Association; www.granitebay.com. Roseville Chamber of Commerce, 650 Douglas Blvd., Roseville 95678; (916) 783-8136; www.rosevillechamber.com.

Local events/attractions: Folsom Lake State Recreation Area, 7755 Auburn-Folsom Rd., Folsom; (916) 988-0205; www.parks.ca.gov. Boating, fishing, hiking, and camping are all available in the recreation area.

Lake Natoma Loop

This daylong hike circumnavigates the lower of two reservoirs on the American River. Lake Natoma is smaller, narrower, and mellower than Folsom Lake, with the paved circuit trail never straying far from its shady shoreline.

Start: At the Nimbus Flat entrance station for the Folsom Lake State Recreation Area on Hazel Avenue
Distance: 11.6-mile loop
Hiking time: 6 to 8 hours
Difficulty: Challenging due to trail length
Trail surface: Pavement
Best season: Year-round, though unshaded portions of the trail should be avoided on hot summer days
Other trail users: Cyclists, in-line skaters, dog walkers, trail runners
Trailhead amenities: Large paved parking lot, restrooms, trash cans, picnic sites, information kiosks and interpretive signs, boat launch (for nonmotorized vessels), swimming beach
Canine compatibility: Leashed dogs permitted

Fees and permits: Day-use fee
Schedule: Open daily, year-round. Hours for Nimbus Flat staging area change with the season. Recreation area typically open 6 a.m. to 8 p.m. in summer (during daylight savings time) and 7 a.m. to 6 p.m. in winter (during standard time). Check the website for current times.
Maps: USGS Folsom CA; online at http://parks.ca.gov/?page_id=500 (click on park brochure link); available at park entry stations
Trail contact: Folsom Lake State Recreation Area, 7755 Folsom-Auburn Rd., Folsom 95630; (916) 988-0205; http://parks.ca .gov/?page_id=500

Finding the trailhead: From Sacramento take US 50 east for 19 miles to the Hazel Avenue exit. Go left (north) on Hazel Avenue, over the freeway and through the lighted intersection, to the signed entrance on the right (before the Sacramento State Aquatic Center parking lot). If you go over the Hazel Avenue bridge, you've gone too far. GPS: N38 38.049'/W121 13.025'

THE HIKE

Though better known as a cycling circuit, this long ramble around Lake Natoma is perfect for walking, talking, getting a great workout, and enjoying some of the best lakeside scenery Sacramento has to offer.

Though far from little, Lake Natoma is dwarfed by its larger neighbor to the east, Folsom Lake. Nimbus Dam forms a slender barrier across the American River; below the dam the river flows free, and anglers congregate in the current to see what they can catch. It's likely they'll have good luck, as the Nimbus Fish Hatchery is just below the dam. Chinook salmon and steelhead, which spawned all along the American River before it was dammed, are raised at the hatchery and released into the river; they swim downstream to mature at sea and return to their natal waters when they are grown and ready to spawn themselves—or be transformed into a succulent meal.

On Lake Natoma itself fishing is not the main attraction. Instead, kayakers, rowing teams, and paddle boarders ply the quiet waters, especially on warm days. Motorized watercraft are permitted on the lake north of Negro Bar, but are restricted to a 5 mph speed limit, so even if they are present, conditions are perfect for a leisurely human-powered cruise. A swimming and wading beach runs along

A pedestrian bridge aids hikers and cyclists in their circumnavigation of the shoreline of Lake Natoma on the American River Parkway.

the linear picnic ground and the parking lot at the trailhead, so you're likely to see kids of all ages enjoying a dip in the summer and early fall.

The trailhead proper is in the southeast corner of the 0.4-mile-long parking area, near restrooms and the last picnic area. This is an urban trail, and at this point noise from nearby US 50 is obvious, though it will fade as you proceed. Follow the paved path as it winds through chaparral and beneath broad-leaved sycamores, doing your best to stay left, on the gravel track that parallels the paved route. There is plenty of room for cyclists to pass slower traffic and for oncoming traffic as well, but hikers should stick to the gravel paths, or be prepared to step off the pavement to let speedier travelers pass.

The winding, shady trail loops to join the main American River Parkway trail and passes the access road for a private residence, then arcs across a pedestrian bridge. On the left, toward the lake, side trails lead onto the dirt or crushed gravel track running parallel to the main path used by cyclists. The narrower track is a nice option for hikers, as it winds through thickets of blackberries that ripen in late summer, and offers easier access to the shoreline for rest and refueling stops. In some areas small beaches and sunny rocks offer respite. The dirt track features more ups and downs, and sometimes is boggy and overgrown, so keep that in mind as you choose your route.

After about a mile the dirt track ends on the paved trail. Following the pavement again, pass a couple of junctions with access routes on the right, staying to the left on the obvious primary route. The Willow Creek staging area, at 2.4 miles, makes a nice turnaround point for those seeking a shorter hike.

Cross another pedestrian bridge, and again you'll have the chance to pick up a parallel dirt track between the paved route and the lake. But if you do, you'll miss the mounds of river cobbles that border the trail on the right, partially blocking the views of buildings beyond. The cobbles are tailings left behind by hydraulic mining operations along the American River in the late 1800s. The lake is mostly out of view along this stretch, screened by the thick understory of scrub (including blackberry and poison oak) that thrives beneath the oaks. Pass several paved paths that lead into adjacent neighborhoods and commercial areas; no worries about taking the wrong route, as the parkway trail, with its stripe of yellow separating opposite directions of traffic, is obvious.

A stone marker and plaque, placed by an Eagle Scout in 1996, identifies a spot significant to several eras of Sacramento-area history. Though not exact, it desig-

> *Mining camps and towns were built along the river between 1842 and 1862 and named for the groups that established them: Texas Hill by Texans, Mississippi Bar by Mississippians, Negro Bar by African Americans.*

nates a corner boundary of Rancho Rio de los Americanos, a land grant dating back to the days when Mexico controlled Alta California. It's also near the sites of two mining camps, Negro Bar and Texas Hill, which date back to the gold rush era. And it marks the northwest corner of the modern-day city of Folsom.

Follow either the main trail or the narrowing dirt track: Either way, you'll end up under the Folsom-Auburn Bridge. Bear in mind that the dirt track in this final section can be very muddy and overgrown, depending on the season, but with its tangled bowers of blackberry and little rustic wooden bridges, it feels quite wild.

To cross the bridge and continue the loop on the other side of the lake, climb up a flight of stairs and follow the long sidewalk to the signalized intersection of Greenback Lane and Folsom-Auburn Road. Cross to the east side of the bridge to the sign for the Negro Bar Park Access, and drop down paved switchbacks to the paved path. There are lots of amenities here, including restrooms and parking. If you want to do a shorter hike (about 5.6 miles) and have arranged a shuttle, this (or the boat launch/picnic area on the west side of the bridge, also part of the Negro Bar staging area) is the perfect pickup spot. You can also extend the walk by continuing east to Rainbow Bridge and taking in the sights at the Folsom Powerhouse State Historic Park.

Now on the north shore of the lake, headed back west on the return leg, you'll pass through more Negro Bar amenities, which include restrooms, parking areas, lawns, picnic grounds, and a boat launch. The Pioneer Express Trail intersects the paved path just beyond the picnic area, offering yet another parallel dirt-track option for hikers. The route described here remains on the paved trail, which drops to lakeside and passes below high bluffs composed of clay, sandstone, and river cobbles. As explained in the interpretive signs along the path, the bluffs were exposed by hydraulic mining operations. Other interpretive signs along the trail describe area fauna, including birds living along the shorelines and fish plying the depths, as well as flora, including the makeup of an oak woodland.

Beyond the bluffs the trail climbs a hill (the first and only), passing a horse trail and a pond on the right. Then it flattens out and pulls away from the lake, winding through a more open landscape of annual grasses, widespread oaks, and wildflowers in season. At the signed trail junction with the spur to Main Avenue, stay straight, toward Hazel Avenue. Tailings of river cobble again border the trail, and a pair of horse trails (available for pedestrian use as well) intersect the path, both signed.

By the time you reach the junction with the western end of the Pioneer Express Trail at the 10.2-mile mark, the Nimbus Dam and trail's end are in sight. Follow the paved path around the fenced-off maintenance structures and climb to the Hazel Avenue Bridge. Turn left on the bridge, and follow the sidewalk down to where the path resumes in front of the Sacramento State Aquatic Center. The paved path winds around the center and back into the Nimbus Flat staging area and trailhead.

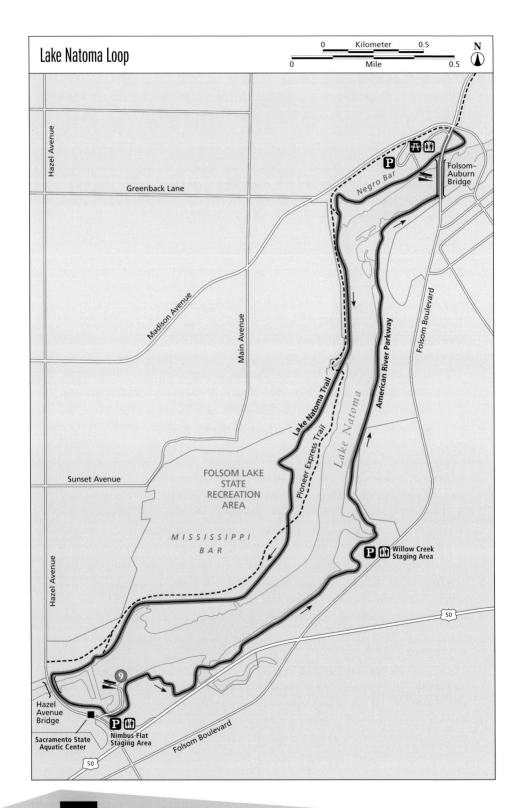

Lake Natoma Loop

Hazel Avenue

Greenback Lane

Madison Avenue

Main Avenue

Negro Bar

Folsom–Auburn Bridge

Folsom Boulevard

American River Parkway

Lake Natoma Trail

Pioneer Express Trail

Lake Natoma

Sunset Avenue

FOLSOM LAKE STATE RECREATION AREA

MISSISSIPPI BAR

Willow Creek Staging Area

Hazel Avenue

50

9

Hazel Avenue Bridge

Sacramento State Aquatic Center

Nimbus Flat Staging Area

Folsom Boulevard

50

0.0 Start in the southeast corner of the parking lot/picnic area, following the paved path east into the greenbelt.

0.7 At the stop sign go left on the American River Parkway trail. Bear right at the drive for a private residence less than 0.1 mile beyond (marked with a sign).

0.9 Cross a pedestrian bridge. You can opt to follow the parallel dirt (sometimes gravel) path that parallels the main trail by heading left on any of the side trails that connect the two.

1.9 Pass a picnic bench and a sign describing the lake's heron rookery.

2.1 Stay left at the junction with an access trail. Stay left again where another trail intersects less than 0.1 mile farther on.

2.4 Reach the Willow Creek staging area, with a parking lot. Stay to the right, crossing the access road.

2.5 Cross a pedestrian bridge. Again, you have the option to take a narrower dirt trail to the left (lakeside) of the paved path.

3.3 Where an access path intersects, stay left.

4.3 Pass an access trail, then a historic marker.

5.0 Pass under the Folsom-Auburn Bridge. Take the staircase up onto the sidewalk alongside Folsom-Auburn Road and proceed across the bridge to the north side and the junction with Greenback Lane.

5.6 Cross to the east side of Greenback Lane and, at the sign for the Negro Bar Park Access, descend to the trail intersection above the parking lot and restroom. Go right on the paved path, beginning the return trip down the north shore of Lake Natoma.

6.1 Pass the boat ramp (with a restroom) and head uphill to the parking area. Pick up the paved trail (or a broad dirt track) heading west from the parking area toward the picnic grounds.

6.7 Just beyond the picnic area, you'll reach the junction with the Pioneer Express Trail. Another nice option for hikers, this path leads back to the Nimbus Dam, running roughly parallel to the paved parkway trail. The route described here remains on the paved trail.

7.1 Pass interpretive signs. The trail is wedged between high bluffs and the lakeshore.

7.8 Pass the horse trail and a pond on the right, then climb a short hill.

8.5 At the signed trail junction with the side trail to the Main Avenue staging area, stay straight, toward Hazel Avenue (3.2 miles away, per the sign).

8.7 Pass a junction with a horse trail, staying on the paved path.

9.6 Pass a second horse trail junction, again staying on the main thoroughfare.

10.2 The Pioneer Express Trail merges into the American River Parkway trail. Stay on the paved path.

10.5 Pass another trail junction, again staying on the main parkway trail. The trail to the right (Middleridge) leads to the Snowberry Creek Assembly Area.

10.9 The trail splits below the dam. Take the right-hand path, climbing to the Hazel Avenue Bridge. Go left on the bridge, past the Sacramento State Aquatic Center, and into the Nimbus Flat staging area.

11.6 Arrive back at the trailhead.

The Folsom Dam Project

Folsom Lake and Lake Natoma are the recreational by-products of a project that harnesses the powerful American River. Folsom Dam was completed in 1955, with Folsom Lake filling behind it, extending 15 miles into the forks of the river. Nimbus Dam and Lake Natoma were completed at about the same time and help regulate releases from the larger Folsom reservoir. Both dams and reservoirs provide flood control, serve as water supplies for households and agriculture, and supply electrical power.

The potential of the American River to supply electricity was the impetus for construction of the Folsom Powerhouse, located on the shoreline of Lake Natoma east of the Folsom-Auburn Bridge, in the last decade of the nineteenth century. Incorporating the original Folsom Dam and a canal, water from the river was converted into electrical power via massive "dynamos," or generators, powered by turbines. The power was transmitted to Sacramento, a feat that was unprecedented in 1895 and was front-page news even in San Francisco.

The Folsom Powerhouse, a landmark listed on the National Register of Historic Places, is the center of a state historic park, located at 9980 Greenback Lane in Folsom. For more information call (916) 988-0205 or visit the website at www.parks.ca.gov/?page_id=501.

HIKE INFORMATION

Local information: Folsom Chamber of Commerce, 200 Wool St., Folsom 95630; (916) 985-2698; www.folsomchamber.com. Check the website for information on area recreation, businesses, and restaurants.

Local events/attractions: Nimbus Fish Hatchery, 2001 Nimbus Rd., Ste. F, Gold River; (916) 358-2884; www.dfg.ca.gov/fish/hatcheries/nimbus. In addition to instructive exhibits in the visitor center, you can also check out the raceway ponds, where salmon and steelhead are raised until ready for release. The hatchery visitor center is open Mon through Fri from 8 a.m. to 3 p.m., and Sat and Sun from 9 a.m. to 3 p.m. It is closed Christmas Day.

Sacramento State Aquatic Center, 1901 Hazel Ave., Gold River; (916) 278-2824; www.sacstateaquaticcenter.com. The aquatic center offers a variety of activities on Lake Natoma, including rowing classes (kayaks or paddle-powered vessels), team-building seminars, and sailing lessons.

Organizations: Friends of Lakes Folsom and Natoma (FOLFAN) assists with trail maintenance and development at Folsom Lake State Recreation Area. The group also promotes trail etiquette and recreational and educational opportunities. Contact the organization at www.folfan.org.

Green Tip:
Walking side by side on an urban trail may facilitate conversation, but it can obstruct the route for other users. The more well loved the route, the more important it is to be aware of your fellow recreationalists. Be courteous by walking single file when necessary.

Beeks Bight Nature Trail at Dotons Point

The oak woodland ecology of Folsom Lake frames this short interpretive trail along the shoreline of a relatively isolated bay.

Start: At the Beeks Bight trailhead, located 3.8 miles from the Granite Bay entrance station to Folsom Lake State Recreation Area (SRA)
Distance: 1.0 mile out and back
Hiking time: 1 hour
Difficulty: Easy
Trail surface: Dirt and gravel singletrack
Best season: Spring for wildflowers; fall and winter for cool temperatures. Hike in the mornings and evenings in summer to avoid the heat of the day. Wait a few days after a heavy winter rain for the trail to dry out.
Other trail users: None, though tracks in the dirt indicate that mountain bikers might sneak onto the trail occasionally
Trailhead amenities: Parking, restrooms, trash cans
Canine compatibility: Leashed dogs permitted
Fees and permits: Day-use fee

Schedule: Recreation area open 6 a.m. to 9 p.m. in summer (during daylight savings time) and 7 a.m. to 6 p.m. in winter (during standard time). Check the Folsom Lake SRA website for specifics, as hours change seasonally.
Maps: USGS Rocklin CA; Folsom Lake State Recreation Area map available at park entry stations and online at http://parks.ca .gov/?page_id=500 (click on park brochure link)
Trail contact: Folsom Lake State Recreation Area, 7755 Folsom-Auburn Rd., Folsom 95630; (916) 988-0205; http://parks.ca .gov/?page_id=500
Special considerations: The loop option is only available when the lake level is low. Avoid contact with poison oak, a staple of the woodland ecology, by staying on the trail.

Finding the trailhead: From I-80 east of Sacramento, in Roseville, take the Douglas Road exit. Go 5.3 miles to the intersection of Douglas Road and Auburn-Folsom Road, then continue on Douglas Road for 1 mile to the Granite Bay entrance station. From the entrance station, follow the park road for 3.8 miles to its end at the Beeks Bight trailhead parking area. The trailhead is in the southeast corner of the parking area, near the information boards. GPS: N38 46.150′/W121 7.957′

THE HIKE

I n the height of the summer season, Folsom Lake attracts recreationalists like the bell of an ice cream truck attracts children. Boaters and swimmers, campers and picnickers, horseback riders and mountain bikers—they all relax and play on the water and along the shoreline, savoring the expansive scenery and whatever is cooking on the outdoor grill.

Hikers may be challenged to find peace and quiet on even the remotest of the park's 95 miles of trail during the summer, and the nature trail at Beeks Bight is no exception. But in the off-season, when temperatures cool and the boats are stored, they stand a good chance of being downright isolated on this short, wooded excursion.

Interpretive panels along the route, placed by local schoolchildren in 2002, offer insight into the human and natural history of the oak woodland ecosystem you'll travel through. They describe how native tribes used the resources of the woodlands. Oak trees, for example, not only provided acorns, a primary element of the native diet, but components could also be used in medicine and dye. Soaproot had a variety of uses, including, of course, as soap. Other signs address aspects of ecology, such as how fire benefits the environment. The trail is lined with numbered markers; check for guides at the Granite Bay entrance station (none were available when this trail was researched). You'll also find benches along the path, perfect spots for rest or a snack.

Oak woodlands frame the trail at Beeks Bight in the Folsom Lake State Recreation Area.

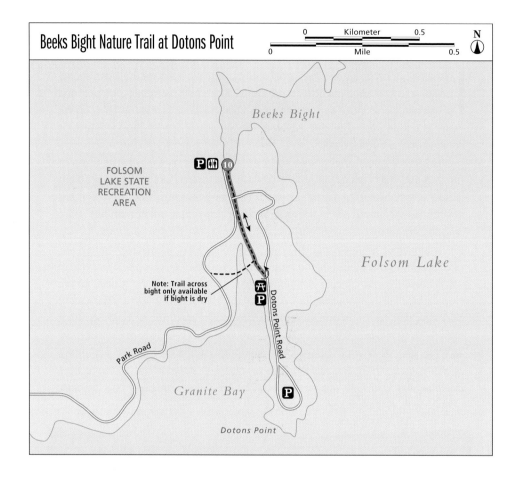

Beeks Bight Nature Trail at Dotons Point

FOLSOM
LAKE STATE
RECREATION
AREA

Beeks Bight

Folsom Lake

Note: Trail across
bight only available
if bight is dry

Dotons Point Road

Park Road

Granite Bay

Dotons Point

The first interpretive panel, encountered at the trailhead, defines "bight" as a bay or cove—in this case a cove named for miller Joe Beek. The bight may be empty or full depending on the lake level. When the bight off Dotons Point at the end of the trail is dry (likely in the late season), hikers can traverse a grassy swale that might otherwise be underwater, linking the nature trail with the park road to make a loop. If the bight is inundated (likely in spring when meltwater fills the reservoir), you'll have to turn around at Dotons Point Road and return as you came.

The path begins by wandering through the oaks that line the edge of the bight. Birds flit in and out of the scrub, and wildflowers bloom in season in pockets of grasslands between thickets of blackberry and scrub. Emerge from the woodland in a clearing with views of Folsom Lake and Folsom Dam, at an interpretive sign describing the dam's purpose. The path merges with a bike trail near the mouth of the cove, climbing gently to trail's end at a small gravel parking area on Dotons Point Road.

MILES AND DIRECTIONS

0.0 Start behind the information board, heading right (south) past the interpretive sign that defines "bight." A mountain biking route departs to the
left. Cross a bridge and head into the woodland.

0.1 Cross Dotons Point Road. Continue straight (south) on the nature trail.

0.3 Pass a bench and some interesting rock outcrops. The trail is graveled for a
stretch.

0.4 Picnic tables overlook a lovely meadow studded with granite outcrops.
Continue south, enjoying views of the lake and dam.

0.5 The nature trail merges with a multiuse singletrack. Go left (southeast) on
the blended trail, climbing to trail's end at Dotons Point Road. A small parking area and trash cans are available here. Return as you came.

1.0 Arrive back at the trailhead.

Option: If the bight is dry, you can return to the trail junction in the meadow and
go left, following the well-worn social trail across the bottom of the empty bay.
You will pass a trail marker on the far side of the inlet. The path then climbs—you
might get your heart rate up—to the park road. Turn right (north) onto the road,
and follow it back to the trailhead. Total mileage for the loop is 1.1 miles.

HIKE INFORMATION

Local information: Granite Bay Community Association; www.granitebay.com.
Roseville Chamber of Commerce, 650 Douglas Blvd., Roseville 95678; (916) 783-
8136; www.rosevillechamber.com.

Local events/attractions: Folsom Lake State Recreation Area attracts millions
of visitors each year and offers a variety of outdoor activities including boating,
windsurfing, swimming, fishing, camping, picnicking, cycling and mountain biking, horseback riding, and lounging on the beach. Much more information is
available on the park website at http://parks.ca.gov/?page_id=500, or call (916)
988-0205.

Camping: Folsom Lake has three developed campgrounds, plus one hike-in
environmental campground. The closest camp to Beeks Bight is at Beals Point,
open year-round. Make reservations by calling (800) 444-7275 or visiting www
.reserveamerica.com.

Sterling Pointe to Rattlesnake Bar

Follow a remote stretch of Folsom Lake's shoreline to a beachhead with lovely lake views. The route is part of the Pioneer Express Trail, used by equestrians for endurance rides, but those on foot need endure nothing more strenuous than a few ups and downs.

Start: At the Sterling Pointe staging area off Auburn-Folsom Road
Distance: 6.8 miles out and back
Hiking time: 4 to 5 hours
Difficulty: Moderate due to distance
Trail surface: Dirt singletrack, some dirt road
Best season: Spring, late fall, and winter
Other trail users: Equestrians
Trailhead amenities: Parking; restrooms; water for humans, horses, and dogs; picnic tables; trash cans; information signboards
Canine compatibility: Leashed dogs permitted
Fees and permits: None
Schedule: Open daily, 8 a.m. to sunset, year-round. The route runs through the Folsom Lake State Recreation Area, but the staging area is not part of Folsom Lake SRA. Recreation area hours change with the season; check the website for current hours.
Maps: USGS Pilot Hill CA; online at http://parks.ca.gov/?page_id=500 (click on park brochure link); available at park entry stations. A map of the Sterling Pointe trails, including the Peregrine Trail and Lake Forest Trail, is posted on an information signboard at the trailhead.
Trail contact: Folsom Lake State Recreation Area, 7755 Folsom-Auburn Rd., Folsom 95630; (916) 988-0205; http://parks.ca .gov/?page_id=500

Finding the trailhead: From I-80 in Roseville take the East Douglas Boulevard exit. Go 5.3 miles east on Douglas Boulevard to Auburn-Folsom Road. Turn left (north) on Auburn-Folsom Road and go 5 miles to Lomida Lane. Turn right (east) on Lomida Lane and drive for about 0.8 mile; Lomida becomes Lake Forest Drive and then Sterling Pointe Court. Signs in the neighborhood point the way. Continue for 0.3 mile on Sterling Pointe Court to the road's end at the staging area. GPS: N38 48.092′/W121 06.666′

THE HIKE

The hike from Sterling Pointe to Rattlesnake Bar begins in a ritzy neighborhood, where the manicured backyards of trophy homes back up to the serenity of a rather remote stretch of Folsom Lake. No need to be envious, however, as you'll share in wealth of a different kind—the kind that money can't buy—along the trail. The views alone are priceless (and are probably what made the area so desirable to the well-heeled residents of the Pointe); add in the lushness of the oak woodland and the sense of well-being that exercise generates . . . well, you don't have to pay a penny for that.

The Sterling Pointe Trail, which you follow down to the Western States Pioneer Express Trail, is part of a hiking and equestrian trail system that offers shorter loops if the longer trek to Rattlesnake Bar is not appealing. The Sterling Pointe path drops past signed junctions with the Peregrine Trail and the Lake Forest Trail before reaching the Pioneer Express Trail, with Folsom Lake hidden by a thick screen of scrub, including poison oak. The abundant foliage of the understory emerges supple and green in the spring, leaves glossy with moisture from the rainy season, and turns brittle and crispy as the dry season progresses.

Tiny hikers march toward the trailhead at the Sterling Pointe staging area, the start of the trek to Rattlesnake Bar.

The Pioneer Express Trail, an endurance route that runs from Sacramento to Auburn and then across the Sierra Nevada, follows the shoreline of both Lake Natoma and Folsom Reservoir as it heads out of Sacramento. It can be traveled in either direction from Sterling Pointe; you'll be headed east, toward the gold fields. Mile markers along the trail testify to its length (though they didn't necessarily agree with the GPS readings taken when the trail was researched). You'll hop on the route at about mile 42. Turn left (north) to reach Rattlesnake Bar (and beyond), passing Long Bar, a small, overgrown picnic area. Social trails branch to picnic sites. Though still out of sight, the drone of boat motors drifting through the trees is a reminder that the lake is below.

Once past Long Bar and its cluster of use trails, route-finding simplifies. The well-traveled singletrack weaves northward along the lakeshore, tucking in and out of ravines where blackberries thrive even after the streamlets that nourish them have dried up. Generally ripe in August, the berries are a delicious trailside snack.

By the 1-mile mark, lake views open. Side trails drop to the shoreline, which rises and falls based on rainfall, snowmelt in the Sierra, and releases from Folsom Dam. The glitter of sunlight reflecting off the windows of trophy homes in the wooded hills on the opposite shoreline catches the eye, as do the boats zooming by on the water.

The trail fractures again at Horseshoe Bar, with unsigned use paths branching right to the lakeshore and to overlooks. Stay left, hooking up and over a short, steep hill and past the gated access point from Horseshoe Bar Road (follow the horse poop and hoofprints if you are uncertain). Continue on the broad dirt road as it arcs around a cove, then narrows to singletrack and continues north.

The trail roller-coasters through the scrub, and is deeply grooved in sections, chiseled by horse hooves. A large power-line tower sits atop one hill, then the route drops, bending right at a trail junction, to cross one of several little bridges that make negotiating stream gullies easy. The landscape opens to meadow as you approach Rattlesnake Bar, with springtime wildflower displays a lovely addition to widening lake views. Stay right at the trail junctions beyond the meadow—the route identified with trail markers—until you reach the signs, picnic areas, and parking lot at the eastern edge of Rattlesnake Bar.

Popular and sometimes busy, you can follow paved Rattlesnake Road to the most developed areas of Rattlesnake Bar, including the boat launch. A web of dirt roads knots around the lakeshore and the small point that juts into the lake. Find a quiet spot along the shoreline to rest and have a snack, enjoying expansive views south across the blue waters of the lake. When you are ready, return as you came.

> *The term "bar," as in Rattlesnake Bar and Horseshoe Bar, was given to bends in the river where forty-niners were likely to find placer gold.*

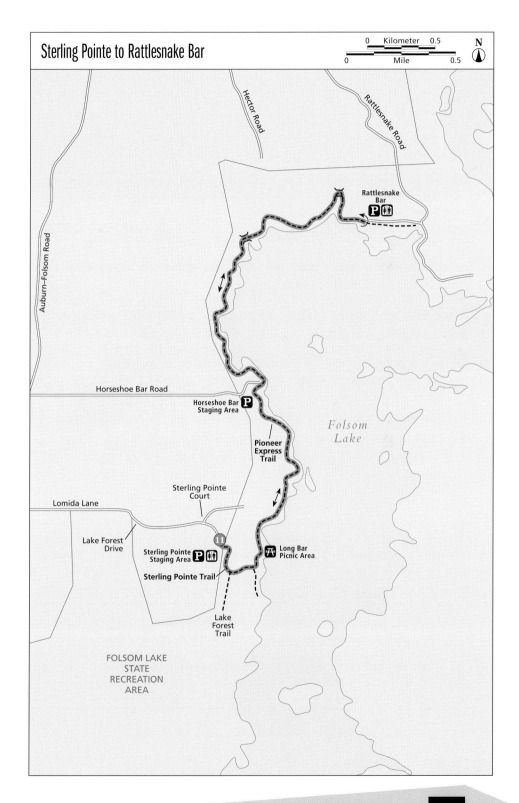

0   Kilometer   0.5

0   Mile   0.5

N

Hector Road

Rattlesnake Road

Rattlesnake Bar

Auburn–Folsom Road

Horseshoe Bar Road

Horseshoe Bar Staging Area

Folsom Lake

Pioneer Express Trail

Sterling Pointe Court

Lomida Lane

Lake Forest Drive

11

Sterling Pointe Staging Area

Sterling Pointe Trail

Long Bar Picnic Area

Lake Forest Trail

FOLSOM LAKE STATE RECREATION AREA

0.0   Start at the signed trailhead at the Sterling Pointe staging area, taking the Sterling Pointe Trail.

0.1   Pass the junction with the Peregrine Trail. Stay straight on the Sterling Pointe Trail.

0.25   At the intersection of the Lake Forest Trail, stay left on the Sterling Pointe Trail. After about 500 feet, meet the lower end of the Peregrine Trail. Stay right and downhill, passing a couple of fences as you drop.

0.4   Reach the signed Pioneer Express Trail. Go left toward Rattlesnake Bar.

0.6   The trail splits before reaching the signed Long Bar picnic area. Stay left (on the high road) to skirt the picnic area.

0.8   Pass endurance trail mile marker 43.

1.3   Pass endurance trail mile marker 43.5.

1.5   Arrive at Horseshoe Bar. Stay left (up and over the hill) on the unsigned, broad, roadlike track to continue on the Pioneer Express Trail. On the other side of the hill, the broad track bends around a cove.

2.0   Pass endurance trail mile marker 44; the trail begins to climb.

2.3   Pass a section of chain-link fence, then endurance trail mile marker 44.5.

2.4   Pass a power-line tower.

2.5   At the trail junction, stay right, passing a trail signpost. Cross a little bridge over an inlet stream.

2.7   Cross a meadow.

2.8   Pass endurance trail mile marker 45 and a side road that leads left. Stay right on the Pioneer Express Trail.

3.1   Cross a bridge over a year-round stream. Pass another trail marker and stay right.

3.4   Reach Rattlesnake Bar. Take a break, then head back the way you came.

6.8   Arrive back at the Sterling Pointe staging area.

HIKE INFORMATION

Local information: Granite Bay Community Association; www.granitebay.com. Roseville Chamber of Commerce, 650 Douglas Blvd., Roseville 95678; (916) 783-8136; www.rosevillechamber.com.

Local events/attractions: Folsom Lake State Recreation Area attracts millions of visitors each year and offers a variety of outdoor activities including boating, windsurfing, swimming, fishing, camping, picnicking, cycling and mountain biking, horseback riding, and lounging on the beach. Much more information is available on the park website at http://parks.ca.gov/?page_id=500, or call (916) 988-0205.

Camping: Folsom Lake has three developed campgrounds, plus one hike-in environmental campground. The closest camp to Sterling Pointe is at Beals Point, open year-round. Make reservations by calling (800) 444-7275 or visiting www.reserveamerica.com.

Other resources: The Wendell & Inez Robie Foundation, PO Box 714, Foresthill 95631; (530) 367-4332; http://robiefoundation.org. The Robie Foundation is dedicated to preserving and maintaining historic trails for equestrians and hikers. The Pioneer Express Trail is one of the foundation's projects.

The Western States Pioneer Express Trail skirts the shoreline of Folsom Lake as it stretches from Sterling Pointe to Rattlesnake Bar and beyond.

12

Sweetwater Trail

A popular route with mountain bikers and hikers alike, the Sweetwater Trail follows the southern shoreline of Folsom Lake below the inflow of the South Fork American River. Mostly shaded, the trail winds through oak woodland and small meadows, with side trails leading waterside.

Start: Signed trailhead in Salmon Falls raft take-out parking lot

Distance: 5.6 miles out and back

Hiking time: 2 to 3 hours

Difficulty: Moderate due to distance

Trail surface: Dirt singletrack

Best season: Spring for wildflowers; late fall for cooler weather

Other trail users: Mountain bikers

Trailhead amenities: Parking, restrooms

Canine compatibility: Leashed dogs permitted

Fees and permits: Day-use fee

Schedule: Open daily, year-round. The trail is in the Folsom Lake State Recreation Area, and hours of operation change with the season, roughly opening near sunrise and closing at sunset. Check the website for current hours.

Maps: USGS Pilot Hill CA; online at http://parks.ca.gov/?page_id=500 (click on park brochure); available at park entry stations

Trail contact: Folsom Lake State Recreation Area, 7755 Folsom-Auburn Rd., Folsom 95630; (916) 988-0205; http://parks.ca .gov/?page_id=500

Special considerations: This trail is popular with mountain bikers. Be prepared to share. If you absolutely can't tolerate wheeled travelers, try the trail from Sterling Pointe to Rattlesnake Bar instead. While trailhead etiquette requires bikers to yield to hikers, it is often easier for a hiker to step off the trail to let a cyclist pass. Be courteous and use common sense.

Finding the trailhead: From Sacramento head east on US 50 for about 25 miles to Eldorado Hills. Take the Eldorado Hills Boulevard exit. Go north on Eldorado Hills Boulevard for about 4.2 miles to the junction with Green Valley Road, where the road's name changes to Salmon Falls Road. Continue north on Salmon Falls Road for 5.6 miles to the Salmon Falls raft take-out parking lot, which drops off to the left and is not easy to see from the eastbound lane. If you reach the Salmon Falls Bridge, you've gone too far. GPS: N38 46.284'/W121 02.583'

THE HIKE

O n the Sweetwater Trail, it's not all about the setting. Granted, that's the trail's greatest asset—it winds through a healthy oak woodland, sports views through the trees across a long arm of Folsom Lake, and includes passage through moist, shady drainages and across open meadowlands. But the successful comingling of diverse trail interests is also highlighted on the Sweetwater.

Conflicts between mountain bikers and other trail users, arguably more with equestrians than with hikers, have plagued public trails since the 1970s, when the popularity of fat-tired bikes boomed. No multiuse route has been immune, but nowadays sharing trails with other users is commonplace. Cooperation among the three groups, when it exists, also extends to building and maintaining trails, and mountain bikers have stepped up in the case of the Sweetwater. The immaculate, winding, roller-coaster singletrack is superlative for both hiking and cycling, and hikers should go forth with gratitude when they venture onto this path.

Fortunately there are enough mountain biking routes in this neck of the woods to thin out the wheeled population, so unless you hit the trail at the same time as a pack of cyclists (during an organized ride, for example), you are unlikely to cross paths with anyone but other hikers.

A small stand of oaks marks a great picnic site near the edge of Folsom Lake, and a possible turnaround point for those seeking a shorter hike.

Beginning near the Salmon Falls Bridge, where the south fork of the American River broadens into the lake, the dirt singletrack heads into scrub and dips through the first of several stream crossings—this one little more than a trickle in late season. Tangles of brush thrive along the waterway, including the noxious, if native, poison oak. Stay on the path and you should be able to avoid contact with its leaves and stems, which carry the rash-producing oil.

Ups and downs, twists and turns, and flickering views of the lake through thick chaparral that includes ceanothus, scrub oak, and burgundy-skinned manzanita characterize the first mile of trail. Though generally quiet and remote in feel, noise from boats on the blue to the right is constant on busy summer days. Hike in late fall, winter, or early spring, and the noise is more intermittent. Pass trails that lead down to lakeside as you proceed, with the views improving the farther you head down the path.

Broader vistas open at the halfway point of the outward leg of the hike. Birds flick through bushes, bees buzz on wildflowers in the grasses in season, and boats zip across the water, presenting a classic tableau of fun in the sun. A bit farther along, side trails lead down to a cove that makes a nice stopping point for a snack or to wet your feet. A stand of oaks provides some shade on the otherwise exposed stretch of shoreline.

Beyond the cove, the trail curls around a finger of the lake. After crossing a culvert in the shade of more oaks, the trail borders a tributary of Sweetwater Creek, which has dug a trench into the soft sediments deposited by the lake as it rises and falls with snowmelt and releases from the distant Folsom Dam. As the path nears its junction with Salmon Falls Road, noise from passing cars becomes noticeable.

Cross a metal bridge that spans the tributary of Sweetwater Creek. Sedges, discernable by the edges on their stalks, line the path. At 2.5 miles the trail empties onto a dirt roadway at a junction; a Sweetwater sign marks the spot. Head left to complete the outbound portion of the hike at the gate and small parking area off Salmon Falls Road. If you don't want to make the last short hitch to the roadside endpoint, you can bear right at the sign and follow any of several trails / old dirt roads (one is signed for use by bikes and horses) that lead across an open, grassy area. Pick a rest spot in the sun or shade, depending on the season, and then retrace your steps to the trailhead.

🌿 Green Tip:
Consider citronella as an effective natural mosquito repellent.

How to Share a Trail

Growing up in Fairfax, California, I was lucky enough to be part of the first wave of mountain bikers. We were a motley crew, riding in jeans instead of padded Lycra bike shorts and rocketing down legendary off-road downhill runs, including the iconic Repack (which earned its name because you'd have to repack your brakes after you burned through them on the descent).

In those early days there were no trail restrictions and mountain bikers rode where they pleased. Unfortunately the hills where we rode had long been the territory of horseback riders and hikers, who were startled and upset by our speed. Not only that, but we were mostly silent, so horses and hikers were spooked when we suddenly appeared. Some of us were also rude, ignoring hikers who asked us to slow down when we approached, and horseback riders who asked us to dismount so we wouldn't startle their animals.

The conflicts that erupted—usually shouting matches but sometimes worse—led to mountain biking bans on many of the singletrack paths that inspired wheeled trailblazers in the first place. Most mountain bikers realized the impact the new sport was having on fellow outdoorspeople and began to abide by the commonsense rules that are now part of the trail-use credo: They yielded to all other trail users. A few did not, however, and these thoughtless cyclists nearly spoiled it for all.

To this day mountain bikers are still dispelling the bad feelings engendered by arrogant cyclists who wouldn't compromise for the benefit of all. Organizations such as IMBA (International Mountain Biking Association) were formed to educate all trail users about trail etiquette once it became apparent that mountain biking was here to stay. Mountain biking clubs, like FATRAC on the Sweetwater, adopted trails (or built new ones) and maintain them for all users. Their goodwill has gone a long way toward mending the breach.

Silent and speedy, mountain bikers bear the responsibility to let hikers know when they are coming, and to travel at reasonable speeds when they know hikers (and horseback riders) share a route. With years on the trail, and hundreds (maybe thousands?) of miles under my wheels and my feet, I can honestly say that I've encountered only a handful of rude riders. Trail users—regardless of their mode of travel—are a peaceful bunch by nature. A little common sense has been exercised by all parties, and now we all play nicely together.

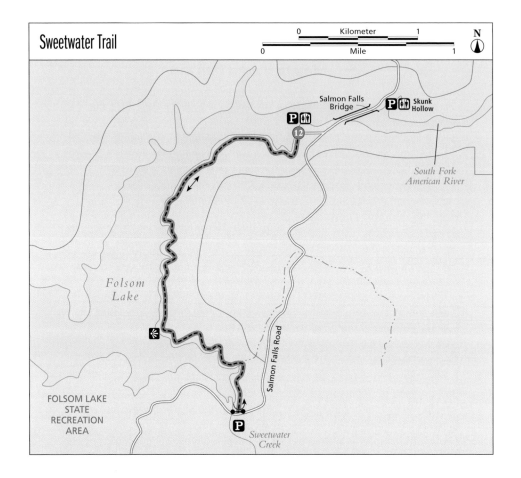

Sweetwater Trail

Salmon Falls
Bridge

Skunk
Hollow

South Fork
American River

Folsom
Lake

FOLSOM LAKE
STATE
RECREATION
AREA

Salmon Falls Road

Sweetwater
Creek

MILES AND DIRECTIONS

0.0 Start at the signed trailhead next to the restroom in the southernmost corner of the parking area. Cross a seasonal stream.

0.6 Cross a second stream, dry in late season.

1.0 Pass a Sweetwater trail marker.

1.1 Pass a trail post. A side trail breaks right to the shoreline. Stay left on the
obvious main track.

1.2 Cross the first of a pair of seasonal stream drainages. The second is at 1.3
miles.

1.6 Lake views open.

1.8 Buoys mark a cove where a large oak provides the only shade. This is a nice spot for a snack or picnic and can be the turnaround point for a shorter hike.

2.1 Cross a culvert in an oak grove.

2.3 Pass a Sweetwater trail marker (lots of poison oak here).

2.4 The trail skirts a tributary of Sweetwater Creek, which has dug its bed into the silt. Cross a metal bridge spanning the creek.

2.5 Reach the end of the singletrack at a Sweetwater sign. Bear left to head up to the small parking area at Salmon Falls Road.

2.7 Arrive at the turnaround at the small parking area off Salmon Falls Road. A gate spans the trail. Retrace your steps to the last junction, at the Sweetwater sign.

2.8 Bear left to explore the meadow if you choose. Otherwise, go right on the Sweetwater Trail to return to the trailhead.

5.6 Arrive back at the trailhead.

HIKE INFORMATION

Local information: Eldorado Hills Chamber of Commerce, 2085 Vine St., Ste. 105, El Dorado Hills 95762; (916) 933-1335; www.eldoradohillschamber.com. The chamber provides information on community activities and businesses.

Camping: Folsom Lake has three developed campgrounds, plus one hike-in environmental campground. The closest camp to the Sweetwater Trail is the Peninsula Campground, which is at the end of Rattlesnake Bar Road and may be closed seasonally. Make reservations by calling (800) 444-7275 or visiting www.reserveamerica.com.

Organizations: The Sweetwater Trail was built by, and is maintained by, the Folsom-Auburn Trail Riders Action Coalition (FATRAC). Visit www.fatrac.org to learn more about this cycling organization.

13

Yolo Bypass Wildlife Area Loop

Follow elevated maintenance roads on a long loop through the 16,700-acre Yolo Bypass Wildlife Area on Sacramento's west side, sharing the wetlands, grasslands and rice fields with countless birds.

Start: At the trailhead in parking lot F
Distance: 4-mile loop
Hiking time: About 2 hours
Difficulty: Easy
Trail surface: Elevated dirt and mown roadways
Best season: Year-round
Other trail users: None. Cyclists are permitted only on the causeway located in the northern part of the wildlife area, between I-80 and the railroad tracks.
Trailhead amenities: Gravel parking area, restrooms, picnic table
Canine compatibility: Dogs not permitted. Within the wildlife area, leashed dogs are allowed on the trails between I-80 and the railroad tracks.
Fees and permits: None

Schedule: Open daily, sunrise to sunset, year-round. Seasonal daylight hours are posted at the entry.
Maps: USGS Sacramento West CA; online at www.yolobasin.org
Trail contact: California Department of Fish and Game, Yolo Bypass Wildlife Area Headquarters, 45211 Yolo CR 32B (Chiles Road), Davis 95618; (530) 757-2461; www .dfg.ca.gov/lands/wa/region3/ yolo/index.html
Other: This route is closed during hunting seasons. Trails in the wetlands area accessed from lots B, C, and D are accessible during hunting seasons.
Special considerations: There is little shade on this route, so avoid hiking during the heat of a summer's day.

Finding the trailhead: From downtown Sacramento head west on I-80 for about 8 miles, through West Sacramento and out toward Davis. Take the E. Chiles Road/Yolo CR 32A exit. Head under the freeway to the signed Vic Fazio Yolo Bypass Wildlife Area entrance. Climb atop the levee, then drop right onto the signed auto tour route at parking lot A. Follow the unpaved auto route south, past lots B and C, for about 1.6 miles to the T junction near parking lot D, with a hunter check-in station. Turn left onto the dirt road and head east toward parking lots H and F, driving up and over the slough. Parking lot F and the trailhead are at the end of the dirt road, 1.4 miles from the hunter check-in station. GPS: N38 31.790'/W121 35.397'

THE HIKE

For decades the levee-bound rice fields and remnants of wetlands on the south side of the interstate on Sacramento's western border were little more than a curiosity for motorists speeding by. Now they are a destination for hikers, birders, and hunters.

The Yolo Bypass Wildlife Area's seasonal and permanent wetlands, grasslands, and riparian zones are also a destination for birdlife of all descriptions, from the commonly seen mallard duck and red-winged blackbird to the more exotic peregrine falcon, great blue heron and Swainson's hawk. It is a major waypoint on the Pacific Flyway, so no matter the season, venturing into the wildlife area will involve bird watching, birdcall, and bird wonder.

The levees that contain ponds and fields in the wildlife area were originally designed for flood control, and their primary purpose remains containment of overflow from the Sacramento River, Putah Creek, and other tributary streams feeding into San Francisco Bay's sprawling delta region. Wildlife and habitat management is another focus and includes agriculture, restoration of wetlands, and limited permitted hunting. The last purpose, which also receives priority and focus, are recreational and educational uses, including hiking trails and guided tours.

A great egret enjoys the cool greenery of a pond at the Yolo Bypass Wildlife Area.

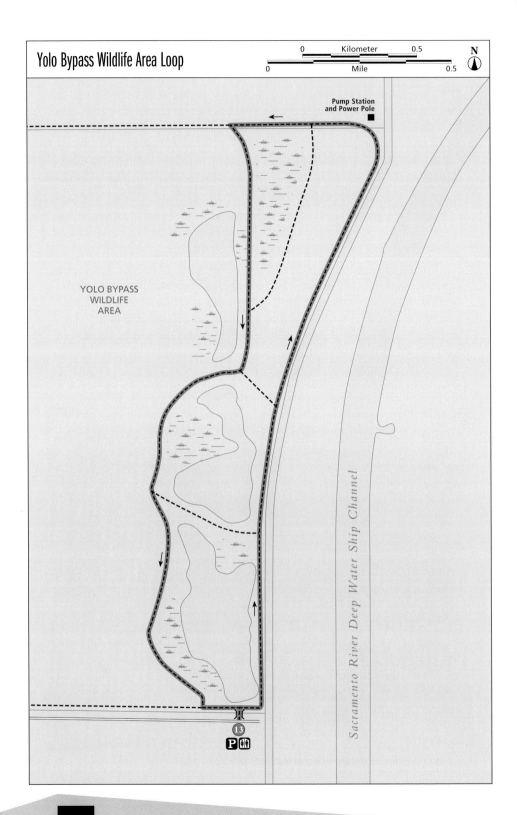

Yolo Bypass Wildlife Area Loop

Pump Station
and Power Pole

YOLO BYPASS
WILDLIFE
AREA

Sacramento River Deep Water Ship Channel

0   Kilometer   0.5

0   Mile   0.5

N

13

P

The wildlife area, which was established by President Bill Clinton in 1997, is owned and operated by the state Department of Fish and Game. Congressman Vic Fazio, for whom the wildlife area is named, worked to ensure that the wetlands restoration and preservation project came to fruition—no small feat considering the divergent interests of the hunters, hikers, flood-control management agencies, businesses, educators, and environmentalists that were (and still are) interested in the project.

Begin by crossing the concrete bridge over the slough. Go right on the wide track, traveling the loop in a counterclockwise direction; you'll return on the path to the left. With sloughs and ponds all around, and water present even in the driest season, the foliage is always lush, even if some of it dries brittle and blond at the end of the dry season. Wildflowers, weeds, and willows crowd the margins, with stands of native sunflowers reaching nearly 5 feet tall in late summer.

The birds are always present, with songbirds, bitterns, and great blue herons camouflaged in the brush; ducks paddling on the ponds and in the calm sloughs; and the occasional raptor surveying the scene from above. The snow egret and great white egret don't hide so well, their white plumage stark against the browns and greens of the landscape. Crickets and dragonflies, as well as peskier blackflies, bees, and wasps, are also present.

The route is flat and easy to travel, following mown roadways perfect for walking and talking. None of the trails or roadways are signed, which can make route-finding a bit of a challenge, but given the wide-open nature of the area, it's fairly simple to stay on track.

Several paths break left from the slough-side track, offering links to shorter loops around the three ponds that are the centerpieces of this loop. Stay right, heading north toward the barely visible interstate. The low hum of cars on the freeway is a constant, but the birds do a great job of drowning it out. The vistas are expansive, given the flatness of the terrain, stretching over wetlands, ponds, grasslands, and rice fields. Signs of civilization—power lines, farm buildings, the straight-line humps of levees—are mostly distant, on the horizon, though at the apex of the loop you'll come in close contact with a pump station and power pole, and an industrial complex dominates the eastern skyline.

The return leg of the loop brings you in closer contact with the ponds and seasonal wetlands. Watch for ducks on open water in the wet season, and a variety of songbirds and shorebirds sheltering in the reeds alongside the ponds. At one point the route slides between the willow-lined shores of two of the ponds, with the foliage offering a natural blind for bird watching.

MILES AND DIRECTIONS

0.0 Start by crossing the concrete bridge. Turn right on the path, traveling the loop in a counterclockwise direction. A wide slough is on the right, and a pond is barely visible through the brush on the left.

0.5 At the unsigned trail junction, stay right on the mown path alongside the slough.

0.9 At the second unsigned trail intersection, stay right again. Two trails branch left, on either side of a waterway that may be dry in late season, presenting an opportunity to shorten the hike.

1.5 Reach a pump station and power pole. Turn left here on the service road, which is lined with willows.

1.8 Pass a junction with a mown path, staying straight (right) on the roadway.

2.0 At a large willow (the only shade in the area), leave the service road and go left on the old mown roadbed, which heads south, back toward the trailhead.

2.5 Trails merge at an unsigned junction. Stay right on the more traveled path.

2.7 Reach a T junction at a slough. Go right on the doubletrack into the willows with ponds on either side.

2.9 Several roads converge at the edge of a field. Go left along the field's edge, then stay right at the junction about 50 yards beyond, continuing south-bound toward the trailhead.

3.2 At the trail junction marked with numbered signs, go left on the unsigned doubletrack that heads southeast.

3.3 Reach another junction marked with numbered signs. Stay straight, continuing south. At the sign for the BLIND, go left on the two-track roadway, with the slough running alongside on the right. The bridge across the slough, and the trailhead, are visible ahead.

4.0 Arrive back at the trailhead.

🌿 **Green Tip:**
Go out of your way to avoid birds and animals that are mating, resting, or taking care of their young.

HIKE INFORMATION

Local information: Sacramento Convention & Visitors Bureau, 1608 I St., Sacramento 95814; (800) 292-2334; http://discovergold.org. Plentiful information about activities and services in the Sacramento region are provided by the chamber.

Local events/attractions: Duck Days is a midwinter festival of educational tours and presentations. Contact the Yolo Basin Foundation (see "Organizations" below) for more information.

Hike tours: Wildlife viewing tours are organized by the Yolo Basin Foundation on the second Sat of each month from Sept to June. For more information call (530) 757-3780 or visit www.yolobasin.org.

Organizations: Yolo Basin Foundation, PO Box 943, Davis 05617; (530) 757-3780; www.yolobasin.org. This nonprofit foundation is dedicated to the stewardship and preservation of Yolo Basin wetlands. It publishes a newsletter, available online, highlighting the people and events that make the basin great.

> *More than 4,000 local schoolchildren, their teachers, and their parents participate in learning activities in the Yolo Bypass Wildlife Area annually.*

A loop through the Yolo Bypass Wildlife Area follows levees bordering ponds and rice paddies that provide habitat for a plethora of birds.

14

Mather Nature Loops

A pair of short loops ramble alongside Mather Lake, offering hikers a chance to stretch their legs, learn about the local habitat, and visit vernal pools in spring.

Start: Trailhead near the dam in Mather Rotary Regional Recreation Area
Distance: 1.5-mile double loop
Hiking time: About 1 hour
Difficulty: Easy
Trail surface: Wide dirt and gravel trails
Best season: Winter and spring to view the vernal pools; fall for color; spring for birds
Other trail users: None
Trailhead amenities: Parking, restrooms, water, tot lot, lawns, trash cans, fishing pier
Canine compatibility: Leashed dogs permitted
Fees and permits: Parking fee
Schedule: Open daily, sunrise to sunset, year-round

Maps: USGS Carmichael CA. Trails around the lake are short and straightforward, so no map is needed.
Trail contact: Sacramento County Regional Parks Department, 4040 Bradshaw Rd., Sacramento 95827; (916) 875-6961; www.msa2.sac county.net/parks
Special considerations: Summer temperatures may preclude use of these trails at midday, and winter rains may render the trails muddy.
Other: Mather Lake is stocked with black bass and trout. No motorized boats are allowed. The vernal pools fill in winter, bloom in Apr and early May, and are gone by late May.

Finding the trailhead: From US 50 take the Sunrise Boulevard exit. Head south on Sunrise Boulevard to Douglas Road and turn right (west). Follow Douglas Road for 1 mile to Zinfandel Drive and turn left (south). Follow Zinfandel Drive for 0.3 mile to the signed park entrance on the left (east). The trailhead for the first loop is on the south side of the dock, behind the gate on the dam; the interpretive loop begins to the left, behind the picnic pavilion. GPS: N38 33.415'/W121 15.572'

THE HIKE

Planes may come and planes may go, but some things stay the same at Mather Field. The sprawling grasslands that insulated this former air force base—a major source of employment and activity during World Wars I and II for a burgeoning Sacramento—are now part of a compact regional park. The meadowlands, along with the lake and its surrounding wetlands, provide space for migrating and resident birds to nest and feed, support rare and fragile creatures in vernal pools, and allow appreciative hikers to walk and observe.

Though suburbia encroaches on all sides, and the roar of aircraft engines and freeway traffic nixes this as a wilderness experience, the abundance of color and wildlife makes a visit more than worthwhile. It's the perfect outing for a family: Mix a hike with fishing, a picnic, a romp on the tot lot . . . or, for older "kids," perhaps a round of golf.

Ducks and geese abide on the lake year-round, but visit during spring or fall if you are interested in species that migrate along the Pacific Flyway. Autumn is lovely, as the foliage of willows, cottonwoods, and other riparian plants around the lake turns to gold. Spring is even more colorful: That's when the vernal pools bloom, blankets of meadowfoam and goldfields thrown across depressions in the grasslands. The display is short-lived, however, with the blooms disappearing within weeks.

The vernal pools also enliven a winter visit to the park. A unique and precious environment, the plants and animals that inhabit the pools are, in many cases, rare and endangered. These include fairy shrimp, which survive the long dry season as cysts, then hatch and reproduce in the brief time the pool is full.

A pair of short trails explores the riparian and vernal habitats of the Mather Rotary Regional Recreation Area.

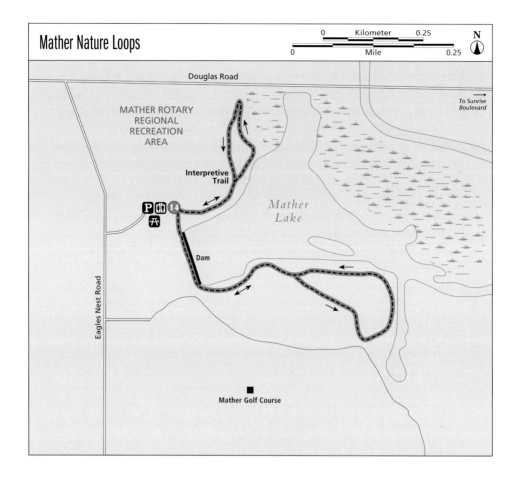

Mather Nature Loops

Douglas Road

MATHER ROTARY REGIONAL RECREATION AREA

Interpretive Trail

Eagles Nest Road

Dam

Mather Lake

To Sunrise Boulevard

Mather Golf Course

Named for World War I test pilot Carl Mather, the airfield at Mather Air Force Base dates back to 1918. It didn't stay open very long: When the war ended, the base was closed. But the advent of World War II prompted its revival, and it continued to operate during the Cold War and the Vietnam War as a training facility for navigators and as a Strategic Air Command base. Military downsizing targeted the facility in the late twentieth century, along with nearby McClellan Airfield. The base closed in 1995, and the property was divided into a county airport and parkland. Development of the 1,600-acre park is ongoing, with a coalition of community groups, including the Audubon Society and the Rotary Club, balancing preservation of open spaces with more intensive uses like ball fields.

The tour of trails around Mather Lake is described beginning with the loop on the south shore, then with the nature trail on the northwest shore. The first loop explores the riparian zone and grasslands on the south side of the lake, with access to waterside picnic sites. The second loop follows a short interpretive trail, where signs describe the area's creatures, from frogs to rodents, and the habitat that nurtures them.

MILES AND DIRECTIONS

0.0 Start behind the gate that blocks vehicle access to the dam. Follow the dam south, with the lake on your left and meadowland to the right.

0.1 At the end of the dam (which borders the fenced Mather Golf Course), go left (east) on the dirt track, dropping through a picnic site.

0.3 The trail splits; stay right (east). At the second split stay right (east) again, heading into the meadow.

0.5 Swing north as the trail approaches the fence that separates the golf course from the natural area. Marshland thick with cattails and reeds borders the route on the right (north), and birdcall emanating from the bush almost overcomes the rumble of traffic.

0.7 The trail loops back on itself along the lakeshore. Retrace your steps back to the trailhead.

1.0 Arrive at the parking area. Pick up the self-guided nature trail on the northwest shore of the lake, passing the fishing pier and a series of benches set in the trees at waterside. You'll also pass an information sign that details the history of Mather Field.

1.1 The nature trail splits. Go right on the lakeside track, following the line of interpretive signs through the riparian thickets.

1.3 The trail merges onto a wider track near a gate that bars access to nearby Douglas Road. Turn left (south) on the gravel road, heading back toward the picnic area through a grassland dotted with adolescent oaks and sycamores.

1.4 Reach the split in the nature trail and, unless you want to do laps, retrace your steps toward the trailhead.

1.5 Arrive back at the trailhead and parking area.

HIKE INFORMATION

Hike tours: Sacramento Splash offers tours of the Mather Field vernal pools during the peak of the wildflower bloom. Visit the website at www.sacsplash.org/our-programs/public-programs/vernal-pool-tours for more information.

Organizations: Sacramento Splash, 4426 Excelsior Rd., Mather 95655; (916) 364-2437; www.sacsplash.org. This nonprofit organization is dedicated to helping Sacramento's schoolchildren better understand their environment.

Honorable Mention

Maidu Regional Park

Another compact parcel in the midst of suburbia, 152-acre Maidu Regional Park is geared toward the ball player, whether soccer or baseball or basketball, with grass fields, batting cages, basketball courts, and plenty of parking for spectators. It also sports a skate park, tot lots, and picnic areas. But hikers are accommodated at the park too. The Maidu Indian Museum features exhibits on the native Nisenan people and a short trail that leads past artifacts. Venture between the museum and the ball fields to explore the small trail system that winds through grasslands and oak groves. The paved path links the soccer complex to the neighborhood; dirt tracks reach into the woods that grow along a stream. The park is located off Rocky Ridge Drive in Roseville. Call (916) 774-5200 for more information, or visit the website at www.roseville.ca.us/parks.

Leave No Trace

Trails in the Sacramento area and neighboring foothills are heavily used year-round. We, as trail users and advocates, must be especially vigilant to make sure our passage leaves no lasting mark. Here are some basic guidelines for preserving trails in the region:

- Pack out all your own trash, including biodegradable items like orange peels. You might also pack out garbage left by less considerate hikers.
- Don't approach or feed any wild creatures—the ground squirrel eyeing your snack food is best able to survive if it remains self-reliant.
- Leave wildflowers, rocks, antlers, feathers, and other treasures where you find them. Removing these items will only take away from the next hiker's experience.
- Avoid damaging trailside soils and plants by remaining on the established route. This is also a good rule of thumb for avoiding poison oak and stinging nettle, common regional trailside irritants.
- Don't cut switchbacks, which can promote erosion.
- Be courteous by not making loud noises while hiking.
- Many of these trails are multiuse, which means you'll share them with other hikers, trail runners, mountain bikers, and equestrians. Generally, hikers yield to equestrians, and mountain bikers yield to all trail users. Familiarize yourself with the proper trail etiquette but use common sense. Often it's easier for a hiker to step aside than for a mountain biker to dismount and move off the path.
- Use outhouses at trailheads or along the trail.
    For more information, visit www.LNT.org.

Shingle Falls drops into the inkwell at its base (Hike 16).

The region north of the Sacramento metropolitan area is fundamentally rural, with small country towns separated by sprawling agricultural parcels, many planted in rice. The defining landmark is the Sutter Buttes, an anomalous eruption of rounded peaks that juts from the valley floor. A landmark visible for miles, the Buttes are on private land, but they form a spectacular backdrop to the public open spaces that surround them.

Fields separating small towns, rivers and creeks, and a historic mining town

The Yuba and Feather Rivers and their tributaries water the region, eventually emptying into the Sacramento River. The twin towns of Yuba City and Marysville straddle the confluence of the two rivers and are the largest communities in the region. The towns offer a variety of amenities, including historic downtown districts that date back to the gold rush days. Yuba City is the Sutter County seat and has been since the mid-1800s.

Trails in this part of the Sacramento Valley are hitched to the area's rivers and creeks, from the braided Feather as it flows through the Bobelaine Audubon Sanctuary to the ponds of the Gray Lodge Wildlife Area. Shingle Falls Dry Creek belies its name, flowing year-round and spilling spectacularly into a deep pool. In the foothills, the historic mining town of Grass Valley offers up Empire Mine State Historic Park: Here the water is underground, having flooded hundreds of miles of underground tunnels after the famed gold mine was closed down.

Directions to trailheads in this region are given from the Sacramento metro area. Marysville and Yuba City are approximately 41 miles (or 50 minutes) north of Sacramento via CA 99 and CA 70. You can access the trails at Bobelaine, Gray Lodge, and Shingle Falls from these routes. Empire Mine State Historic Park is in the foothills northeast of the metro area, and is reached via scenic CA 49.

Hollow-doored concrete buildings stand on the site of the Pennsylvania Mine, one of many mine sites now protected within Empire Mine State Historic Park (Hike 18).

Bobelaine Audubon Sanctuary

Rustic paths lead through a wildlife sanctuary on the banks of the Feather River, where you'll share the trail with foxes, deer, and a complete Audubon guidebook of birds.

Start: At the signed trailhead in the small sanctuary parking lot
Distance: 4.6-mile double loop
Hiking time: About 3 hours
Difficulty: Moderate due to trail length and route-finding challenges
Trail surface: Mowed 10-foot trails, dirt pathways
Best season: Winter, spring, and fall for bird watching; spring for wildflowers; fall for color
Other trail users: None
Trailhead amenities: Small parking area, information kiosk
Canine compatibility: Dogs not permitted
Fees and permits: None
Schedule: Open daily, sunrise to sunset, year-round
Maps: USGS Nicolaus CA; Bobe- laine Audubon Sanctuary map available at the preserve (when the mailbox next to the interpretive board is stocked) and online at www.sacramentoaudubon.org/ bobelainesanctuary.html
Trail contact: Sacramento Audubon Society, PO Box 160694, Sacramento 95816-0694; www .sacramentoaudubon.org. Phone numbers and e-mail addresses for society officials are available on the website.
Special considerations: Remain on trails to avoid contact with poison oak and to protect fragile wildlife habitat.
Other: Bring drinking water. Groups of 10 or more are asked to contact the Sacramento Audubon Society before hitting the trail.

Finding the trailhead: From downtown Sacramento take I-5 north to the CA 70/99 junction. Go right (north) on CA 70/99 for 19.3 miles toward Marysville and Yuba City, staying left on CA 99 where it diverges from CA 70. Pass over the Feather River bridge and continue to Laurel Avenue. Turn right (east) on Laurel Avenue and drive 0.9 mile, past the END sign (the last 0.1 mile is unpaved) to the trailhead parking area. GPS: N38 55.852'/W121 35.441'

Bobelaine Audubon Sanctuary encompasses a long strip of riparian habitat and oak woodland on the western banks of the Feather River. About 2.5 miles in length, a third of a mile wide, and totaling 430 acres, the ecological preserve is relatively small, but with frontage on the river and a wildlife population of amazing variety, it packs a scenic wallop.

Shorebirds, songbirds, and waterbirds all flock to the Bobelaine Audubon Sanctuary, making this a popular destination for birders as well as hikers.

Since this is an Audubon Society site and is located on the Pacific Flyway, you should expect to see a huge number of both resident and migratory birds. And, given its location amid the flat farm fields north of the Sacramento metro area, the wilderness atmosphere of the place is unexpected and appealing.

The Feather River runs broad and unfettered along the boundary of the sanctuary, weaving through sandbars and deposits of river rock, skimmed by bleached-white great egrets and clusters of diving ducks. The bigleaf maples and sycamore trees that thrive in the riparian zone sport leaves of prehistoric size, large enough that you could wear one as a mask, completely hiding your face. Fields of sinuous tule crowd sections of the route and erupt from the trail beds

Wide trails of mown grass wind through the riparian zone along the Feather River in Bobelaine Audubon Sanctuary.

themselves, a bounty that would have kept local Native Americans well stocked in basket-weaving materials.

You'll share the trail with birders carrying binoculars and scopes. Whether you're an enthusiast or not, you'll be hard-pressed not to be charmed and entertained by the kinglets, purple finches, and California towhees that jitterbug through the brush; the green herons that hunker on the riverbanks and on bare tree limbs; and the hawks swinging on thermals overhead. Deer and squirrels scurry through the scrub, and on hot days lizards practice pushups on the paths.

Most of the trail intersections in the sanctuary are marked with signs, but some are not. Coupled with intertwining social trails—stay on the main routes to avoid damaging the ecology and coming into contact with poison oak—the sometimes sparse signage can render route-finding a challenge. Maps may or may not be available at the trailhead, so print one off the website (or keep this guide handy). In a pinch, the information board at the trailhead has a map of the trail system and sanctuary boundaries. Keep the river to the east and stay on the clear, mowed tracks—you may stray from your planned route, but you won't get lost.

The tour describes a loop circling counterclockwise around the sanctuary, incorporating sections of the Oak, Grassland, North, and Center Trails. Begin on the levee, which offers views down onto an orchard on the right (west) and the undeveloped sanctuary, a tangle of wild grapes, figs, willow, and oaks, on the left (east). A parallel trail runs along the foot of the levee; slide down onto this where the grassy face of the levee allows. As you near the 0.5-mile mark, pick up the trail that leads into the sanctuary at a gate, with a sign that prohibits horses, hunting, and fishing in the preserve.

Pick up the South Trail just inside the sanctuary; the trail passes through a gully and meadow before reaching the signed intersection with the Oak and Center Trails. Follow the Oak Trail through the woodland, then branch off onto the Center Trail. The bigleaf maples along this track sport preternaturally large leaves, and a broad meadow opens to the right (east). As you near the 2-mile mark, take the side path that branches right toward the Feather River. The trail stretches across a meadow to a bluff overlooking the waterway, which in late season is broad, dark, clear, and curdled with current. When you have taken in the views, retrace your steps back to the main trail and turn right to meet the Grassland Trail.

The Grassland track narrows as it passes through stands of tule, then curves away from the river through a thicket of encroaching coyote bush. Meet up with the North Trail, which you'll follow to the Otter Trail, which leads back to the Center Trail, which in turn leads back to the levee.

Climb onto the levee and follow the trail back toward the trailhead, enjoying great views across farmlands on the right (west) and placid Lake Crandall on the left (east). The levee trail leads back to the parking area and trailhead.

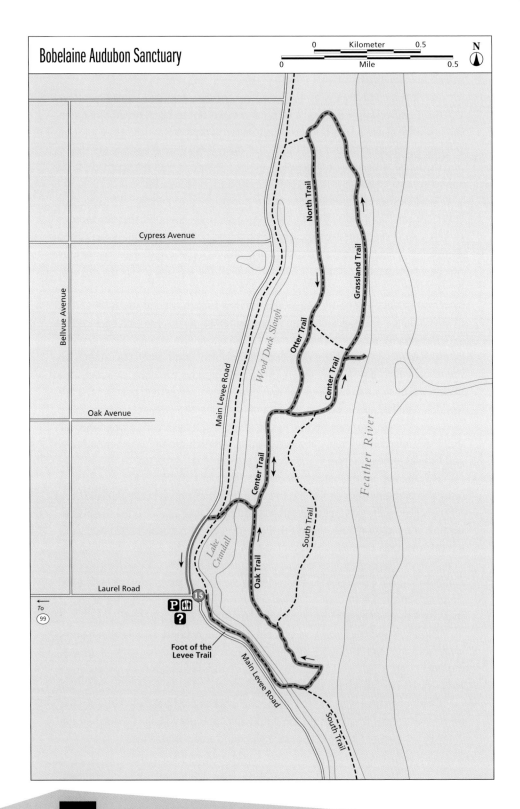

Kilometer
0   0.5
Mile
0   0.5

N

Cypress Avenue

Bellvue Avenue

Oak Avenue

Laurel Road

To
99

Main Levee Road

Wood Duck Slough

North Trail

Grassland Trail

Otter Trail

Center Trail

Feather River

Center Trail

South Trail

Oak Trail

Lake Crandall

15

P

Foot of the
Levee Trail

Main Levee Road

South Trail

MILES AND DIRECTIONS

0.0   Start by passing through the gate and onto the levee, heading right (south). Pick a social trail to follow down onto the parallel trail that runs along the foot of the levee.

0.4   Reach a junction with a trail that drops off the levee and a singletrack trail that breaks left (east) into the preserve proper. Go left (east), around a gate, then right (south) on a singletrack trail.

0.5   At the unmarked trail intersection, go left (east). This is the South Trail. Ignore side trails that wander into the brush.

0.9   Reach the signed trail intersection with the Oak Trail. Go left (north) on the Oak Trail.

1.4   Arrive at the unsigned trail intersection of the Oak Trail and the Center Trail. Stay straight (northeast) on the Center Trail.

1.6   At the unmarked trail junction, stay right (east) on the Center Trail.

1.9   Take the side trail that branches right (east) to the riverside. Check out the river, then return to the main trail and turn right (north).

2.2   Meet the signed Grassland Trail. Go right on the Grassland Trail.

2.7   The Grassland Trail curves away from the river.

2.9   Reach the unmarked junction with the North Trail. Go left (south) on the first trail (the second trail is in a large clearing and leads to the Foot of the Levee Trail).

3.6   Arrive at the junction with the Otter Trail. Go right (southwest) on the singletrack Otter Trail.

4.0   Arrive at the signed junction of the Otter Trail and the Center Trail. Go right (south) on the wide Center Trail.

4.2   At the trail intersection stay right (west) on the unsigned Center Trail. The levee rises ahead.

4.3   Pass the gate and climb onto the levee. Turn left (south), heading back toward the trailhead. A parallel trail runs along the foot of the levee, but the high road offers better views.

4.6   Drop off the levee to the trailhead and parking area.

HIKE INFORMATION

Local information: Yuba-Sutter Chamber of Commerce, 1300 Franklin Rd., Yuba City 95993; (530) 743-6501; www.yubasutterchamber.com. Find information about the Yuba City/Marysville area and local events through the chamber.

Hike tours: The Sacramento Audubon Society offers periodic tours of the Bobelaine sanctuary and other birding sites in the Sacramento Valley and beyond. Check out the website at www.sacramentoaudubon.org for more information and a schedule of field trips.

Citizen Scientists for the Birds

Birds are bellwethers of a healthy environment. Populations may be adversely impacted by environmental and habitat degradation, whether by climate change, the use of pesticides, or the transformation of a wetland into a shopping mall.

Tracking birds through time, using annual bird counts, is key to determining whether populations are flourishing or diminishing, and thus if the environments they rely on are healthy. Citizen scientists are crucial to gathering data during bird counts. You don't need to be a birder to help out: Minimum requirements are the ability to count and the willingness to stay outdoors for the better part of a day.

A pair of annual bird counts—the Christmas Bird Count and the Great Backyard Bird Count—offer hikers and others the chance to be citizen scientists and to help ensure that the environment remains healthy for those on the wing as well as those on foot. Learn more about the Christmas Bird Count at http://birds.audubon.org/christmas-bird-count. More information about the Great Backyard Bird Count is at www.birdsource.org/gbbc.

Shingle Falls

Ramble through rolling woodlands in the foothills east of Marysville to a vigorous waterfall in a small gorge on Dry Creek. A swimming hole and sunny rocks below the falls are perfect for a swim and sunbathing on a hot summer's day.

Start: At the gated bridge at the end of Spenceville Road
Distance: 5.2-mile lollipop (includes exploration of trails around falls)
Hiking time: 2 to 3 hours
Difficulty: Moderate due to trail length and the steepness of trails around the falls
Trail surface: Well-maintained gravel road, dirt singletrack
Best season: Spring for wildflowers; summer and early fall for swimming
Other trail users: Equestrians, hunters in season
Trailhead amenities: Parking
Canine compatibility: Leashed dogs permitted
Fees and permits: None
Schedule: Open daily, sunrise to sunset, year-round. The area closes to all public use for nine days beginning the last Saturday in March, except to those individuals possessing a special permit issued by the California Department of Fish and Game.
Maps: USGS Camp Far West CA and Wolf CA; online at www.dfg .ca.gov/lands/wa/region2/spence ville.html
Trail contact: Oroville/Spenceville Wildlife Area, California Department of Fish and Game, 945 Oro Dam Blvd. W., Oroville, CA 95965; (530) 538-2236; www.dfg.ca.gov/ lands/wa/region2/spenceville .html
Special considerations: Hunting is allowed in the Spenceville Wildlife Area from Sept 1 to Jan 31. If hiking in hunting season, be sure to wear bright colors, such as blaze orange.

Finding the trailhead: From Sacramento head north on I-5 to CA 99. Continue north on CA 99 for about 12 miles to CA 70. Make a slight right onto northbound CA 70 toward Marysville. Travel another 22 miles to the Feather River Road exit. Go right (east) on Feather River Road to the first intersection, then right again onto North Beale Road (no obvious street signs at these junctions). Travel 0.2 mile to a signalized arterial, and go left to continue on North Beale Road. Go another 0.8 mile on North Beale to Hammonton-Smartville Road. Go left on Hammonton-Smartville Road, staying right at the signalized Y intersection with Simpson Lane, which leads to downtown Marysville. Drive for about 15 miles to the intersection with Chuck Yeager Road. Go right on Chuck Yeager Road for about 4 miles to Waldo Road (no sign). Go left on Waldo Road, a graded dirt road, for nearly 2 miles, across the single-lane bridge, to Waldo Junction and the signed intersection with Spenceville Road. Go left on Spenceville Road, traveling about 2.3 miles to the parking area on the left, past the camping area and near the road's end. The trailhead is at the yellow gate at the old stone bridge; a small sign identifies the Fairy Falls Trail. GPS: N39 06.824'/W121 16.245'

THE HIKE

They are Shingle Falls according to the US Geological Survey, Fairy Falls on trail signs, and Beale Falls in some printed and online guides. Being "also known as" may create some confusion, but no matter what you call them, these falls are a stunning destination.

No worries about confusion getting to the falls. They are reached via well-maintained wildlife area service roads, which are perfect in width and grade for family outings, with the option of taking an engaging, well-signed singletrack for the last mile. A web of social trails leads from the access road to the top of the falls—and to the creek below the spill, where a swimming hole awaits. These smaller trails may be challenging in steepness and footing, especially for little ones, but standing at the overlook and watching the whitewater dive into the inkwell below is ample reward for your effort.

The trail begins at the site of the Spenceville mine. For more than fifty years copper and other mineral resources were removed from the site. After the mine became part of the Spenceville Wildlife Area, the California Department of Fish and Game (DFG) and the California Department of Conservation (DOC) worked to reclaim the land so that its residual toxicity would not pose significant danger to the fish populations in Dry Creek—or threaten the well-being of other critters in the area, including humans. The result is what you see today: essentially nothing, except the stone bridges that aid stream crossings at the trailhead, a chain-link fence, and low-key signage that indicates the area is closed. The mitigation was so successful that the DOC earned the Governor's Environmental and Economic Leadership Award for its work.

As with other wildlife areas under the purview of the DFG, hunting and fishing are permitted in the area, as is grazing. The terrain is ideal for both. Rolling hills support a healthy blue oak–gray pine woodland, home to deer and other game such as wild turkeys. Open meadows provide ample forage for cattle. The grasslands are often cropped close, but where they aren't (and even after they've been grazed), wildflowers bloom in profusion. Encompassing almost 12,000 acres, there is plenty of space for all users to enjoy the wildlife area without bumping into one another.

The trail begins by crossing the stone bridge over Dry Creek, then heads right at the fence line on the dirt roadway, crossing two smaller bridges over side streams.

Follow the road up into the hills. A couple of prominent side trails diverge from the main trail in the first 0.5 mile, the first heading north through a gate, and the second dropping south from the roadway into the creek drainage (neither is signed). Stay on the dirt roadway at both. Beyond these the route is straightforward and marked with signs for Fairy Falls, so there is no chance of straying.

After a long, gentle climb, with scattered oaks offering scanty shade on hot summer days, the trail hooks sharply right at a white gate (a FAIRY FALLS sign points the way). Pass a second white gate, then climb through a sloping meadowland, with views stretching down into the Dry Creek drainage and north across more rolling pastureland into the foothills.

A cattle guard spans the road at the hilltop. You have a choice here: You can either follow the trail to the right or the road beyond the cattle guard to the left. Both meet within sight at the edge of the woods. At the second signed trail junction,

A scenic stretch of trail leads through remote pastureland on the way to Shingle Falls.

Shingle Falls

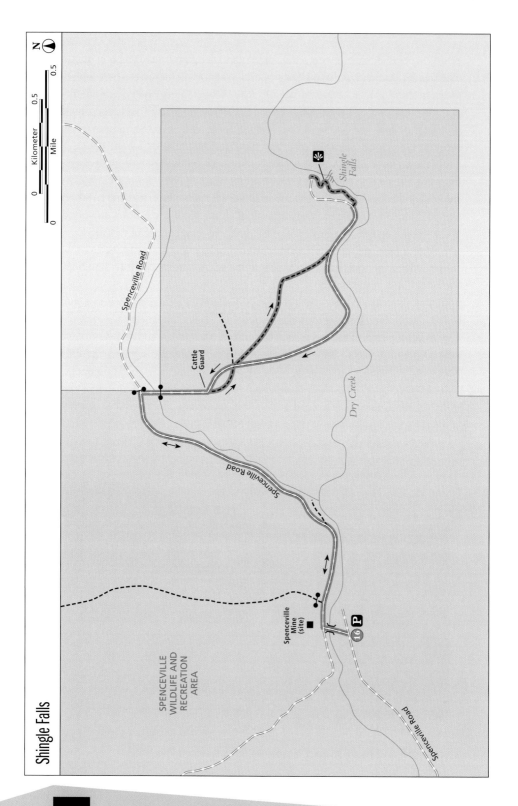

you again have a choice: The described route heads up on singletrack into the oaks and returns via the roadway to the right. The road is signed for Upper Falls and the trail for Fairy Falls, but again, the falls are one and the same. Take the trail signed for Fairy Falls, climbing into the woodland.

The singletrack is mildly challenging, with occasional downed trees forcing hikers onto social trails that skirt the obstacles. It dips through several drainages, then traverses a grassy hillside before hitching up with the dirt roadway. Go left on the road, which runs alongside Dry Creek, now rollicking in its rock-bottomed bed. A riparian corridor shades the waterway, thick with brambles, poison oak, and maples that fire yellow and orange in late fall.

After passing a streamside clearing, the roadway hitches uphill. A use trail breaks right just before a gate, away from the road and down toward the creek, offering access to a large swimming hole fed by two short falls, each no higher than 2 or 3 feet.

A web of use trails climbs the hillside between the swimming hole and the falls themselves. These are steep and winding, with rocky footing, but are easy to follow. The paths merge onto a narrow track running alongside the rickety chain-link fence that separates hikers from the 100-foot drop into the steep-walled chasm below the falls. The fence looks like it could be pushed over with a gentle shove, and certainly can be climbed, but take care to stay on the safe side of the barrier. Though a long jump into the chocolate waters of the inkwell may look inviting to an adventurous soul, it's better to approach from below and simply observe from above.

The falls themselves are a stair-step spill and run year-round, though they are fullest in spring when swollen with snowmelt, or after rainstorms begin in the fall. The second drop is the longest, at least 50 feet and perhaps more. The inkwell gives the impression of bottomlessness, which makes it as mysterious as the falls are invigorating.

Once you've cooled your heels in the swimming hole and enlivened your senses at the falls overlook, return to the roadway, which you will follow back to the trailhead. Stay left then right on the roadway where the trail meets the narrow Fairy Falls path, and make a gentle climb back to the upper trail junction and then to the cattle guard on the hilltop. From there, retrace your steps to the trailhead.

MILES AND DIRECTIONS

0.0   Start by crossing the stone bridge with the yellow gate. On the far side of the bridge, turn right and follow the dirt roadway over two smaller bridges.

0.1   Pass a singletrack trail behind a gate on the left. Stay right on the service road.

0.5 At the unsigned junction, stay left on the roadway. The path to the right drops into a blackberry hedge along a tributary stream.

1.2 At the first white gate, a FAIRY FALLS trail sign directs you right. Pass a second white gate and head up through the meadowland.

1.5 Reach a cattle guard and go right on the trail. You can also follow the roadway down to the next trail junction.

1.7 At the five-way junction, a trail sign indicates that Fairy Falls is 1 mile ahead via a singletrack path, and that Upper Falls is 0.9 mile distant via the roadway. Take the signed FAIRY FALLS trail.

2.2 The trail ends on the dirt road. Go left on the broad track.

2.4 Take the well-worn use trail that breaks right, toward the creek, just before a twisted open gate. This leads down to the swimming hole.

2.6 Wander up via social trails to the falls overlook. Check out the falls and basin below, then pick a social trail to follow back to the service road, and retrace your steps to the junction with the Fairy Falls singletrack and the service road. Stay left on the service road, which winds up to the cattle guard on the hilltop. From here, retrace your steps to the trailhead.

5.2 Arrive back at the trailhead.

HIKE INFORMATION

Local information: Yuba-Sutter Chamber of Commerce, 1300 Franklin Rd., Yuba City 95993; (530) 743-6501; www.yubasutterchamber.com. Find information about the Yuba City / Marysville area and local events through the chamber.

Camping: A rustic campground is about 0.5 mile from the trailhead. Camping is permitted from Sept 1 through the end of the spring turkey hunting season. Visit www.dfg.ca.gov/lands/wa/region2/spenceville.html for more information.

> **Green Tip:**
> *When you just have to go, dig a hole 6 to 8 inches deep and at least 200 feet from water, camps, and trails. Carry a ziplock bag to carry out your toilet paper, or use a natural substitute such as lichen or leaves instead (but not poison oak!). Fill the hole with soil and cover with natural materials when you're done.*

Gray Lodge Wildlife Area

Thousands of migrating and resident waterfowl forage, rest, and nest in the restored wetlands of Gray Lodge Wildlife Area, on the north side of the Sutter Buttes. Two trails, both featuring observation blinds (and one being interpretive), wind through the complex of ponds and marshes that offer the birds shelter and sustenance throughout the year.

Start: At the wildlife area's parking lot 14
Distance: 2.25-mile loop
Hiking time: 1 to 2 hours
Difficulty: Easy
Trail surface: Gravel levee roads, wheelchair-accessible paved path
Best season: Spring and fall, during migration seasons
Other trail users: None
Trailhead amenities: Parking, restrooms, information signboard, picnic tables, self-serve fee station
Canine compatibility: Leashed dogs permitted
Fees and permits: Parking fee
Schedule: Open daily, sunrise to sunset, year-round
Maps: USGS Pennington CA; maps and nature trail guides available at information kiosk at trailhead
Trail contact: California Department of Fish and Game, Gray Lodge Wildlife Area, 3201 Rutherford Rd., Gridley 95948; (530) 846-7505 (naturalist office), (530) 846-7500 (general information); www.dfg.ca.gov/lands/wa/region2/graylodge
Other: Visit the tiny exhibit room, located near the entrance to parking lot 14. You'll find fine examples of taxidermy inside—birds of the marsh great and small, as well as other residents including beavers, muskrats, and weasels. A 3-mile auto tour route also begins at parking lot 14.
Special considerations: Travel as lightly and quietly as you can so that you don't startle the wildlife. Also keep in mind that the trail described is only a small segment of the more than 70 miles of trails located within the wildlife area. Additional options are open to hikers during the spring and summer months. Trail closures are subject to the needs of wildlife, which change with the season, food availability and local conditions. Check online or by calling for more information about whether longer routes are open at the time of your visit.

17

Finding the trailhead: From Sacramento head north on I-5 to CA 99. Go 44 miles north on CA 99 to Live Oak, where a sign for the Gray Lodge Wildlife Area directs you left onto Pennington Road. Follow Pennington Road for 8.1 miles to the signed junction with Almond Orchard Road (also Pennington Road) and turn right. Follow Almond Orchard / Pennington Road for 1.6 miles to the signed entrance to the wildlife area on the left. Turn left on Rutherford Road (the park road) and go 2.4 miles to parking lot 14. The trailhead is in the southeast corner of the lot. GPS: N39 19.400'/W121 50.319'

THE HIKE

On a sunny day in early November, the marshes of Gray Lodge Wildlife Area clamor. Rafts of ducks paddle on the ponds, too many to count. When they take off, their wings thump the surface, sounding like an old motor turning over. In the reeds the songbirds sing, but they are well camouflaged—ubiquitous little brown birds whose identities typically elude the amateur birder. Acres of wetland north of the interpretive trail observation deck are blanketed with hundreds—maybe thousands—of geese, ducks, swans, and sandhill cranes, a gray and brown and white patchwork of wings and water.

Walk slowly and silently, and the resting birds won't be disturbed. Many are making a long migration along the Pacific Flyway, some traveling thousands of miles from summer territories in the far north to winter grounds down south. Gray Lodge, with its abundant water and forage, is the perfect way station.

The birds are easily spooked. One group of ducks, sunning on a sandy island amid the reeds, senses danger and takes flight, squawking warnings into the clear blue sky. Those ducks set off another collection of ducks, which sets off another, which sets off the geese, which sets off the cranes . . . and before you know it, the air is turbulent with wing beats and raucous cries of alarm—and, quite possibly, scolding. The cacophony may take a while to subside, and the tongue-lashing will follow you as you retreat.

This tour of the wildlife area, which takes in two of its trails, begins on the Flyway Loop Trail. A good gravel levee-top road, bordered by a slough and edged with reeds and sedges, stretches south toward the Sutter Buttes, an island of distinctive peaks stranded in the flats of the Sacramento Valley. Near the 0.5-mile mark, trail signs direct you west, along a second levee road and past the Betty Adamson Observation Hide, a cement-block structure with a bay of windows looking out over the wetlands. Benches and counters have been installed inside the hide, which aid birders viewing the wildlife, making notes, and referring to field guides. The birds remain undisturbed, chirping and quacking and crowing and singing outside like a bunch of elementary school kids in a cafeteria at lunchtime.

Cross the auto tour road to reach a second blind, this one named for Harry Adamson. The same amenities await, only with a different aspect over a different pond. From the second blind the levee-top trail continues north, wedged between ponds and sloughs, to a hub where levees and sloughs meet. Follow the signed Flyway Loop Trail to the east, again bounded by water on both sides, and with great Sutter Butte views to the right (south).

The Flyway Loop Trail intersects the paved, wheelchair- and stroller-accessible interpretive Wetland Discovery Trail amid towering cottonwoods. Two more informal viewing platforms can be accessed from the interpretive trail. The first is atop a little rise, and the blind consists of reeds that have been woven together. The second is the viewing platform that faces north, open to the birds, where being careful and quiet is paramount.

Returning to parking lot 14 from the last blind, a triad of benches offers one last opportunity to gaze out over a pond before arriving back at the trailhead.

The quiet waters of Gray Lodge Wildlife Area, sheltered by the rugged Sutter Buttes, are calming for migratory fowl and hikers alike.

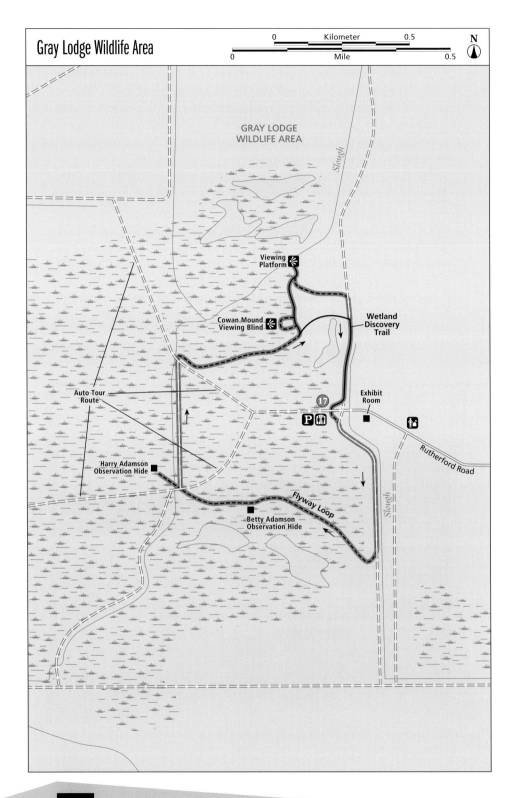

Gray Lodge Wildlife Area

0   Kilometer   0.5

0   Mile   0.5

N

GRAY LODGE
WILDLIFE AREA

Slough

Viewing
Platform

Cowan Mound
Viewing Blind

Wetland
Discovery
Trail

Auto Tour
Route

17

Exhibit
Room

P

Harry Adamson
Observation Hide

Rutherford Road

Betty Adamson
Observation Hide

Flyway Loop

Slough

MILES AND DIRECTIONS

0.0   Start on the Flyway Loop Trail, following the gravel levee-top road.

0.4   At the signed junction, go right on the Flyway Loop.

0.75   Arrive at the Betty Adamson Observation Hide. Duck inside to check it out, then continue on the levee-top trail.

0.9   Reach parking lot 18, and cross the auto tour road. The Harry Adamson hide is on the other side, down a side trail to the left. Visit, then continue north on the straight-shot levee road.

1.25   Several levee roads meet at slough gates that are clustered in a circle. The auto tour route crosses here, too. Follow the signs around the hub to a levee road signed as the hiking trail, heading northeast. About 20 steps beyond, go right again.

1.6   Meet the paved Wetland Discovery interpretive trail near post 7. Go left.

Ducks take flight from a pond in Gray Lodge Wildlife Area, with the Sutter Buttes forming a smoky backdrop.

1.7 Take a short unpaved detour to the Cowan Mound viewing blind, which is reached via a short flight of stairs. The unpaved trail loops back to the paved route.

1.9 Go left onto the short trail that leads to the viewing platform. Check out the show, then return to the Wetland Discovery Trail and go left. The trail is now dirt.

2.0 Meet a levee road and go right, as the sign directs.

2.1 Rejoin the paved trail. Go left, back toward the trailhead parking area.

2.25 Pass benches overlooking a last pond, then arrive back at the trailhead.

HIKE INFORMATION

Local information: Yuba-Sutter Chamber of Commerce, 1300 Franklin Rd., Yuba City 95993; (530) 743-6501; www.yubasutterchamber.com. Find information about the Yuba City / Marysville area and local events through the chamber.

Local events/attractions: The Sutter Buttes, those tempting mountains just south of the Gray Lodge Wildlife Area, can only be explored as part of guided hikes offered by the Middle Mountain Foundation. Call (530) 755-3568 or visit www.middlemountain.org for more information.

Hike tours: Guided tours along the interpretive Wetland Discovery Trail to the viewing platform are offered on weekends throughout the year. No reservations are necessary. Rain cancels. Contact the Gray Lodge Wildlife Area's naturalist office at (530) 846-7505 or visit the website at www.dfg.ca.gov/lands/wa/region2/graylodge/events.html for more information.

Camping: There is a trailer campground at the Gray Lodge Wildlife Area, but use is restricted to the waterfowl season. Contact the wildlife area at (530) 846-7500 or visit www.dfg.ca.gov/lands/wa/region2/graylodge for more information.

Keep on Hiking!

The route described here is only a small segment of the more than 70 miles of trails located within the wildlife area. Additional options are open to hikers during the spring and summer months. Trail closures are subject to the needs of wildlife, which change with the season, food availability, and local conditions. Check online or by calling for more information about whether longer routes are open at the time of your visit.

Empire Mine State Historic Park

Beneath your feet, 367 miles of carefully constructed tunnels wind through the ore beds of the Empire Mine. Aboveground, Empire Mine State Historic Park maintains a much smaller system of trails that, instead of burrowing through rock, winds through a mature mixed evergreen forest and accesses remnants of California's gold rush legacy.

Start: At the signed trailhead at the south end of parking lot

Distance: 3.9-mile double loop

Hiking time: 2 to 3 hours

Difficulty: Moderate due to some hill climbing

Trail surface: Dirt and gravel paths, dirt roadway

Best season: Spring and fall

Other trail users: Mountain bikers, equestrians

Trailhead amenities: Large paved parking lot and picnic facilities at the trailhead proper. Restrooms, information, and trail maps are available in the visitor center.

Canine compatibility: Leashed dogs permitted

Fees and permits: Use of the trails is free, but tours of the Bourn cottage and grounds, as well as admission to the museum, require a fee. There is no charge to check out the visitor center and museum.

Schedule: Trails and visitor center are open daily, 10 a.m. to 5 p.m., year-round; closed Christmas Day, New Year's Day, and Thanksgiving. The gift shop is operated by Empire Mine Association volunteers and hours vary.

Maps: USGS Grass Valley CA; online at www.parks.ca.gov/?page_id=25137; available for a small fee at gift shop in visitor center

Trail contact: Empire Mine State Historic Park, 10791 E. Empire St., Grass Valley 95945; (530) 273-8522; www.empiremine.org

Other: The small museum inside the center includes a scale model of the Empire Mine and adjacent mines, as well as collections of mining paraphernalia and precious and semiprecious stones and metals. Be sure to purchase the interpretive guide and map, which identifies sites along the Hardrock Trail.

Special considerations: Some of the trails on Osborn Hill were undergoing renovation when this guide was researched in 2011. Though some rerouting may occur, necessitated by mitigation of toxic mine wastes, trails will essentially cover the same ground. Exact mileages may be different, signage may be upgraded, and other improvements may be in place at the time of your visit.

Finding the trailhead: From Sacramento head west on I-80 for about 24 miles to the exit for CA 49 (Placerville / Grass Valley) in Auburn. Go left (north) on CA 49 for 22 miles to the Empire Street exit. Follow Empire Street right for 1.3 miles (it becomes E. Empire Street) to the park entrance and parking lot on the right. GPS: N39 12.423′/W121 02.737′

THE HIKE

To get an idea of the amazing catacomb that exists under your feet when you hike at Empire Mine State Historic Park, spend some time in the visitor center. The displays are fascinating and informative, but it's the scale model of the mine's guts—and tangled intestines are an apt description—that will blow your mind. The woodland above does not begin to hint at the complex man-made maze below, but knowing that a labyrinth weaves through the depths is a unique and provocative enhancement to a walk in this park.

The main attraction in Empire Mine State Historic Park is the estate of the Bourn family, which made its fortune with the Empire. William Bourn Sr. arrived in San Francisco seeking riches, like the rest of the forty-niners, and got lucky (unlike many of his fellow argonauts) when he acquired what would turn out to be, literally and figuratively, a gold mine. He also prospered from his interests in the Comstock Lode, which spurred a silver boom on the other side of the Sierra in Nevada.

His son, William Bourn Jr., took over the Empire in 1878 and advanced the family fortune. But the younger Bourn had other interests as well, including serving as president of the San Francisco Gas Company (predecessor to today's Pacific Gas & Electric Company, primary provider to much of northern California). Bourn Jr. was also fond of grand housing: His Empire Cottage is hardly a cottage (a tour is well worth the price of admission); Greystone, his home in St. Helena, is a Wine Country showcase; and his residence outside San Francisco, Filoli (a public site maintained by the National Trust for Historic Preservation), boasts a ballroom where more than 200 ounces of gold leaf from the Empire Mine was used as decoration.

In addition to the Bourn home and surrounding grounds, Empire Mine State Historic Park encompasses almost 800 acres of prime foothills real estate, with a couple of trail systems exploring the mixed coniferous and oak woodlands. This double loop explores the Hardrock and Osborn Hill areas. If you'd like to see more, check out the trails on Union Hill.

A word about route-finding: Mining is a necessary but toxic business, and some of the terrain covered by this hike bears evidence of this toxicity. If a section of trail is posted for mitigation, please take the recommended detours.

Begin on the east edge of the parking lot adjacent to the mining yard, with its rusting, picturesque equipment protected behind a stone wall. The trail heads south and splits almost immediately: Head right toward Penn Gate on the service road, passing the A-frame and following the gravel road down into the woods. The left fork leads to Union Hill.

Enveloped almost immediately in the scent of the surrounding pines, the trail also promptly immerses you in mine remnants. Rusting remains from the Orleans mine and stamp mill, which competed with the Empire Mine until the Empire absorbed it, litter the forest floor—coils of cable and piles of metal scrap. Signs indicate points of interest and also the route to Wolf Creek and Osborn Hill beyond.

Wolf Creek is a placid little stream, flowing through a deep, dark green woodland. In the hollow the trees are more mixed, with some broad-leafed species of oak and maple giving the forest depth and color. This is a great spot to reconnoiter: If you want a really short hike, retrace your steps to the trailhead. A longer loop keeps you on the Hardrock Trail, which heads out toward Penn Gate. The longest option, described here, takes in Osborn Hill before heading out to Penn Gate and then back to the trailhead.

Heading up the Osborn Hill Trail, described traveling clockwise, you will pass a couple of intersections with paths to the Prescott Hill Mine Trail, which break off to the left. The Prescott mine site itself is just off the Osborn trail; its tailings piles are mounded to the left. The legacy of those tailings was in evidence at the junction

The flotsam and jetsam of the Orleans mine and stamp mill lie just off the trail in Empire Mine State Historic Park.

just beyond the Prescott Hill mine, where in 2011 signs warned hikers out of an area contaminated with arsenic, lead, and manganese. The site may be mitigated by the time of your hike, but again, be aware that trail diversions will occur when park officials determine a detour is necessary for safety.

Continue the gentle climb to the power line, where trails collide in the clearing. Take the middle track (unsigned in 2011), which continues up into the woods. The trail to the left leads out to Osborn Hill Road, whose road noise spills into the woods along this stretch. Hiking uphill, a couple of left turns lead to a switchback with a fenced-off mine adit tucked in the crook of its elbow. A bit more climbing leads to the top of the hill, where you go left to visit the modern remnants of the Conlon Mine, near the park's boundary alongside Osborn Hill Road.

From the Conlon Mine site, head downhill on the return leg of the Osborn Hill Trail. Construction and trail work was under way in 2011; the exact alignment of the downhill leg may vary when you visit. Regardless, the downhill stretch begins by running along the highline of Osborn Hill. A sign indicates a scenic overlook, but the manzanita has grown so tall and thick you'll have a hard time taking in the views.

Drop to the power line, then continue down through the woods to close the loop at the junction above Wolf Creek. Back in the hollow, go left on the Hardrock Trail toward Penn Gate, following a broad trail/roadway shaded by overarching stands of bigleaf maple. This is a lovely stretch, with blackberry, broom, and poison oak (negative qualities aside, a handsome shrub or vine) mingling on the verge and the scent of incense cedar strong in the air.

The Hardrock narrows to singletrack at a trail sign that directs you right. Cross a diversion dam and continue alongside a fence that encloses an area protected to preserve its historic significance and artifacts. The Hardrock ends at the Pennsylvania Mine, a large clearing with several concrete structures along the right side. Penn Gate, with a parking area and information sign, is just beyond.

The Empire Street Trail, which takes you back to the trailhead, begins behind the Pennsylvania Mine structures. The narrow, unsigned singletrack climbs into the woods, skirts a historic mule corral, and passes a junction with the WYOD Loop Trail before paralleling noisome Empire Street.

The last leg of the trail runs alongside busy Empire Street and skirts the Magenta Drain settling ponds, which help mitigate damage from mining activities. Cross a park service road: The path, wedged between the stone fence protecting the Bourn estate grounds and the roadway, leads directly back to the trailhead.

Empire Building (In Brief)

It all started in 1850, when enterprising gold seekers sunk "coyote holes"—20 to 40 feet deep—to extract the riches promised by the discovery of gold-bearing quartz in present-day Grass Valley. More than a century later, the deepest point in the Empire Mine complex was 11,000 feet belowground. In this part of gold country, the men went as deep as the Sierra Nevada are high.

In the end the underground workings of the Empire and its forty-eight companion mines encompassed 5 square miles and more than 360 miles of shaft. In addition to the maze of shafts and tunnels, a dam was constructed down below, to prevent water from flowing from the neighboring Bullion Mine into the Empire. The water backed up instead into the Bullion and eventually forced its closure.

Though travel in the mine would later be improved by rail and motor, at first men and muck moved up and down the shaft in buckets. Cornish men, called "the world's best hard rock miners," were employed at the Empire and its sister operations, starting as young as age seven, according to displays in the Empire Mine State Historic Park museum.

The mine complex encompassed all aspects of ore processing, from blasting it out of the ground to crushing it and running it through the stamp mill, where it was washed with water and quicksilver. The quicksilver bonded to the gold and made it sink into sand, where it could be more easily extracted. Cyanide was also used in the refining process, hence the toxicity of the waste products from the mine. Retort was the last step, where the mercury was removed and the gold "sponge" that remained melted into ingots.

The production record of the mine is astounding: About 5.6 million ounces of gold, worth an estimated $40 million, was extracted from the earth over the one-hundred-year life of the mine.

The mine ceased operation in 1956, and the shafts and tunnels are now filled with water.

Wallace Stegner's Pulitzer Prize–winning novel, **Angle of Repose,** *describes the lives of several generations of a mining family. A fabulous read, the book takes you to the mines of New Almaden in San Jose, as well as to mines in Leadville, Colorado; Michoacan, Mexico; and rural Idaho. Stegner's protagonist, Lyman Ward, speaks to the reader from the mining town of Grass Valley, site of the Empire.*

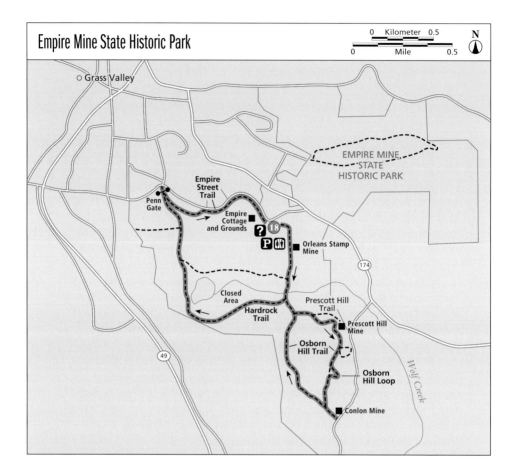

Empire Mine State Historic Park

MILES AND DIRECTIONS

0.0 Start at the signed trailhead at the east side of the parking area, heading south. At the trail Y just beyond the gate, stay right, following signs for Penn Gate.

0.1 A trail sign directs you left down a paved road that quickly becomes gravel again.

0.25 Pass the Orleans Stamp Mine. A series of trail junctions follows. Remain on the signed Hardrock Trail toward Penn Gate, staying left at the first junction, left at the second, and then right to cross the creek.

0.3 Cross Wolf Creek. Head straight (uphill) on the signed Osborn Hill Trail. The start of the Osborn loop is less than 0.1 mile up from the creek; stay left to travel in a clockwise direction.

0.5 Pass the first junction with the Prescott Hill Mine Trail, staying right on the Osborn Hill Trail.

0.7 At the second junction with the Prescott Hill Mine Trail, continue again on the Osborn Hill Trail. The intersection with the Prescott Crosscut Trail is about 30 yards farther; again, remain on the Osborn Hill Trail.

0.8 Arrive at the power-line clearing. Take the middle trail (unsigned) uphill; the left-hand trail leads out to Osborn Hill Road.

0.9 At the unsigned junction, go left onto the dirt roadway. A short distance uphill, go left again onto the gravel path. Switchback around the fenced-off mine adit.

1.0 At the unsigned intersection, stay left.

1.1 Reach the top of Osborn Hill. Go left to visit the Conlon Mine site.

1.2 Arrive at the Conlon Mine site. After exploring, retrace your steps to the previous trail intersection.

1.3 Back at the junction, stay straight and downhill to continue the loop. A sign indicates the Hardrock Trail lies ahead.

1.6 Drop to a second junction with the Prescott Crosscut Trail at the power-line clearing. Continue downhill on the signed loop trail.

1.8 An unsigned trail merges; continue downhill on the Osborn Hill Trail.

1.9 Close the loop and drop to the junction with the Hardrock Trail in the Wolf Creek drainage. Go left on the Hardrock Trail toward Penn Gate.

2.4 Where an unsigned trail merges, remain on the Hardrock Trail. Less than 0.1 mile farther, go right on the signed Hardrock, which narrows to singletrack and crosses a diversion dam.

2.8 The fence surrounding the historic area ends.

2.9 At the junction with the trail to Stacey Lane, stay right on the signed trail to Penn Gate.

3.1 Pass the Pennsylvania Mine buildings and reach Penn Gate. Pick up the Empire Street Trail, a narrow unmarked singletrack that begins behind the mine buildings.

3.3 Pass the mule corral as you climb toward Empire Street.

3.4 At the junction with the WYOD Loop Trail, stay left, following signs directing you to the visitor center.

3.5   The trail reaches Empire Street and skirts the Magenta Drain reclamation ponds. Cross a park road and continue uphill on the roadside pathway.

3.6   Pass a garden gate; you can peek into the estate from here.

3.8   Pass a second garden gate.

3.9   Arrive back at the trailhead.

HIKE INFORMATION

Local information: Grass Valley/Nevada County Chamber of Commerce, 248 Mill St., Grass Valley 95945; (530) 273-4667 or (800) 655-4667; www.grassvalley chamber.com. Get information about local communities, area history, and more on the chamber site.

Nevada County Gold, 14520 Lynshar Rd., Grass Valley 95945; (530) 272-3239; www.nevadacountygold.com. This online guide includes information about sites, events, and visiting Grass Valley and surrounding communities.

Hike tours: Tours of the Bourn cottage and mine yard are offered daily, weather permitting, and are included in the entry fee. During the summer months more tours are scheduled, and Cottage Living History is offered between 12 noon and 3 p.m. on weekends. Visit the Empire Mine Park Association website at www .empiremine.org for details.

Organizations: The Empire Mine Park Association provides financial and volunteer support for operations and tours at Empire Mine State Historic Park. Visit the website at www.empiremine.org for more information.

Green Tip:
Stay on the trail. Cutting from one part of a switchback to another can destroy fragile plant life.

Honorable Mentions

Sutter Buttes

The signature landmark of the Central Valley north of Sacramento, the Sutter Buttes are the eroded remnants of an ancient volcano. What once was a nearly perfect conical peak is now a collection of smaller andesite domes, heavily wooded and resembling the ramparts of a massive castle. The buttes are mostly privately owned, but a nonprofit organization, dubbed the Middle Mountain Foundation in honor of the name bestowed upon the mountains by the native southern Maidu (Nisenan) people, coordinates with landowners to provide limited public access to the land. Organized hikes explore the various peaks, and guides interpret the natural and human history of the area. For more information or to sign up for a guided hike in the Sutter Buttes, contact the Middle Mountain Foundation at (530) 755-3568 or visit www.middlemountain.org. You can sign up online by clicking on the "Hikes" tab.

Malakof Diggins State Historic Park

Located north and east of Grass Valley and Nevada City (and outside an hour's driving distance from downtown Sacramento), this state historic park showcases the largest hydraulic mine in California. Hydraulic mining, in which a high-velocity stream of water is blasted into a mountainside, washing out gold and other precious metals trapped in the sediments, was a relatively short-lived practice in the Sierra Nevada, given its dramatic and harmful effects on landscapes and properties downstream, which were inundated in runoff. The Diggins Loop Trail (3 miles long) explores the Malakof mine, which the park touts as resembling "Bryce Canyon in miniature." At the time this guide went to press, Malakof Diggins SHP was on the list of parks slated for closure due to California state budget cuts. Be sure to contact the park before visiting. For more information contact Malakof Diggins State Historic Park by calling (530) 265-2740, or visit www.parks.ca.gov/?page_id=494.

West Valley

Lake Berryessa lies far below the Blue Ridge, enclosed in the scrub-covered hills of the coastal mountains (Hike 25).

The cities of Davis, Vacaville, Fairfield, and Winters lie west of Sacramento, clustered close to I-80. While Fairfield and Vacaville could best be described as bedroom communities for Sacramento and cities in the San Francisco Bay Area, Davis is a college town with an agricultural bent. Winters, gateway to Lake Berryessa and the Vaca coastal range, is focused on agriculture, though it has a quaint downtown boasting a pair of fabulous restaurants: the legendary Buckhorn and the Putah Creek Café, featured on the Food Network.

Trails in this region highlight two major geologic features: the Coast Range and the Sacramento–San Joaquin River delta. The Coast Range is a buckling of the earth, where faulting along tectonic plates has heaved up and riven the landscape. The resulting steep-sided, relatively low peaks reach from the western boundary of the Great Valley to the Pacific. The steep loop through Cold Canyon and onto Blue Ridge showcases the rugged beauty of this terrain; Rockville Hills Regional Park offers a gentler exploration of the coastal hills.

The delta, where the Sacramento and San Joaquin Rivers flow into San Francisco Bay, was once a vast maze of wetlands and channels. These days the rivers and their tributaries, as well as the tidal influences of the bay, are contained by levees and development. But pockets of wildlands persist and are being restored, offering refuge for a variety of wildlife and for hikers as well. Premier among the delta explorations are hikes at Rush Ranch and Grizzly Island.

Steep-sided low peaks, a river delta, and two urban hikes

A pair of urban hikes in Davis round out West Valley offerings. The Davis Arboretum offers an educational exploration of flora from around the world, while the Covell Greenbelt epitomizes the potential of a linear park corridor, linking neighborhoods with open space and local art.

A sunbleached bedrock mortar once used by Native Americans overlooks the marsh at Rush Ranch (Hike 22).

Putah Creek Loop Trail

Tucked along an out-of-the-way stretch of Putah Creek, amid agricultural parcels outside the city of Davis, this loop trail offers seclusion, bird watching, and a chance to monitor the progress of an effort to restore agricultural land to native habitat.

Start: At the main trailhead for the South Fork Preserve on South Putah Creek

Distance: 1.4-mile loop

Hiking time: 1 hour

Difficulty: Easy

Trail surface: Wide dirt trail

Best season: Spring and fall. Summertime heat may limit trail use to mornings and evenings. Winter rains may render trails muddy; wait a couple of days for the surface to firm up.

Other trail users: None

Trailhead amenities: Parking, information board with trail map, picnic table, trash cans

Canine compatibility: Leashed dogs permitted

Fees and permits: None

Schedule: Open daily, sunrise to sunset, year-round

Maps: USGS Davis CA; trail map on information board at trailhead

Trail contact: City of Davis Parks and Community Services, 1818 Fifth St., Davis 95616; (530) 757-5626; www.cityofdavis.org

Finding the trailhead: From downtown Sacramento head west on I-80 toward Davis. Take the Mace Boulevard exit. Travel 2.3 miles south on Mace Boulevard to the trailhead, which is on the left (east) side of the road. GPS: N38 31.038'/W121 41.703'

THE HIKE

The south fork of Putah Creek flows east from Lake Berryessa in the coastal mountains into the Yolo Bypass Wildlife Area, and then into the Sacramento River delta. The flow seems backwards, seeing as the Pacific Ocean lies in the opposite direction. But the creek does eventually reach that goal, providing water for farms and fields in the western reaches of the southern Sacramento Valley along the way.

While Putah Creek is constrained by levees throughout the agricultural bottomlands, in this little preserve it is allowed to flood, as it did before the arrival of Europeans, when Native Americans (possibly Patwin) lived and foraged along its banks. In this way it waters the wetlands and riparian zones that are being restored along its banks.

The man-made forces that have shaped the surrounding landscape for decades still envelop the 84-acre preserve and its trails, with orchards neatly planted at its eastern boundary and an enormous levee bounding the south side. But as the information sign at the trailhead describes, the creek also supports a complex "riparian ribbon" that includes habitat for chinook salmon, prickly sculpin, California quail, and a variety of raptors. If all goes as planned, those creatures and

A stretch of Putah Creek flashes fall colors within a small preserve undergoing restoration between Davis and west Sacramento.

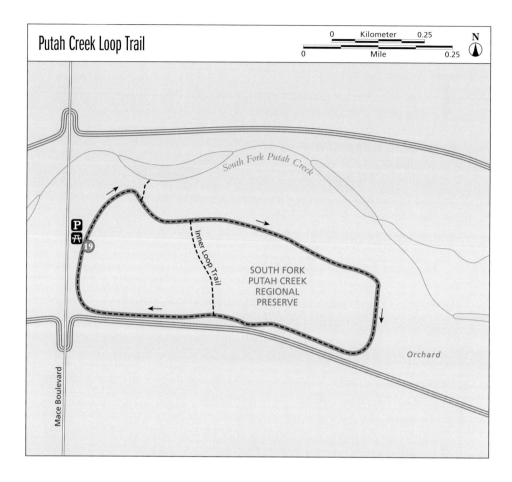

the sycamores, willows, and oaks that shelter them will find permanent renewal in this preserve.

The riparian corridor along the creek itself, thick with berry brambles, cottonwoods, and willows, is healthy and complete—green, and ringing with birdsong. The meadow between the creek banks and the levee is still a bit stark, with oaks that were fledgling in the early part of the millennium beginning to gain vigor and size amid the grasses, the majority of which are native perennials.

This pocket of parkland is isolated and little used, a huge bonus for the hiker seeking solitude. Visit in the morning or evening, or on any weekday, and you'll likely be alone with the birds chirping in the brush and the wind humming through the grasses. But the trail is wide enough to be a walk-and-talk affair, perfect for families or friends seeking a quiet outing to catch up and, if so inclined, do a little bird watching.

The route is easy to follow. Begin with a visit to the creek, following a narrow path that leads a short distance down to the broad, quiet waterway. The bank is choked with berry brambles and poison oak, so while it's lovely to look at, it's not picnic-friendly.

Once you return to the main trail, go left and head east through savanna that blooms with wildflowers, sage, wild rose, and chamise in season. You'll pass the junction with the Inner Loop (unsigned), which offers an opportunity to shorten the hike if desired. The Outer Loop bends south along the fence line that marks the interface of the shaggy preserve and the orderly rows of a manicured orchard. Continuing the circumnavigation, the route turns west, returning toward the trailhead in the shadow of the levee, a sloping grassy wall that rises to the left (south). Make a final turn, now headed north again, and you are back at the trailhead.

MILES AND DIRECTIONS

0.0 Start by heading left (north) on the gravel trail, taking the loop in a clockwise direction.

0.1 At the trail intersection go left (north), toward the creek. Return to the trail junction and continue on the broad main trail.

0.3 Reach a junction with a road/trail at a fence line. Go left (east). At a second trail intersection (with the unsigned Inner Loop), stay straight (east), remaining on the unsigned Outer Loop.

0.6 At the junction stay straight (east) on the Outer Loop Trail. A rusted water trough sits outside the fence.

0.7 Circle south toward the levee. The property boundary is fenced on the left (east).

0.8 Head westward along the foot of the levee.

1.0 Pass the junction with the Inner Loop and a gated roadway that leads up onto the levee. Stay straight (west) on the Outer Loop Trail.

1.3 Round the last curve of the loop, heading north parallel to Mace Boulevard toward the trailhead.

1.4 Arrive back at the trailhead and parking area.

HIKE INFORMATION

Local information: Davis Chamber of Commerce, 604 Third St., Davis 05616; (530) 756-5160; www.davischamber.com. Community events and other information can be found on the Davis chamber website.

UC Davis Arboretum Trail

Walk from an environment you might find in Australia to an oak grove that includes exotic species from Spain and the Middle East, all while following the UC Davis Arboretum Trail. This winding interpretive path follows Putah Creek through downtown Davis and the adjacent university campus.

Start: Signed trailhead behind Davis Commons shopping center

Distance: 4.25-mile lollipop

Hiking time: 2 to 3 hours

Difficulty: Easy

Trail surface: Pavement, crushed gravel

Best season: Year-round

Other trail users: Cyclists, dog walkers, joggers

Trailhead amenities: Parking at the trailhead; abundant amenities, including restrooms and water, in the adjacent shopping center

Canine compatibility: Leashed dogs permitted

Fees and permits: None

Schedule: Open daily, 24 hours a day, year-round

Maps: USGS Davis CA and Merritt CA; online at http://arboretum .ucdavis.edu

Trail contact: UC Davis Arboretum, 1 Shields Ave., Davis 95616; (530) 752-4880; www.arboretum .ucdavis.edu

Finding the trailhead: Head west on I-80 for about 14 miles to Davis. Take the Richards Boulevard exit and turn right (north) onto Richards. Drive 0.1 mile to the junction with First Street. Turn left on First, at the Davis Commons shopping center. Go 1 block and turn left again onto D Street. Park in the shopping center lot. The signed Davis Arboretum trail begins across the road from the lot's southwest corner. GPS: N38 32.489'/W121 44.413'

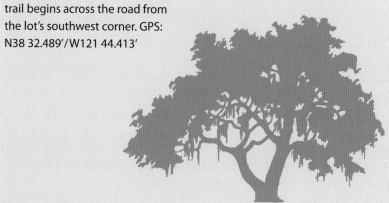

THE HIKE

Take a botanical tour of the world without ever leaving California's Great Valley by exploring the trail through the Davis Arboretum. Interpretive signs along the winding urban path, which borders a tame stretch of Putah Creek, identify the stunning variety of plants that have been nurtured here. It's a chance to get educated while you exercise.

The arboretum, a scenic greenbelt that transects the UC Davis campus, serves a variety of purposes. Recreation is premier among them, with cyclists, joggers, and walkers using the path at all hours. But the 100 acres of gardens are also integral to university research and are the site of guided tours led by university experts for school groups and families. The arboretum also hosts horticultural sales, during which local residents can pick up plants best suited for sustainable gardens in the region.

The trail is accessed from the Davis Commons parking lot, but take the time to visit the arboretum's Terrace Garden, located on the east side of the shopping center, before you set off on your hike. In the garden you'll find a fountain, plantings identified with discreet signage, and tables and chairs from which to enjoy it all. A brief exploration of the garden is a nice prelude to what you'll find along the trail proper.

Arboretum trails run on either side of Putah Creek, with footbridges spanning the waterway to link them: The described route alternates sides. A number of side

The Davis Arboretum's Redwood Grove provides a quiet, shady place to take a break from hiking or to study for an exam.

trails break away from the main path to access Arboretum Drive and campus service roads, but as long as you remain creekside, you won't get lost. Sounds from the nearby freeway are muffled but present for much of the walk. Those sounds, coupled with a variety of other trail users—cyclists, dog walkers, researchers, and students—are a constant reminder that this is an urban trail, albeit one of the finest in the area.

The paved path begins by dropping into the Australian Collection. Well signed and maintained, the collection includes a wide variety of eucalyptuses and other species native to the continent Down Under. It is the perfect introduction to the caliber of exhibits you'll walk through along the route.

Staying on the north side of the creek, follow signs toward the Redwood Grove and the Wyatt Deck. The Redwood Grove is a popular destination, offering benches in perpetual shade, cool temperatures even in the heat of summer, and interactive interpretive signs. Just in case you've forgotten that you are in a college town, students gathered in clusters socializing or sitting singly with textbook or computer are clear reminders.

The path continues through the East Asian Collection and skims the shores of Lake Spafford, where green lawns and benches offer more room for study and reflection. Campus halls are visible on either side of the creek corridor.

Cross a bridge to the Mary Wattis Brown Garden of California Native Plants and continue west, now on a crushed gravel path that is still suitable for wheelchairs and strollers. The trail proceeds through several garden rooms focused on California natives, including foothills botanicals and valley oaks. The Acacia Grove and Mediterranean Collection follow, before the trail enters the manicured environs of the Putah Creek Lodge. Verdant lawns, an amphitheater, a boathouse and launch, and the Early California Garden are on the grounds. The path winds along the south shore of a small lake, then climbs a hill and bends right, passing an equestrian center on the left.

Pass the Carolee Shields White Flower Garden and the arboretum gazebo, then turn left onto the gravel Oak Discovery Trail. Oaks from around the world grow along these winding crushed-stone paths—Persian oak, cork oak, oak of Tabor, cozahuatl, and English oak, as well as California natives—and are identified with mosaic tile signs. Loop through the grove, then check out the Valley Wise Garden before following the paved path back down to the lake and the Putah Creek Lodge.

After crossing the bridge back to the lodge, retrace your steps to the bridge at the Valley Oak Collection. Cross to the north side of the creek, exploring garden rooms including the conifer and redbud collections. The UC Davis water tower rises above. The Native American Contemplative Garden is just before Mrak Hall Road; in this garden you'll find native plantings mingled with standing stones that invite you to reflect on the legacy of the native Patwin people who once thrived on the shores of Putah Creek.

After passing under Mrak Hall Road, follow the north-side path back to Lake Spafford. Cross the bridge to the south side of the creek to explore the sages, ceanothus, and buckeyes of the California Natives Garden. You'll arrive back at the Wyatt Deck, and from there retrace your steps to the trailhead at Davis Commons.

MILES AND DIRECTIONS

0.0 Start at the trailhead behind Davis Commons, descending into the Australian Collection.

0.3 Cross the footbridge, following signs for the Redwood Grove and Wyatt Deck.

0.4 Pass a side trail that offers street access, staying right and passing through an underpass painted with a mural depicting insects and their habitat. Enter the Redwood Grove.

0.5 Arrive at the Wyatt Deck, with restrooms. Cross the bridge back to the north side of the creek and turn left, following signs for Lake Spafford and the East Asian Collection.

0.75 Cross the bridge to the left, entering the California Natives Garden. Turn right on the garden path, which becomes crushed gravel. Cross Mrak Hall Road and pick up the obvious paved path on the opposite side, marked with a California Foothill Collection sign.

0.9 Pass a bridge, staying left on the paved path.

1.0 Stay right on the obvious main trail where two paved walkways access a service road to the left. Walk through another underpass and enter the Valley Oak Collection.

1.1 Pass another bridge, staying left on the paved path and entering the Acacia Grove. Stay right where a side path to the parallel roadway intersects.

1.25 Proceed into the Mediterranean Collection, passing yet another access path. Cross a campus service road and pass a sprawling lawn on the left.

1.4 Arrive at the Putah Creek Lodge. Continue on the obvious paved path around the south shoreline of the adjacent lake, passing the amphitheater and boat launch.

1.7 Pass another access road, staying right.

1.8 Climb a short hill to the east end of the loop. The trail curls right.

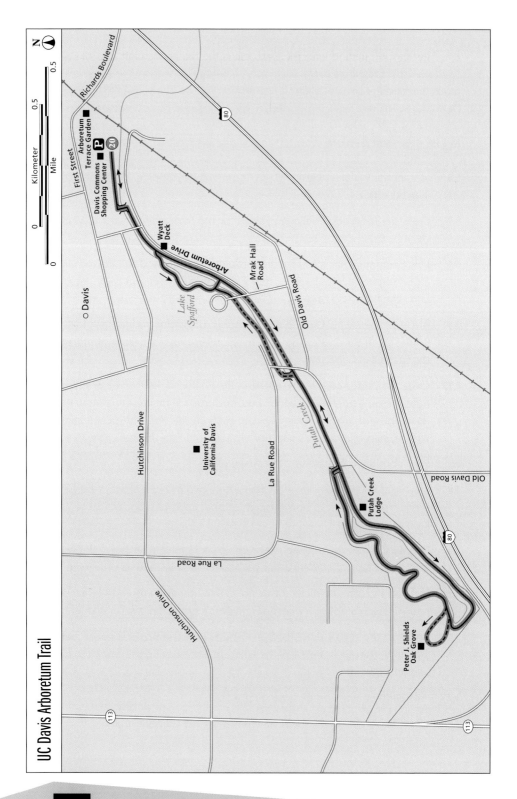

UC Davis Arboretum Trail

N

0   0.5   Kilometer   0.5
0   Mile

Richards Boulevard

First Street

Arboretum
Terrace Garden

P 20

Davis Commons
Shopping Center

Davis

Wyatt
Deck

Arboretum Drive

Lake
Spafford

Mrak Hall
Road

Old Davis Road

80

Hutchinson Drive

University of
California Davis

La Rue Road

Putah Creek

La Rue Road

Putah Creek
Lodge

Old Davis Road

Hutchinson Drive

80

Peter J. Shields
Oak Grove

113

113

2.0   Reach the junction with the Oak Discovery Trail and go left into the oak grove. Circle through the oaks in a counterclockwise direction, exiting at the gazebo. Turn left, pass the restroom, and visit the Valley Wise Garden. Turn left when you leave the Valley Wise Garden and follow the path down toward the lake.

2.6   Go left on the asphalt path that lies above the lake. Enter the Mediterranean Collection.

2.7   Stay left where paths merge at lakeside.

2.9   Cross the bridge at the signed South American Collection to return to the Putah Creek Lodge. Turn left to retrace your steps back to the bridge spanning Putah Creek at the Valley Oak Collection.

3.25 Cross the bridge at the Valley Oak Collection to the north side of the creek, then turn right, passing through the Conifer and Redbud Collections.

3.5   After exploring the Native American Contemplative Garden, cross Mrak Hall Road, rejoining the arboretum trail on the other side. Where trails lead left onto the campus, stay right, alongside the creek.

3.6   Cross the bridge back to the California Natives Garden on the south side of Lake Spafford.

3.8   Return to the Wyatt Deck. Retrace your steps from here.

4.25 Arrive back at the trailhead.

HIKE INFORMATION

Local information: Davis Chamber of Commerce, 604 Third St., Davis 05616; (530) 756-5160; www.davischamber.com

Local events/attractions: Putah Creek Lodge, UC Davis Conference and Event Services; (530) 752-2675; www.events.ucdavis.edu/events/html/arboretum/putah_creek_lodge.html. The Putah Creek Lodge, located on the UC Davis campus adjacent to the arboretum trail, is a lovely location for events, lectures, and ceremonies.

Hike tours: UC Davis experts lead guided tours of the arboretum, as well as host workshops, classes, and family programs. To access the calendar of events, visit the website at www.arboretum.ucdavis.edu or call (530) 752-4880.

Restaurants: Mikuni Sushi, 500 First St., Ste. 11, Davis; (530) 756-2111; www.mikunisushi.com. Located right in Davis Commons, adjacent to the arboretum trailhead, this urban sushi bar offers delicious, refreshing bites that will satisfy before or after a hike.

Covell Greenbelt

Stroll along pleasant paved paths in a leisurely loop that encompasses ponds, wild-life viewing platforms, and novel sculptures depicting man's best friend at play.

Start: At Davis Community Park on Covell Boulevard, at the pedestrian bridge
Distance: 2.75-mile lollipop
Hiking time: About 1 hour
Difficulty: Easy
Trail surface: Pavement
Best season: Year-round
Other trail users: Cyclists, joggers, in-line skaters
Trailhead amenities: Parking, restrooms, playing green, tot lot
Canine compatibility: Leashed dogs permitted

Fees and permits: None
Schedule: Open daily, 24 hours a day, year-round
Maps: USGS Davis CA and Merritt CA; online (along with other greenbelt trails in Davis) at http://cityofdavis.org/gis/bikemap.pdf
Trail contact: City of Davis Community Services Department, 1818 Fifth St., Ste. 5, Davis 95616; (530) 757-5626; http://cityofdavis.org/cs

Finding the trailhead: From Sacramento head west on I-80 for about 14 miles to the Richards Boulevard exit. Head north for 0.1 mile on Richards to First Street. Turn right on First Street and go 1 block to F Street. Turn left on F Street and drive 1.2 miles to E. Covell Boulevard. Turn left on Covell and drive 1 long block to the Davis Community Park parking lot on the left (south) side of the road. GPS: N38 33.628'/W121 44.816'

THE HIKE

This looping tour along paved paths links Davis Community Park, a hub of activity next to Davis Senior High School, with quieter Covell and Northstar neighborhood parks. The paths run through green spaces that back up to suburban homes, with links to residential streets and cul-de-sacs. Ideal for a Sunday outing with the family or easy-access exercise after a long day at work, the trail is a local favorite.

Though you can jump on the route at a number of access points along the way, and can extend the hike by linking to other bike and walking routes in the area (check out the city of Davis's online bike map for options), this loop begins and ends at Community Park. Start by crossing the pedestrian bridge that spans Covell Boulevard, which deposits you immediately into 5.2-acre Covell Park. The

> 🍃 **Green Tip:**
> *Please keep your dog on leash on public walkways and trails. Tying a waste bag around the leash is a sure way to guarantee you can clean up after your pet no matter where you walk.*

A viewing platform overlooks the small wildlife area in Northstar Park along the Covell Greenbelt loop.

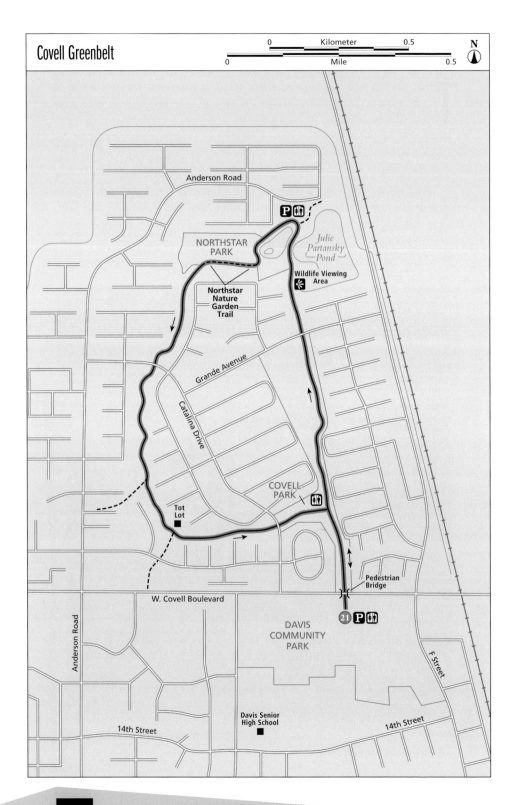

Kilometer

Mile

N

Anderson Road

NORTHSTAR
PARK

*Julie
Partansky
Pond*

Wildlife Viewing
Area

Northstar
Nature
Garden
Trail

Grande Avenue

Catalina Drive

COVELL
PARK

Tot
Lot

Pedestrian
Bridge

W. Covell Boulevard

Anderson Road

DAVIS
COMMUNITY
PARK

21

F Street

Davis Senior
High School

14th Street

14th Street

linear park encompasses benches, broad green lawns, playground areas, restrooms, and tennis courts. The first major trail intersection, located just inside Covell Park, marks the start of the loop: Stay right (heading north) to travel in a counterclockwise direction.

The next major junction is near the tennis courts; again stay right. Parallel paths continue north, one dirt and one paved, alongside an open field. Cross Grande Avenue and travel through quiet neighborhoods, past a lovely sidebar garden planted by path patrons and a number of signed access paths.

Next up is 13.5-acre Northstar Park, which encompasses soccer fields and Julie Partansky Pond. Named for a former Davis city council member and mayor, the pond functions both as the centerpiece of a wildlife viewing area and as a stormwater retention basin. Thickets provide cover for songbirds such as warblers, swallows, and sparrows; and larger birds, including great egrets, great blue herons, and a variety of ducks, can be seen at water's edge and on the surface of the pond. A pair of observation decks border the pond, offering opportunities to break from walking and just watch instead.

The path circles a second, more developed pond in the center of a huge green, then links with a gravel path that leads through the Northstar Nature Garden. A series of arbors arc over the path, which is planted with drought-resistant species. The path is very short and ends back on the paved greenbelt trail near a tot lot and soccer fields. The greenbelt trail bends southward, back toward downtown Davis, skirting backyards as it proceeds.

The green space around the trail widens, and at the 1.6-mile mark you'll pass the first of the Art in Public Places installations along the trail. Titled *Three Frolicking Dogs,* the bronze statues depict lifelike canines doing the ordinary (sniffing a sprinkler) and extraordinary (riding a tricycle). The sculptures were created by Jean van Keuren and installed in 2005. You could call the statues whimsical, evocative, and playful, but a quote from the Davis Wiki website offers another point of view: "They are, as are most works of dogs behaving like humans, thoroughly creepy."

The greenbelt trail eventually bends east and reenters Covell Park, where the loop closes at the trail sign and tot lot. Turn right and retrace your steps to the trailhead.

MILES AND DIRECTIONS

0.0   Start by crossing the pedestrian bridge that leads into Covell Park.

0.25   At the Y junction near the Baja Avenue tot lot, stay right to begin the loop, traveling in a counterclockwise direction.

0.4   The trail splits; you can walk either way, picking up the path heading north on the other side of the tennis courts.

0.7 Cross Grande Avenue.

0.8 Enter Northstar Park and pass the wildlife area.

0.9 At the junction with the trail leading out to Anderson Road, stay left, circling the pond in the center of the green and passing the Northstar parking lot and restroom.

1.25 At the intersection with the signed Northstar Nature Garden Trail, turn right onto the gravel path (the paved path runs parallel).

1.6 Pass the first of the Three Frolicking Dogs sculptures.

1.8 Pass the second dog sculpture.

1.9 At the third dog sculpture, the trail splits. Take the left-hand fork, remaining in the greenbelt. At the tot lot stay left again, avoiding the path that leads to the tunnel.

2.3 Cross Catalina Drive and reenter Covell Park. Close the loop at the trail that leads south toward Davis Community Park, turning right to retrace your steps.

2.75 Arrive back at the trailhead.

HIKE INFORMATION

Local information: Davis Chamber of Commerce, 604 Third St., Davis 05616; (530) 756-5160; www.davischamber.com

Restaurants: The Hotdogger, 129 E St., A-1, Davis; (530) 753-6291; www.the hotdogger.com. Where better to satisfy your hunger after visiting the Covell Greenbelt, with its canine statuary, than at a hot dog joint? Kraut dogs, chili dogs, Chicago dogs—even tofu dogs—are served up at this local favorite.

The first of the **Three Frolicking Dogs** *sculptures along the Covell Greenbelt is called* **Gallifornia Dreaming** *and depicts a dog looking at a wild turkey. The second is* **Cool Canine:** *The pooch is intently inspecting a sprinkler. The third,* **Winged Furry***, shows a dog riding a tricycle, tongue trailing out of its mouth.*

Rush Ranch

Two trail loops showcase very different ecosystems on Rush Ranch. The first loop takes you through delta salt marsh and freshwater marsh, thick with rushes, reeds, and birdcall. The second loop crosses grasslands typical of those that blanket the surrounding hills, with views extending west to Mount Diablo.

Start: Signed Marsh trailhead behind museum and visitor center
Distance: 4.1-mile double loop
Hiking time: 2 to 3 hours
Difficulty: Easy
Trail surface: Dirt ranch roads
Best season: Spring for wildflowers; late fall and winter for migrating birds
Other trail users: None
Trailhead amenities: Large gravel parking area, picnic tables, restrooms, signboard with information and maps. Restrooms and information are in the visitor center and exhibit room.
Canine compatibility: Dogs not permitted

Fees and permits: None
Schedule: Open daily, sunrise to sunset, year-round
Maps: USGS Fairfield South CA; online at www.rushranch.net; map in interpretive trail brochures available at visitor center
Trail contact: Solano County Land Trust, 1001 Texas St., Fairfield 94533; (707) 432-0150; www.rush ranch.net; www.solanolandtrust .org/RushRanch.aspx
Special considerations: Insects, including wasps, can be pesky at Rush Ranch. Wear repellent.

Finding the trailhead: From Sacramento head west on I-80 for about 38 miles to the CA 12 / Abernathy Road exit. Turn left on the Suisun Highway and cross over the freeway; the name changes to Chadbourne Road. After about 0.5 mile, turn left onto CA 12, heading toward Rio Vista. Go 3.5 miles on CA 12 to Grizzly Island Road and turn right (a left turn at this arterial will put you on Sunset Avenue). Follow Grizzly Island Road for 2.4 miles to Rush Ranch, on your left. GPS: N38 12.530′/W122 01.537′

A t Rush Ranch—where salt marsh meets freshwater marsh, coastal plain meets Central Valley prairie, shady eucalyptus groves meet open ranchland—the emphasis is on the ecotone. A quote from Richard Louv's *Last Child in the Woods,* displayed on the wall in the exhibit hall of the ranch's visitor center, explains why:

> Look for the edges between habitats;
> Where the trees stop and a field begins;
> Where rocks and earth meet water.
> Life is always at the edges.

The edges along the ranch's two loop trails are very different. Follow the Marsh Trail over a hilltop covered in grasses that typically blanket the uplands of the coastal ranges, then slide down to the salt marsh. Walk from there through brackish marsh into the managed freshwater marsh. Follow the South Pasture Trail around a finger of the marsh, where Native Americans (possibly Patwins) used a large stone as a bedrock mortar, then into the uplands, where grazing cattle crop the annual grasses before they crisp into a fire hazard in the summer sun.

From grassland to marshland the flora varies widely—bunchgrass is just a stone's throw from pickleweed, which in turn is a few paces from cattail, which backs up to hedges of nonnative blackberry. The fauna, which include a variety of songbirds, shorebirds, waterfowl, and raptors, as well as river otters, coyotes, and raccoons, transition from habitat to habitat as instinct or opportunity dictates.

But the creatures of Rush Ranch often find what they need—and thus can be most easily observed—at the edges. Among the unique (and sometimes endangered) species that can be found on the ranch's more than 2,000 acres are the Suisun shrew and the Suisun Marsh song sparrow; rare plants include the Suisun aster and Jepson's tule pea. The delta smelt, a species of some controversy because the protection of its freshwater-saltwater habitat has allegedly resulted in job losses within California's agricultural community, is also present in the waterways of the ranch.

The Suisun Marsh, one of the largest contiguous estuarine marshes in the western United States, is a fragment of what was once a sprawling wetland delta system that reached well into the Central Valley. About 90 percent of that vast marshland has been eroded by the activities of humankind in the 250 years or so since European contact. The water has been corralled by levees and channeled into sloughs; vast tracts have been drained for farmland, and other areas have been filled to provide a foundation for residential and commercial development. At Rush Ranch you will walk on levees that restrict tidal action on all but 5,000 of the marsh's 85,000 acres.

Both the Marsh and the South Pasture Trail are described, but one can be taken without the other. At about 2 miles each, and given their different emphases, it's a nice combination. Be sure to pick up interpretive guides for the trails at the visitor center; return them for the next user when you're done.

Begin on the Marsh Trail, which starts directly behind the visitor center in a grove of eucalyptus. Fairly common on ranch properties, the Australian native was intended to serve as a timber crop, but the wood proved unsatisfactory as lumber. The eucalyptus trees were better employed as windbreaks than as furniture or floorboards.

The first highlight on the Marsh Trail is the top of Overlook Hill. Take a seat on a bench and survey the marsh, which stretches north toward the Vaca range and west toward the steep flanks of Mount Diablo. To the south and east are the Potrero Hills, completely treeless, emerald green in the wet season and hot gold in summer and fall.

At the base of the hill are re-creations of a Patwin tule house, shade shelter, and granary, used as part of the ranch's educational program. The trail then leads into the wetland, following a mown path that threads through reeds and tules; tall, thick hedges of blackberry; and wild fennel that can tower to 8 feet. The dense

Old farm implements in the "boneyard" attest to Rush Ranch's history.

foliage provides shelter and sustenance for ducks, red-winged blackbirds (who chatter incessantly in the reeds), and other resident and migrating birds. Cross a tidal gate, which helps regulate the inflow and outflow of salt water, carefully managed to provide optimum habitat for wildlife. Typically the marsh is drained in summer and allowed to refill in winter.

As you swing east, Suisun Slough, looking much like a lazy river, comes into view. Beyond the water you can see some of the development around Fairfield (likely you've already been buzzed by a plane taking off or landing at nearby Travis Air Force Base), with the Vaca Mountains rising behind. Interpretive marker 12 (this one is easy to spot; other trail markers are hidden in brush) identifies Goat Island and Japanese Point, but you won't know you're on an island unless the marsh has water in it. Pass the tidal gate and go left on the ranch road, circling the hill to a gate. If you visit in winter or early spring, you'll see the wildlife pond off to your left; this dries up later in the year. Climb the two-track trail and cross the grassland back to the main ranch, where you'll pick up the South Pasture Trail at the signed trailhead under the water tower.

The South Pasture Trail begins in the boneyard, where ranch implements are labeled and being left to do what a rancher would let them do when they were no longer of use: rust and decay. The trail follows a ranch road east toward Mount Diablo; the interpretive guide directs your attention to the summer homes of thousands of solitary native bees that burrow into the ground along the road, creating distinctive "chimneys." Look right to the Notch, a cleft in the rise where dirt was excavated for use in levee building. Pass an interpretive sign that describes the ongoing research being conducted on the ranch.

At Spring Branch Creek the marsh extends across the trail up into the swale on the left. Trail signs indicate the crossing with the Spring Branch Creek Cutoff, which is an option for a shorter loop. Stay right instead, heading out a short distance to the Indian grinding rock, where Native Americans processed the foodstuffs they harvested from the marsh, leaving rounded holes in the soft pale rock. An arrow directs you up to an overlook, then down through a gate, where the route launches into the grazed pastureland.

The views across the tidal plain to the peaks of the coastal ranges, which include the Vacas to the north and Mount Diablo to the west, are spectacular and unimpeded. The trail curls around to the east and then the south, a peaceful, remote-feeling stroll. You might see cattle grazing or a horse at the water tank; keep your distance and the livestock will do the same. Off in the distance, through a gap in the Potrero Hills, you can see wind turbines slowly spinning in the nearly constant breeze.

Follow the low trail markers as they direct you across the uplands, then down into the swale and across Spring Branch Creek again. Beyond the boardwalk that spans the marsh, the trail rolls back to the boneyard and trailhead.

History of Rush Ranch

Before it was a ranch, the Suisun Marsh area served as winter hunting and gathering grounds for natives known as the Suisunes (which translates as "people of the west wind"), a subgroup within the larger Patwin tribe. The indigenous people left one lasting mark on the land: the grinding stone overlooking the marsh. The depth of the holes worked into the rock attests to the many meals prepared there before the arrival of settlers from Spain, then Mexico, then the eastern United States. All other signs of the Suisuns—their tule canoes, their shelters, and their granaries—have been reclaimed by time.

The settlers have left a much more lasting mark on the land. Ranch founder Hiram Rush came to California in 1849—not to seek gold, like so many others, but to run cattle. He arrived with a seed herd and started out with a holding of about 5,000 acres, which he eventually parlayed into more than 50,000 acres on properties in the Suisun Valley and Monterey County. At Rush Ranch he ran thousands of head of cattle and sheep. After amassing both wealth and influence, Hiram Rush met a tragic and unexpected end on the ranch when he was killed in a buggy accident. He was 60 years old.

Hiram's son, Benjamin Franklin Rush (1852–1940), took over ranch operations, and he too achieved great success. He ran as many as 5,000 head of cattle and sheep on the land. He and his wife, Anna, raised seven children; he also became a publisher and a bank director and was active in valley agricultural societies. Significantly, neither the junior nor the senior Rush did much to alter the natural tidal ebb and flow in the Suisun Marsh, leaving the basic underpinnings of the landscape and its rich habitats untouched.

It was the pristine nature of the ranch and its unique niche in the shrinking San Francisco Bay delta region that attracted preservation efforts. The signboard in the parking area says it best: The ranch may be "40 miles from the Golden Gate . . . but it's still the edge of the bay."

Rush Ranch was acquired by the Solano Land Trust in 1988, with a grant from the California Coastal Conservancy. Its remarkable attributes, including its status as part of one of the largest estuarine marshes in the western United States, have also resulted in its inclusion in the San Francisco Bay National Estuarine Research Reserve.

MILES AND DIRECTIONS

Marsh Trail

0.0 Start at the signed trailhead behind the visitor center.

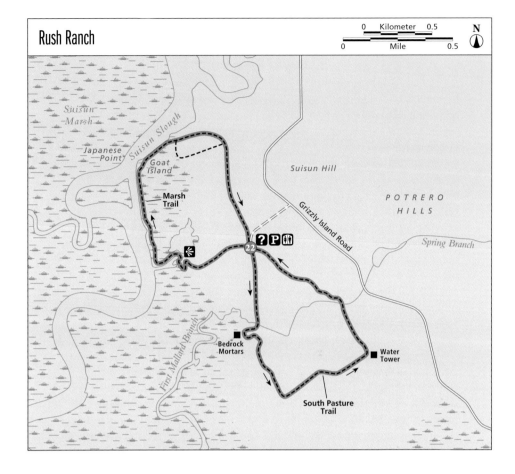

0   Kilometer   0.5

0   Mile   0.5

N

0.1   Trails merge; proceed toward the hill on the broad dirt ranch road.

0.2   Pass through a fence. Go left, then quickly right, to pick up the trail that climbs onto Overlook Hill.

0.3   Reach the top of Overlook Hill. Take in the views, then descend left (to the west), following signs down to the trail at the base. Go right on the Marsh Trail, passing the mock native structures.

0.4   At the signed trail junction, go left into the marsh.

0.5   Cross the tidal gate.

1.0   At interpretive marker 12 the trail arcs east over a rise, then south toward the Potrero Hills.

1.25   Pass through a gate at marker 14 and go left, circling the hill on the ranch road.

1.5 At the gate, continue straight up the hill on the two-track road toward the ranch.

2.0 Arrive back at the ranch and trailhead.

South Pasture Trail

0.0 Start at the signed trailhead under the water tower in the boneyard. The trail splits immediately; stay right to complete the loop in a counterclockwise direction.

0.3 Reach the junction with the Spring Branch Creek Cutoff and the signed trail to the Indian grinding rock.

0.4 Visit the grinding rock, then continue around the base of a small hill and climb to its apex, where you'll find a bench and overlook. The South Pasture Trail continues to the right.

0.8 A bench affords great views of Mount Diablo.

1.0 Reach the water tank. Stay right, on the ranch road that leads to another viewing bench. Go sharply left at the bench (an arrow points the way), heading downhill on the mown track.

1.5 Cross the swale and pass through a stile at a break in the fence line. At the junction with the Spring Branch Creek Cutoff, stay right, following the path across the boardwalk.

1.7 Pass a second fence line via a stile. Follow the ranch road up and over the small hill.

2.0 Reach the boneyard.

2.1 Arrive back at the trailhead.

HIKE INFORMATION

Local information: Fairfield-Suisun Chamber of Commerce, 1111 Webster St., Fairfield 94533; (707) 425-4625; www.ffsc-chamber.com. The chamber provides resources for visitors and local residents alike.

Organizations: The Rush Ranch Educational Council, an all-volunteer nonprofit organization, develops and administers educational programs at Rush Ranch for schoolchildren and adults alike. The programs focus on local native history and culture, native wildlife, marsh biology, and Rush Ranch history, among other themes. Write to the council at PO Box 2088, Fairfield 94533; call (707) 422-4491; or visit www.rushranch.net.

A circuit through this wildlife refuge in San Francisco Bay's marshy delta region offers views of Mount Diablo, opportunities for bird watching, and the chance to see one of California's rare tule elk herds.

Start: Across Grizzly Island Road from parking lot 4

Distance: 4.75-mile lollipop

Hiking time: About 3 hours

Difficulty: Moderate due to distance

Trail surface: Gravel and dirt levee roads

Best season: Spring, during bird migrations; late Sept, during the tule elk rut

Other trail users: None

Trailhead amenities: Dirt parking area, porta-potty. Information and restrooms are also available at the wildlife area's headquarters.

Canine compatibility: Dogs not permitted Mar through June. Dogs must be on leash.

Fees and permits: Fee is charged. You must get a permit and sign in and out at the California Department of Fish and Game entry station; there is a self-registration booth. Carry the permit with you while you are on the trail.

Schedule: Open for hiking Feb through July and the last 1 to 2 weeks of Sept. The area is closed for general public use, including hiking, during special tule elk hunts in Aug and early Sept, and Oct through Jan during waterfowl hunting season. Contact the wildlife area for precise dates of hunting seasons, as they vary. When open for hiking, hours are from sunrise to sunset.

Maps: USGS Honker Bay CA; online at www.dfg.ca.gov/lands/wa/region3/grizzlyisland; available at the entrance kiosk

Trail contact: California Department of Fish and Game, Grizzly Island Wildlife Area, 2548 Grizzly Island Rd., Suisun 94585; (707) 425-3828; www.dfg.ca.gov/lands/wa/region3/grizzlyisland/index.html

Other: Grizzly Island may close in winter due to flooding. Contact the wildlife area before your visit to check on conditions and access.

Special considerations: Insects, including wasps, can be prolific in season. Use repellent.

Finding the trailhead: From Sacramento head west on I-80 for about 38 miles to the CA 12 / Abernathy Road exit. Turn left on the Suisun Highway and cross over the freeway; the name changes to Chadbourne Road. After about 0.5 mile, turn left onto CA 12, heading toward Rio Vista. Go 3.5 miles on CA 12 to Grizzly Island Road and turn right (a left turn at this arterial will put you on Sunset Avenue). Follow Grizzly Island Road for 5.3 miles to Belden's Landing, a Solano County park and boat launch. Turn right, staying on Grizzly Island Road, and cross the Montezuma Slough Bridge. Stay left on the other side of the bridge, following Grizzly Island Road for another 3.5 miles to the Grizzly Island Wildlife Area entry station. Check in at the station, then continue another 5.8 miles to parking lot 4. The trailhead is across the road from parking lot 4. GPS: N38 06.461'/W121 55.634'

THE HIKE

When the Spaniards arrived in California, in the late eighteenth century, herds of tule elk roamed the region's grasslands. But the arrival of the Europeans nearly spelled extinction for the smallest members of the elk family, which were driven to the brink by poaching and loss of habitat to ranching and agriculture.

The story goes that the population dwindled to a single breeding pair, but there were others (though not many). Protected by landowners with a mind toward preservation, the sparse population was allowed to propagate unmolested, and now several herds roam public properties within the state, including a herd at Grizzly Island.

The area is managed by the California Department of Fish and Game for the benefit of the tule elk, as well as for other wild animals including river otters and a bonanza of resident and migrating birds. Ponds between the area's many levees are filled and drained to suit the needs of wildlife, providing forage for whatever species is targeted and enabling hikers to experience different seasons in different ways.

An estimated 500,000 tule elk roamed the grasslands of California prior to the gold rush. More than 3,200 tule elk now thrive in the state, mostly in protected wildlife areas.

Paying attention to the seasons is critical if you want to see the tule elk. They rut in the fall, making September a prime time to see males with full racks in velvet. February is another prime time, as the males still have their antlers. Birds are present year-round, but species change with the time of year. The wildlife area is along the Pacific Flyway, so migrating species can be seen as well as year-round residents.

Some critters do not need intensive management—just a place to live and breed and thrive unhindered. Grizzly Island is one such place. Songbirds find shelter in the cattails and brush that thrive on the borders of ponds and sloughs. Crickets hop crazily from underfoot during the late summer, and dragonflies scour the shorelines for mosquitoes and other prey. Fish jump in the slow waters of Howard Slough, a soft plop followed by rings that spread lazily to the brushy banks. The wings of ducks thrum the surfaces of ponds as the birds take flight en masse.

Begin by crossing Grizzly Slough. The distinctive dark silhouette of Mount Diablo rises above the lower folds of Coast Range hills. Follow the levee road straight west toward the hills, ignoring other roads that border ponds and ditches on either side. Since the ponds are filled and drained as required by wildlife, what is full dur-

Names notwithstanding: The Roaring River Slough hardly roars, and Mount Diablo hardly looks devilish, and there isn't a grizzly to be found at Grizzly Island Wildlife Area. But the hiking and wildlife viewing are divine.

ing one visit may be empty the next. Given the variations, while this route is a good choice for a leg-stretching hike in late summer, another tour in another part of the area might be better in a different season. Stopping by the Grizzly Island office and checking with officials is a good way to get oriented and obtain information about elk, shorebird, and river otter sightings.

After a relatively long run westward, the levee road bends to the south. Now Mount Diablo is on the right, and the white-winged towers of a wind farm stud the hills to the left. The gray towers to the south are part of a refinery near Benicia. A lazy S curve swings the trail westward, between ponds and the slough that waters them, with noxious star thistle and sweet-smelling wild fennel crowding the road's edge in late season. Birdcall rings from the brush, white egrets and pelicans take wing when startled, and the hairy scat of carnivores dots the roadway.

The levee road curves to the east again, spilling onto River Road, which runs alongside the Roaring River Slough. Turn right and follow the broad roadway north (you may encounter a vehicle or two on this stretch). The Roaring River is hardly that: Placid and wide, it is bordered by cattails, reeds, and ceanothus, which provide the perfect cover for even the largest shorebirds, including great blue herons, which may be so well camouflaged that you'll only spot one if it takes flight. The roadway is perfect for walking and talking with friends, scanning the waterways for otters, and searching the reeds and brushlands for shorebirds.

Follow the river northward, toward the Vaca range. Just beyond the 3-mile mark, take the levee road that branches right (east). It points toward the wind farm, the great white blades spinning or still depending on the wind and the whim of the energy grid. The road is slightly overgrown, bending right where it meets water. A bit farther you'll meet the roadway along Howard Slough, which you follow back to the levee road you came in on. A left turn on the original levee path, and it's an easy walk back to the trailhead and parking area.

MILES AND DIRECTIONS

0.0 Start by crossing Grizzly Slough and heading west down the levee road.

0.25 The trail reaches Howard Slough, with water on either side (depending on whether ponds are full).

0.4 At the junction stay straight (west) on the obvious primary levee road.

0.5 At Steve's Ditch (no sign), with trails on either side of the waterway, again stay straight (west) on the levee road.

1.5 After curving southeast, then west, then east again, the trail empties onto the gravel River Road, alongside Roaring River Slough. Go right on the broad, well-maintained River Road.

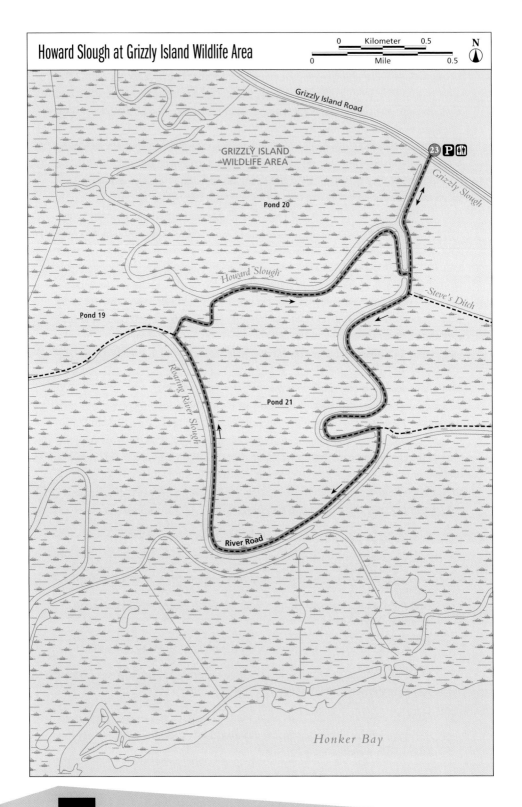

Howard Slough at Grizzly Island Wildlife Area

Grizzly Island Road

GRIZZLY ISLAND
WILDLIFE AREA

Pond 20

Howard Slough

Grizzly Slough

23 P

Steve's Ditch

Pond 19

Pond 21

Roaring River Slough

River Road

Honker Bay

0   Kilometer   0.5
0   Mile   0.5

N

2.3 The river road curves northward, skirting Pond 21 on the right.

3.1 Take the levee road that branches to the right off River Road.

3.2 The levee road bends right where it meets the water.

3.4 Meet the Howard Slough road. Go right, keeping the slough on the left.

4.3 The levee road hitches back westward, then intersects a connector path that leads over the slough and onto the levee road that links to the trailhead. Turn left on the levee road and retrace your steps.

4.75 Arrive back at the trailhead.

HIKE INFORMATION

Local information: Fairfield-Suisun Chamber of Commerce, 1111 Webster St., Fairfield 94533; (707) 425-4625; www.ffsc-chamber.com. The chamber provides resources for visitors and local residents alike.

Restaurants: Quick, easy, and delicious, Yo Sushi is a great pre- or post-hike stop. Located at 1430 North Texas St., Fairfield; (707) 425-1100; www.getyosushi.com.

Hulking Mount Diablo hovers on the western skyline above the ponds at Grizzly Island Wildlife Area. The ponds are filled by wildlife managers via sloughs and gates to meet the needs of resident and migratory birds.

Rockville Hills Regional Park

A network of fine trails winds through a regional park located on the western fringe of Fairfield. This exploration of Rockville Hills leads to a lake and cave, and through a portion of a natural rock garden.

Start: At the Rockville Hills park trailhead on Rockville Road
Distance: 3.1-mile lollipop
Hiking time: About 2 hours
Difficulty: Moderate due to elevation changes
Trail surface: Dirt road, dirt singletrack
Best season: Spring for wildflowers; mid to late autumn when temperatures are moderate
Other trail users: Mountain bikers
Trailhead amenities: Gravel parking lot, trash cans, information signboard with map
Canine compatibility: Leashed dogs permitted
Fees and permits: Entrance fee
Schedule: Open daily, dawn to dusk, year-round

Maps: USGS Cordelia CA and Mount George CA; online at www .fairfield.ca.gov/gov/depts/pw/ rockville_hills_regional_park_n_ open_space/rockville_hills_ regional_park/rockville_trail_ map.asp
Trail contact: City of Fairfield Public Works, 1000 Webster St., Fairfield 94533; (707) 428-7614 (park ranger); www.fairfield.ca.gov/gov/ depts/pw/open_space/rockville_ hills_regional_park/default.asp
Other: The park has been improving the trails and signage to make route-finding even easier than it is now.

Finding the trailhead: From Sacramento head west on I-80 for about 40 miles to the Suisun Valley Road / Green Valley Road exit. Head north on Suisun Valley Road for 1.4 miles to Rockville Road. Turn left on Rockville Road and go 0.7 mile to the signed trailhead parking area on the left. GPS: N38 14.907′ / W122 07.959′

THE HIKE

Sometimes the best trails are the backyard trails, the ones that locals turn to when they need an afternoon escape. Yes, having a historical site or a spectacular destination might be the best reason to seek out a trail, but sometimes the point is simply the pleasure of the walk.

That's what Rockville Hills has to offer. Sure, there's a lake, there's a cave, there's a naturally occurring hilltop rock garden—there are even wonderful views. But much of this 633-acre park's appeal lies in the perfect condition and pitch of its trails, its calming oak woodlands and open meadows, and its all-around friendliness.

The route begins by climbing the wide, dirt Rockville Trail up and away from the trailhead parking area. The path, part of the Bay Area Ridge Trail, winds upward through a woodland of broadly spaced oaks, buckeyes, and bays. As you gain altitude via the gentle grade, views open out across the Suisun delta region, reaching south all the way to Mount Diablo on a clear day.

> *In a park with lots of mountain biking traffic, such as Rockville Hills, staying on the broader trails (fire roads and service roads), where it is easier to pass, helps minimize potential user conflicts.*

An earthen dam forms part of the trail loop at Rockville Hills Regional Park.

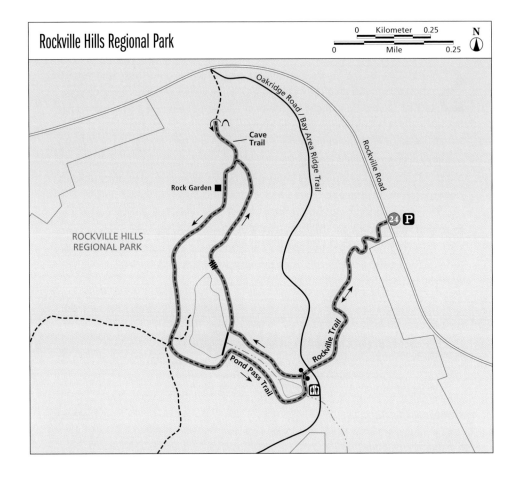

The trail tops out at the junction with Oakridge Road. Pass the gate and the information signboard, and then skirt the pond, which is nearly dry in late season, on the right-hand side. Even when there is no water visible in the shallow basin, herons and other waterbirds find sanctuary in the reeds and rushes of its marshy edges. The trail proceeds through an oak-studded swale to the dam of the small lake that is at Rockville's heart.

The lake is a congregation point for park visitors, who picnic on the shores. The power lines that run through the park are most visible in this great open depression, but in spring wildflowers dominate the viewscape and the wetlands circling the lake clamor with birdlife, including red-winged blackbirds singing in the reeds, ducks plying the calm waters, and the occasional hawk that may, on a slow day, use the dam as a roost.

Proceed around the lake to the north and east, following signs for the lookout/overlook. A boardwalk spans the wetland surrounding the lake's inlet stream. Pass through the fence via a stile, then turn right and follow the singletrack trail along the fence line. A number of singletracks pour off the hillside to the left, indicative of the park's popularity with mountain bikers. The trails are numbered and graded much like ski slopes, with green trails being easy, blue trails moderate, and black trails difficult.

A second little boardwalk marks the end of the fence-line trail. A moderate climb leads up to Paradise Pass—more of a saddle—then a rather steep descent through burgundy-trunked manzanita takes you down and around a high point to where you can check out the cave. There is no marker, so keep an eye out on the uphill side of the slope once you reach the open stretch of trail overlooking Rockville Road. The cave is not easily explored: It sits high above the trail, only the most rugged of use trails leads up the rock slope, and its narrow, dark mouth is not inviting. Check it out, then retrace your steps to the pass and go right, up onto the rock garden ridge.

A maze of paths explores the rock garden, jumbles of lichen-stained boulders crowding a long ridgetop. Pick your way through the garden, staying to the left side (lake side) of the ridge and enjoying views down over the reservoir and out across the hills to the south and west. All trails merge with a broad dirt track. Once on the track, go left and downhill, back toward the lake.

At the bottom of the hill you'll encounter a massive intersection, with nine trails converging. Fortunately there is a trail sign to help you decipher which one goes where. Better still, there is the lake: Simply take the path that leads left, along the shoreline and back to the dam. Pick up the signed Pond Pass Trail, which will lead you around the south side of the pond and back to the junction with the Rockville Trail at Oakridge Road. From there, retrace your steps to the trailhead.

MILES AND DIRECTIONS

0.0 Start by climbing away from the parking area on the Rockville Trail. The trail splits almost immediately; stay left and uphill (there were no trail signs here in 2011).

0.1 At the second trail split, above the ranch buildings, stay straight on the main (unsigned but obvious) path.

0.25 A pair of unsigned trails intersect the trail. Stay on the broad main path.

0.5 Reach the junction with paved Oakridge Road at the top of the hill. An entrance station with a restroom is down the road to the left. Cross the road to the information signboard and trail sign, passing through the gate and toward the lake. At the trail intersection just on the other side of the gate, stay right on the broad dirt signed Lake Trail. Reach the junction with paved Oakridge Road (aka the Bay Area Ridge Trail) at the top of the hill.

0.6 Where the dirt roadways/trails merge, stay left on the obvious path toward the lake.

0.8 Arrive at the lake. Go right on the wide trail. Where side trails intersect over the next 0.1 mile, stay left, circling the shoreline and following signs for the lookout. Cross the boardwalk through the marsh at the trail's inlet.

1.0 Pass through a stile at a break in a low fence. Singletracks collide on the other side of the fence. Take the unsigned singletrack to the right, along the fence. Pass Trail 19 on the left.

1.2 At the signed junction for Paradise Pass, go left and up on the dirt roadway.

1.3 A series of paths intersect the main dirt road/trail to the pass. Stay left at the trail leading to paved Oakridge Road, left again at the junction with the Lake Front Trail, and right at the junction with the Charmise Loop, climbing straight for the pass, an obvious break in the ridgeline ahead.

1.4 Drop over the pass and down to the cave, which is above the trail to the right. After you've checked it out, return to the pass.

1.6 Back on the pass, go right into the signed rock garden. A maze of trails explores the area. Stay right at the trail post, then left on the lake side of the ridgetop. Where the rock garden path meets the broad dirt road/trail, go left and downhill. Pass junctions with the Rock Garden Trail and the Tower Trail as you begin to descend.

1.8 Pass the May-December Trail, staying on the broad dirt track.

2.0 Reach a mousetrap of trail junctions, with nine paths converging at a trail sign. Take the broad trail leading left to the lakeside. After about 100 yards go left, over a stile at a break in the fence, and onto a shore-line trail leading to the dam.

2.25 Back at the dam, pick up the Pond Pass Trail, which leads down and around the lower pond via single-track and boardwalks.

2.4 Stay left where trails diverge at the dam of the pond, crossing back toward the restroom and the junction at Oakridge Road.

2.5 Back at the start of the loop at the information sign on Oakridge Road, go right to retrace your steps down the Rockville Trail.

3.1 Arrive back at the trailhead.

Local information: Fairfield-Suisun Chamber of Commerce, 1111 Webster St., Fairfield 94533; (707) 425-4625; www.ffsc-chamber.com. The chamber provides resources for visitors and local residents alike.

Hike tours: Interpretive hikes led by park rangers are offered. Contact the park for more information by calling (707) 428-7614.

Restaurants: Quick, easy, and delicious, Yo Sushi is a great pre- or post-hike stop. Located at 1430 North Texas St., Fairfield; (707) 425-1100; www.getyosushi.com.

Organizations: The Rockville Alternative Transportation Society (RATS), a mountain biking organization, performs regular trail maintenance at Rockville Hills Regional Park. Visit the website at www.ratsmtb.com to learn more. Another regular team of volunteers doing park maintenance is known simply as the "Trail Crew," working rain or shine to keep trails in tip-top shape for all users.

Hiking the Ridgetop

A portion of the Bay Area Ridge Trail, a regional path that, as the name implies, follows ridgelines around San Francisco Bay, passes through Rockville Hills Regional Park. The segment is part of 330-plus miles of trail that have been cobbled together since the idea was first discussed back in 1987. The goal is to create a path upon which hikers and other users can circumnavigate the bay. Once complete, more than 550 miles of trail will be incorporated.

Thus far the route primarily consists of trails running through existing parklands. The gaps cross private land, and efforts to secure passage across those parcels are ongoing. Spearheading the effort is the Bay Area Ridge Trail Council, a nonprofit organization formed in 1992 specifically to promote the trail.

A wonderful interactive map of the trail is available at http://ridgetrail .org/interactive_map/&Itemid=99. It shows existing trail segments and designates whether those portions are multiuse or are limited to foot traffic or other specific uses.

For more information on the effort, as well as to find out how you can help, and for specifics of the existing and proposed route, contact the Bay Area Ridge Trail Council by calling (415) 561-2595, or visit the website at www .ridgetrail.org.

Homestead and Blue Ridge Loop
(Stebbins Cold Canyon Reserve)

Steep-walled Cold Creek canyon, on the edge of Lake Berryessa, embraces wildness and adventure. The Homestead Trail leads up alongside seasonal Cold Creek to the remains of an old goat ranch. From there stairs and switchbacks climb to the summits of Blue Ridge, with views down over Berryessa and out across the surrounding ridges of the coastal ranges.

Start: At the unsigned gate across CA 128 from the dirt parking area, just below Lake Berryessa's Monticello Dam

Distance: 4.6-mile loop

Hiking time: 3 to 4 hours

Difficulty: Challenging due to steep and/or rocky stretches and numerous ups and downs. You will gain and lose more than 1,300 feet in elevation on the loop.

Trail surface: Dirt singletrack, unmaintained dirt roadway

Best season: Spring and fall, when temperatures are moderate

Other trail users: None

Trailhead amenities: Dirt parking pullout across the highway from the trailhead

Canine compatibility: Leashed dogs permitted on Blue Ridge Trail but not on Homestead Trail

Fees and permits: None. A small donation is suggested to help maintain the preserve.

Schedule: Open daily, sunrise to sunset, year-round

Maps: USGS Monticello Dam CA and Mount Vaca CA; online at nrs .ucdavis.edu/stebbins/technical/ hiking.pdf; posted on trail signs at trailheads; map in interpretive brochure available at start of Homestead Trail

Trail contacts: Putah Creek Wildlife Area, California Department of Fish and Game; (707) 944-5500; www .dfg.ca.gov/lands/wa/region3/ putahcreek.html. UC Davis Stebbins Cold Canyon Reserve; nrs .ucdavis.edu/stebbins.html.

Other: Mile markers have been placed along the trail loop, but they did not correspond to the GPS readings taken in 2011. Though the markers on the ground, determined with a measurement wheel, may be more accurate, the GPS readings are used in the Miles and Directions for consistency's sake.

Special considerations: The steep, rocky terrain requires good hiking skills and strong legs and lungs. The Cold Creek crossing on the Homestead Trail may be impossible during high water (after significant rains). Other potential hazards, all of which are native to the coastal hills and thrive in this reserve, include poison oak, rattlesnakes, and ticks.

Finding the trailhead: From Sacramento head west for about 11 miles on I-80 to the exit for CA 113 in Davis. Go north on CA 113 for about 2 miles to the Russell Boulevard exit (CR 32) and head west toward Winters. Follow Russell Boulevard / CA 32 for about 11 miles; the road will cross I-505 and enter Winters as Grant Avenue / CA 128. Continue on CA 128 for another 10 miles. Cross the bridge over Putah Creek; the trailhead parking area is 0.2 mile beyond, on the right (west) side of the road as it makes a sharp curve up toward the Monticello Dam. The trailhead is on the left (south) side of the road, at the first gate. The second gate, located less than 0.1 mile uphill from the first, marks the end of the loop. There are no signs at the parking lot or at the gates; signs are located a short distance up the trails. GPS (parking lot): N38 30.564'/W122 05.801'

THE HIKE

The trail begins at a junction just inside the gate, with a map and elevation photo to help you decipher your route. Take the unsigned Homestead Trail straight into the riparian corridor along Cold Creek; the steep Pleasant Valley Trail is to the left, and the connector to the Blue Ridge Trail is to the right. A low post with a *"3"* on it is the first of the interpretive markers along the Homestead Trail; you can pick up a guide from the box at the information sign a bit farther up the path (it's also available on the UC Davis Stebbins Cold Canyon Reserve website). The markers are low and inconspicuous, but worth trying to keep track of, as the interpretive guide provides great information on the natural and human history of the reserve.

Side trails break to the right toward the creek, which is dry in late season and a spirited companion when fed by rainfall in winter and spring. The trail gently ascends for the most part, with a few sets of stairs hinting at the more arduous climb to come. The brush is thick and smells of spice: Bay laurel overhangs the route. Scat on the path is wrapped with hair, indicating a carnivorous depositor—you'll need a guidebook (or an expert) to determine if it is the spoor of a cat or a coyote.

At interpretive marker 22 the trail crosses the creek. Most of the time this is not a difficult proposition: Rock-hop or wade if the water is low and slow-moving; when the creek is dry, it's a walk-across. When the water is high, this might be the turnaround point. Use your good judgment.

Beyond the crossing the trail continues up the narrowing canyon, passing through a bower of overhanging branches. Water flowing down the path has eroded a channel that has been filled with dried brush, forcing you to the high side where erosion is less problematic.

You'll find remnants of the Vlahos homestead at the 1-mile mark. A moss-covered stone wall is the first visible remnant, built on the creek side of the trail at the junction with the path leading left and up onto the Blue Ridge. The trail that continues straight explores the homestead site, where John Vlahos raised goats in the early twentieth century, using the milk for cheesemaking. If you don't want to tackle the climb up to and along the ridge, this is a nice turnaround point for a pleasant 2-mile out-and-back trek.

To continue the loop, climb the short flight of steps leading away from the homestead site. The trail steadily but easily ascends along the side of the canyon, with a narrow, rusted pipeline—perhaps a water line for the old homestead—running alongside the track. Completely shaded by dense bay and oak and parallel to the creek, this section of the route may be the coolest on warm summer days.

Reach the base of a steep flight of steps at the 1.5-mile mark, and the climb begins. One guidebook writer calls these "monster" stairs, and he's got a point: The steps assist in an ascent of more than 500 feet in about 0.2 mile, a rather frightening statistic. The height of some of the steps, where erosion has eaten away the dirt below the thick wooden risers, contributes to the thigh burn. As you slog uphill, you might contemplate the trail designer . . . A masochist? A 19-year-old college athlete? But short traverses between flights and switchbacks allow you to catch your breath, and mercifully it's over swiftly. Once on the ridge, there are no more stairs, but there's plenty more climbing.

An old stone wall is one of the remnants of an old homestead in Stebbins Cold Canyon Reserve.

The Blue Ridge Trail rolls over five steep summits, each seemingly higher than the last. But that's not true, according to the USGS: You'll have reached the apex on the first peak, at more than 1,500 feet above sea level. Vistas unfurl like the leaves of a fern frond, row after row of coastal hills breaking away to the north and west, blue and purple in the distance. The Vaca range surrounds you, cloaked in grassland and dark oak woodlands, its steep folds dropping into dark drainages. Westward rise the Mayacamas, like the Vacas pleated by the fault lines that have crumpled California through the millennia. Beyond the Mayacamas the long broad bulk of Sonoma Mountain hunkers, a former volcano worn to roundness by time and the elements.

Short saddles separate the individual summits along the route. Climbing into and out of these saddles involves negotiating steep, sometimes rocky terrain. Pay particular attention on the third summit, where the hiking involves hands-on concentration as you negotiate steep drops, lever yourself down around boulders, and pick your way across ankle-twisting rocky stretches.

Lake Berryessa comes into view by the summit of the third peaklet, smooth and jewel blue in its mountainous basin. Lake views become more prominent as you continue, and rocky outcrops offer great vantage points, as well as opportunities to rest and take on fuel and water. Arguably the best views come at the beginning of the final descent of the last summit, where a pair of outcrops at openings in the brush look directly down on the reservoir.

The descent is aided by more wooden steps, again with switchbacks and long traverses through the chaparral. As you near trail's end, the route expands to roadway width and reenters the shady oak woodland. Pass the connector trail to the Homestead trailhead and drop to the gate and information signboard just above CA 128. Hitch a few yards down the highway to the trailhead parking lot.

MILES AND DIRECTIONS

Note: Markers and GPS reading do not correspond. GPS is used here for consistency within this guide.

0.0 Start by taking the short access path out of the parking area and crossing CA 128 to the first (lower) gate. Just inside, the trail splits. Take the unsigned Homestead Trail to the right; the Pleasant Valley Trail leads up left. A connector trail to the far right leads to the Blue Ridge Trail.

0.1 Pass another gate and an information signboard. Maps can be found in the small black box.

0.6 At marker 22 cross Cold Creek.

0.8 Cross a small bridge and pass the 0.75-mile marker.

1.0 Arrive at the Vlahos homestead. Go right, up the short flight of stairs, to continue the loop.

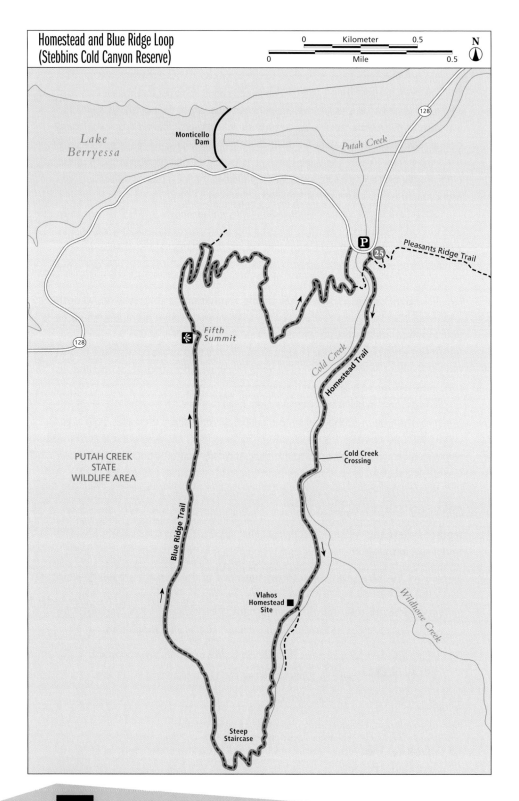

Kilometer
0   0.5

Mile
0   0.5

N

Lake
Berryessa

Monticello
Dam

Putah Creek

128

P

25

Pleasants Ridge Trail

Fifth
Summit

Cold Creek

Homestead Trail

128

Cold Creek
Crossing

PUTAH CREEK
STATE
WILDLIFE AREA

Blue Ridge Trail

Wildhorse Creek

Vlahos
Homestead
Site

Steep
Staircase

1.25   Pass the 1.25-mile marker.

1.5   Take a deep breath. The stair-step climb begins.

1.7   Arrive at the signed junction of the Tuleyome, Homestead, and Blue Ridge Trails. Go right on the Blue Ridge Trail.

1.8   Pass the 2-mile marker and attain the first summit.

2.0   Arrive on the second summit. A short saddle separates the two.

2.1   Atop the third summit, a rock outcrop affords the first views of Lake Berryessa.

2.5   Pass the 2.75-mile marker.

2.8   After passing the 3-mile marker, arrive at the top of the fourth peaklet.

2.9   A quick up and down leads to the top of the final summit. Begin the descent.

3.1   The trail splits at an unsigned junction with a short overlook trail. Stay right, descending toward the Putah Creek drainage.

From the top of Blue Ridge, you can look down on lovely Lake Berryessa and across the coastal hills north of San Francisco Bay.

3.4 Pass the 3.5-mile marker.

4.0 The trail widens into roadway. Brush occasionally encroaches, and the foliage transitions from chaparral to oak woodland.

4.4 The connector trail breaks off to the right. Stay straight on the wide Blue Ridge Trail.

4.5 Reach the end of the trail at the gate.

4.6 Arrive back at the trailhead.

HIKE INFORMATION

Local information: Winters Chamber of Commerce, 11 Main St., Winters 95694; (530) 795-2329; www.winterschamber.com. The chamber provides information on local businesses, events, and activities.

Local events/attractions: Lake Berryessa, a US Bureau of Reclamation property, hosts a variety of recreational activities including boating and other water sports, fishing, and camping. For more information on recreational opportunities at the lake, visit the bureau's field office and visitor center at 5520 Knoxville Rd., Napa; call (707) 966-2111; or go to the website at www.usbr.gov/mp/ccao/berryessa.

Camping: A number of campgrounds circle Lake Berryessa. Contact the concessionaire, Berryessa Shores, at (707) 966-9088 or visit www.lakeberryessashores.com/camping for information.

Restaurants: Putah Creek Cafe, 210 Railroad Ave., Winters; (530) 795-2682; www.putahcreekcafe.com. Featured on Guy Fieri's popular Food Network show, *Diners, Drive-ins and Dives,* this downtown eatery uses an outdoor pizza oven to bake delicious pies.

Buckhorn Steak & Roadhouse, 2 Main St., Winters; (530) 795-4503; www2.buckhornsteakhouse.com. This award-winning bar and restaurant is located on the ground floor of the historic DeVilbiss Hotel in downtown Winters. The steaks are the main attraction, but the sides (especially the fries) are delicious as well.

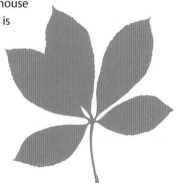

South Valley

A railroad bridge and fall foliage along the Cosumnes River catch the light of the setting sun (Hike 29).

Much like the region north of the Sacramento metropolitan area, the valley to the south is composed of flatlands dedicated to farming and ranching. This region is also influenced by the other big river that spills into the San Francisco Bay delta, the San Joaquin. Like the Sacramento River, the San Joaquin is contained by levees and dams, which allow it to flow tamely through the Central Valley towns of Stockton and Lodi. Its headwaters are in the southern Sierra Nevada, and its tributaries include the Merced River, flowing out of Yosemite National Park, the Kings River, spilling out of Sequoia–Kings Canyon National

Water—a river, sloughs, lakes; flatlands for farming and ranching; bedrock mortars

Parks, and the Cosumnes, the largest free-flowing river coursing out of the mountains.

Water is the focus of many of the trails in this region, whether rivers like the Cosumnes, which is featured on the Cosumnes River Walk, sloughs such as those found in Delta Meadows River Park, or lakes like Camanche Reservoir, focal point of the China Gulch Trail. At Deer Creek Hills Regional Preserve, you'll wander through the foothills on old ranch roads and trails blazed by cattle. Howard Ranch is notable for its skyline, which in addition to distant views of the Sierra front also includes the cooling towers of the decommissioned Rancho Seco nuclear power plant. Up in the foothills, a state park surrounds one of the most remarkable artifacts left by California's native peoples: a grinding rock supporting more than a thousand bedrock mortars.

The major highways heading south from Sacramento are I-5 and CA 99. In the foothills, you'll follow scenic two-lane roads such as CA 88 to access trailheads.

Old ranch roads and cattle paths make up the North Pond loop trail through Deer Creek Hills Preserve (Hike 28).

Stone Lakes National Wildlife Refuge

Once threatened by urban growth sprawling south from metropolitan Sacramento, a short paved loop through restored wetlands at Stone Lakes National Wildlife Refuge focuses on education and expanding awareness of what came before shopping malls and freeways.

Start: At the trailhead on the east side of the parking lot
Distance: 0.5-mile loop
Hiking time: About 30 minutes
Difficulty: Easy
Trail surface: Pavement; wheelchair and stroller accessible
Best season: Year-round
Other trail users: None
Trailhead amenities: Parking, restrooms, information signboards
Canine compatibility: Dogs not permitted

Fees and permits: None
Schedule: Open daily, sunrise to sunset, year-round
Maps: USGS Bruceville CA; online at www.fws.gov/stonelakes/hq .htm. The trail is straightforward enough that no map is needed.
Trail contact: US Fish & Wildlife Service, Stone Lakes National Wildlife Refuge, 1624 Hood-Franklin Rd., Elk Grove 95757; (916) 775-4420; www.fws.gov/ stonelakes

Finding the trailhead: From Sacramento head south on I-5 to the Hood-Franklin Road exit. Go right (west) on Hood-Franklin Road for about 0.8 mile to the refuge entrance on the left. GPS: N38 22.198′/W121 29.728′

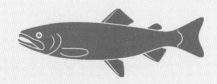

This one is for the kids.

Though the Stone Lakes National Wildlife Refuge has been around since 1994, and guided hikes have been taking place on a small parcel of the 6,500-acre refuge near North Stone Lake for years, the Blue Heron Trails are a new addition, opened to the public in November 2011. The paved paths wind through a restored wetland and circle three small ponds that attract a variety of birdlife, including the stately sandhill crane.

But it's the educational emphasis that makes this little trail sing. Interpretive panels line the paths, focusing on the various attributes and inhabitants of the refuge. And the Little Green Heron Playscape, when complete, will be a major attraction. Plans call for a child-friendly garden, a "messy materials" area, and other stations where kids can climb, dig, make music, create works of art, and otherwise enjoy themselves outdoors and with natural supplies. For youngsters growing up in metropolitan Sacramento, who might be limited by time or money in their opportunities to explore the natural environment that surrounds them, Stone Lakes is the perfect introduction.

A work in progress, the Blue Heron trails at Stone Lakes National Wildlife Refuge are geared toward education.

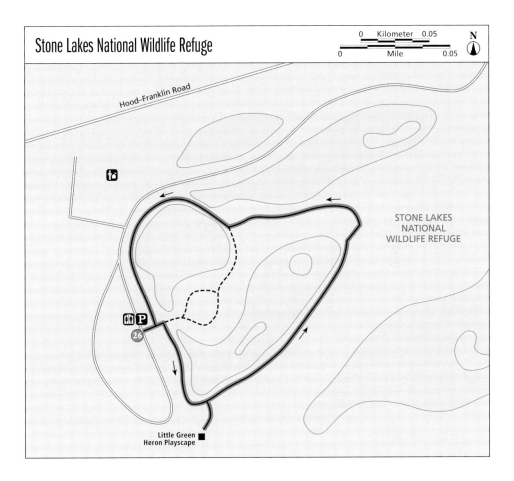

0   Kilometer   0.05

0   Mile   0.05

N

Hood–Franklin Road

STONE LAKES
NATIONAL
WILDLIFE REFUGE

P

26

Little Green
Heron Playscape

Purists may scoff at the inclusion of this trail on a number of scores: It's paved; its surroundings are heavily developed, including the covered amphitheater at its center; power-line towers interrupt the viewscape; noise from I-5 wafts across the flat fields. But this section of the Stone Lakes refuge has undergone an almost miraculous transformation that deserves recognition. The property was planted in grape vines before the restoration began in 2001: The vineyard has been removed, the ponds dredged, and the wetlands around them restored. When the native shrubs and trees that have been planted by schoolchildren from nearby Elk Grove begin to mature, insulating the small park from its agricultural surroundings, a dollop of wilderness will have been revived.

An easy counterclockwise loop around the outermost paved path, decorated with the footprints of birds and imprints of cattails, is described. The path winds past the playscape, then between a pair of ponds, with bridges spanning ditches between the water bodies. Interpretive signs enrich the route. Curl around a power tower to an interpretive kiosk, then head back toward the wildlife refuge headquarters, in the two-story house next to the parking area. Search the reeds around the pond for birds or other critters, check out a last interpretive sign, and arrive back at the trailhead after an easy, informative half-mile stroll.

Docent-led interpretive hikes are regularly scheduled and take place on a 2-mile-long trail that begins at the Elk Grove gate (located off I-5 at the Elk Grove Boulevard exit). The hike leads through seasonal wetlands that are managed for the benefit of resident and migratory birds, including hawks, shorebirds, and song-birds. Visit the national wildlife refuge website for a schedule of guided hikes.

Plans also call for additional hiking trails and more public access to the refuge, which encompasses both North and South Stone Lakes as well as acres of wetlands and seasonally flooded agricultural lands. Among the activities land managers hope to accommodate on the parcel are canoeing, kayaking, and fishing.

MILES AND DIRECTIONS

0.0 Start at the information kiosk, heading right on the paved path toward the playscape.

0.1 Pass a bridge that leads left to the amphitheater, staying right on the outer path.

0.2 Cross a little bridge.

0.4 At the trail junction between ponds, stay right, on the outside path.

0.5 Arrive back at the trailhead.

HIKE INFORMATION

Local information: City of Elk Grove, 8401 Laguna Palms Way, Elk Grove 95758; (916) 683-7111; www.elkgrovecity.org/public-info/index.asp. The public information page on the Elk Grove website provides business, visitor, and community information.

Organizations: Friends of Stone Lakes NWR is a volunteer organization that provides support for the refuge. In addition to funding educational programs, members lead guided hikes on the property. Visit the Stone Lakes NWR website at www.fws.gov/stonelakes or call (916) 775-4421 for more information.

Delta Meadows River Park

This straight-ahead walk follows an old railroad grade through dense riparian habitat along sleepy Railroad Slough. Blackberry, wild grape, and fig are twined with the native willow and cottonwood that thrives along the waterways.

Start: At the white gate behind Chuck Tison Memorial Park in historic Locke

Distance: 3.4 miles out and back, including short detour along a second levee road

Hiking time: About 2 hours

Difficulty: Easy

Trail surface: Dirt and gravel roadway

Best season: Spring through fall. Trail may be muddy in winter.

Other trail users: The occasional mountain biker

Trailhead amenities: Small dirt parking area

Canine compatibility: Leashed dogs permitted

Fees and permits: None

Schedule: Open daily, sunrise to sunset, year-round

Maps: USGS Isleton CA, Courtland CA, and Bruceville CA. A map is not necessary as there is, essentially, only one trail in the park.

Trail contact: California Department of Parks and Recreation, Delta Sector, 17645 CA 160, Rio Vista 94571; (916) 777-7701; parks.ca.gov/?page_id=492

Other: The Delta Meadows park property is unimproved; there are no services. The property is patrolled by California Department of Fish and Game wardens. The park was closed as of this writing, but foot traffic is permitted on the trail.

Finding the trailhead: From Sacramento follow I-5 south about 20 miles to the Twin Cities Road exit. Take Twin Cities Road west about 4 miles to River Road, which is perched on the levee. Turn left on River Road and drive through the historic town of Locke. Look for the sign for Chuck Tison Memorial Park on the left just outside town, before River Road makes a sweeping turn into Walnut Grove. Turn left on the unsigned paved road at Tison park, then quickly left again toward a white gate, where there is parking for about 5 cars. There is a Delta Meadows River Park sign, but it is partially obscured by foliage. GPS: N38 14.832'/W121 30.528'

27

THE HIKE

This obscure little park has been closed since 2010—the result of budget constraints that may result in the closure of many more of California's state parks in 2012—but the single trail, built on a former railroad grade, is still open to foot traffic.

Obscurity lends Delta Meadows a unique feel. Even the most minimal of amenities are missing, and toward trail's end lush, untamed riparian plants and grasses encroach on the route. It could be viewed as a neglected child, a bit sad and a little shabby, but instead it feels content and grandmotherly. Perhaps those very qualities—placidness, gentleness, a sense of hidden depths—drew park planners to acquire the property in the first place.

Obscurity also means the trail is little used. You may find yourself alone on the broad track, or perhaps accompanied by another party or two. But there are no crowds, despite the fact that Locke and Walnut Grove, with their historical sites, quaint shops, and cozy eateries, are nearby.

The trail has a decidedly undistinguished start, with the trailhead and dirt parking area surrounded by rusting shipping containers and other industrial flotsam and jetsam. The former railroad grade shoots straight ahead, with the cottonwoods and willows that line the nearby waterways pushed back so that the sun bakes the surface. The sound of cars driving on nearby River Road wafts into the park, cell towers

An old rowboat lies beached amid the reeds alongside the slough in Delta Meadows River Park.

rise from open meadows to the right, and you can look down on the backyards of trailer park homes through openings in the trailside brush to the left.

But within a quarter of a mile, all that is left behind. Grand old oaks reach boughs over the track, and blackberries, poison oak, wild grape, and other scrubby plants thicken the understory. At your first glimpse of Railroad Slough, take the short path that breaks right: This out-and-back spur dead-ends at a gate and a service road that leads back to the cell tower, but not before passing figs that, instead of growing into majestic trees, have adopted a bush-and-vine form, their giant leaves unmistakable amid the less flashy oak and grape. Where the spur track climbs onto a mound you'll encounter a stand of sycamores—and possibly, if the tides (or the owner) haven't taken it away, a hard-used skiff, its red and white paint chipped and peeling.

Retrace your steps to the junction with the rail-trail and go right, passing a gate and a fenced-off utility station, the last man-made items you'll encounter for a stretch.

The trail becomes more remote feeling the farther you walk. You can glimpse the waterway to your right, but the brush is so dense, it's hard to get a clear shot. Meditative if you are on your own, and an easy walk-and-talk if you have a companion, the setting is quieting.

The landscape opens onto a meadow on the left, and a gate blocks passage onto an intersecting roadway that leads into private property. Farther on ponds can be glimpsed to the left, their surfaces obscured by water plants with vibrant purple blooms.

The trail, now distinctly overgrown, with noxious star thistle erupting along the centerline and thick on the verge, ends not far beyond the ponds. A berm and sign mark the endpoint; beyond the berm the path is overwhelmed by a bank of blackberry. Retrace your steps to the trailhead.

MILES AND DIRECTIONS

0.0 Start by passing the gate and heading down the obvious but unsigned former railroad grade.

0.25 At the junction—the only one in the park—leave the main trail and drop past a gate on a short side spur.

0.4 Arrive at the end of the spur. Ignore the paved roadway that drops right; there is also a gated roadway posted No Trespassing. Retrace your steps to the junction with the railroad grade.

0.6 Back at the junction, turn right onto the rail-trail.

0.7 Pass the gate and utility installation.

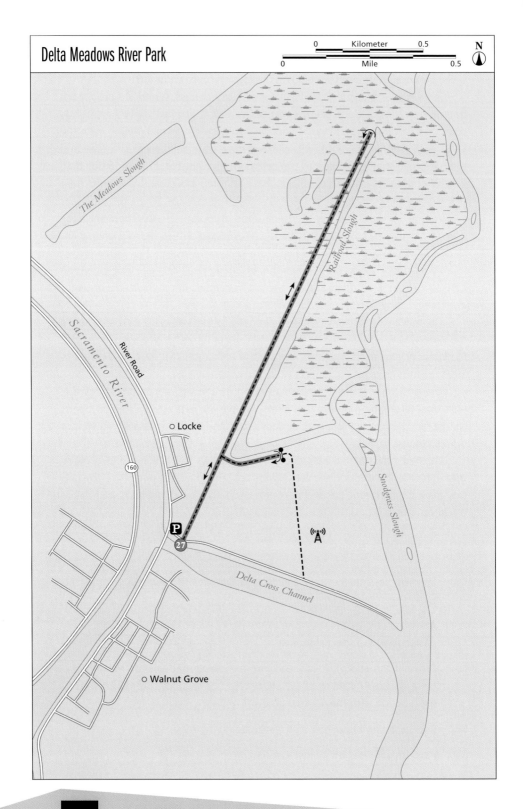

Kilometer

0   0.5

Mile

0   0.5

N

The Meadows Slough

Railroad Slough

Sacramento River

River Road

Locke

160

Snodgrass Slough

P

27

Delta Cross Channel

Walnut Grove

1.25 A meadow opens to the left. Pass a gated dirt roadway, continuing straight on the obvious track.

1.7 Reach the end of the line at a berm and a state park boundary sign. Retrace your steps to the trailhead.

3.4 Arrive back at the trailhead.

HIKE INFORMATION

Local events/attractions: Visit www.locketown.com for information about attractions in historic Locke. For visitor information about Walnut Grove, Locke, and Ryde, go to www.walnutgrove.com. Though the Walnut Grove Chamber of Commerce no longer exists, links on this site describe local history, activities, and events.

Restaurants: There are a number of fun eateries in nearby Walnut Grove. One is the Pizza Factory, at 14127 River Rd.; (916) 776-2626; www.walnutgrove.pizza factory.com. Build your own pie using traditional or gourmet toppings, including anchovies and cashews.

Budgets and Parks

More than seventy sites in the California State Parks system were targeted for closure in 2012, due to the budget crisis brought about by the recession. The closures represent a savings of $22 million to the state.

The state parks system includes more than 270 properties and encompasses more than 1.4 million acres. Potential adverse effects of the closures include increases in fire danger and vandalism and the loss of public access to significant natural and historic resources.

The Sacramento area is not as hard hit by proposed closures as other California communities. At this time, of those in this book, only honorable mention Malakof Diggins State Historic Park is on the chopping block.

The obvious solution to the crisis is to increase revenues for the parks, which is not likely to happen soon in tax-phobic California. In lieu of that, the state parks department is working with private and nonprofit organizations to cooperatively manage and operate parks slated for closure.

Several organizations have been launched to help stave off the closures. Contact the California State Parks Foundation (916-442-2119; www.calparks .org) or Save Our State Parks (www.savestateparks .org) for more information.

Closure is an inadequate descriptor for what will happen in real life: The parks will still be available to folks on foot, but there won't be any services. It'll be interesting to see how that plays out in parks that haven't arranged a private/public partnership. The liability alone, I imagine, could prove astronomically expensive for the state!

Deer Creek Hills Preserve

Follow the North Pond Loop Trail, which rambles along ranch roads and cattle paths through blue oak woodlands and open meadowlands to a small man-made pond, then traces segments of Crevis Creek to a natural seasonal pond.

Start: At the preserve's dirt parking area off Latrobe Road

Distance: 3.1-mile lollipop

Hiking time: 2 to 3 hours

Difficulty: Moderate due to the rolling nature of the terrain

Trail surface: Dirt ranch roads, narrow cattle trails

Best season: Spring for wildflowers and vernal pools; late autumn for cooler temperatures

Other trail users: Guided horseback and mountain bike rides are permitted on the property, but mostly you'll only encounter other hikers.

Trailhead amenities: Gravel parking lot, picnic shelter, restroom

Canine compatibility: Dogs not permitted

Fees and permits: None

Schedule: The self-guided North Pond Loop is open Sat from 9 a.m. to 1 p.m.; Sacramento Valley Conservancy docents are on hand. The preserve is closed to public access at all other times. Guided hikes are held at other times on the weekends; sign up on the Sacramento Valley Conservancy website.

Maps: USGS Folsom SE CA; online at www.sacramentovalley conservancy.org/admin/upload/DCHTrailGuide_web.pdf

Trail contact: Sacramento Valley Conservancy, PO Box 163351, Sacramento 95816; (916) 731-8798; www.sacramentovalley conservancy.org

Other: The North Pond Loop Trail opened as a self-guided route in 2012. Other trails in the preserve are available via docent-led hikes. Visit the preserve website at www.sacramentovalleyconservancy.org and click on the calendar tab for a schedule of guided tours.

Special considerations: Though Latrobe Road can be navigated by an ordinary passenger vehicle, there is a substantial creek crossing that some drivers may not wish to negotiate. Use a high-clearance vehicle to access the trailhead if available, or carpool.

Finding the trailhead: From downtown Sacramento head east on US 50 to the Sunrise Boulevard exit in Rancho Cordova. Head south on Sunrise Boulevard, traveling about 7.3 miles to the junction with CA 16 (Jackson Road). Go left (southeast) on CA 16 for 7.7 miles, toward Rancho Murieta, to the junction with Stone House Road. Turn left on Stone House Road and go 1.4 miles to the junction with Latrobe Road. Latrobe Road is gravel; follow it for 0.9 mile to the Deer Creek Hills Preserve gate and parking area, which are on the left. GPS: N38 31.611'/W121 05.218'

THE HIKE

Deer Creek Hills Preserve is remarkable for a number of reasons. First there is the setting: Straddling the ecotone between the ranchland/grassland of the southern Sacramento Valley and the mixed woodlands of the Sierra foothills, the property is composed of gentle hills cloaked in annual grasses and wildflowers, and shaded by widely spaced blue oaks.

Then there is the preserve's environmental significance. Within its boundaries flow watershed streams for Deer Creek, which flows into the Cosumnes River, which flows into the San Joaquin River, which flows into San Francisco Bay. Little Crevis Creek may not seem all that impressive (though it has carved out a nice miniature canyon near the end of the loop), but it plays a part in a larger scheme with widespread implications for environmental health.

And then there is the story of the ranchland's unlikely preservation, spearheaded by a small conservancy that, before Deer Creek Hills presented itself, had only protected much smaller pieces of property that required a lot less funding.

To hear Aimee Rutledge, executive director of the Sacramento Valley Conservancy, tell the story, you can't help but be inspired. The conservancy was fledgling when the Deer Creek Hills property came to the fore. The script runs like this: A small group of like-minded citizens with a love of wildlands, a preservation bent, and not a whole lot of money encounter a developer whose ambitious residential and commercial project has been rejected by the county of Sacramento and local voters. Seizing the opportunity, the citizens meet to discuss the possibilities. They are upping the ante by thousands of acres and millions of dollars. They take it on

🌿 Green Tip:
Use phosphate-free detergent—it's less harmful to the environment, especially sensitive waterways.

. . . they contact the investors behind the beleaguered developer to see if they can purchase the land . . . they partner with public agencies to augment their effort . . . and they win!

That was back in 2002 and 2003. These days the conservancy manages the 4,060-acre Deer Creek Hills property (held in co-ownership with Sacramento County and the California Departments of Fish and Game and Parks and Recreation), conducting youth programs, stewardship programs, and restoration projects on the former sheep ranch. A new master plan calls for trail improvements, winter grazing to control weeds and damper fire danger, and continued public access.

For most of its history, Deer Creek Hills Preserve was accessible only on guided hikes led by docents. As of 2012 the lollipop loop to the North Pond was opened on Saturday mornings as a self-guided trail. The route follows old ranch roads and cattle trails. It is well signed, but the cattle sometimes use the trail markers as rubbing posts, knocking them flat. If, by chance, a preserve volunteer hasn't been out to replace/restore the markers, no worries: The route is relatively easy to navigate if you have a trail map in hand.

Begin by following the ranch road, which leads clear to the North Pond. The roadway, gently climbing and wide enough to walk side by side, leads up into the

The trail through Deer Creek Hills Preserve borders sections of Crevis Creek, part of the watershed for Deer Creek and, ultimately, the San Joaquin River.

rolling hills, which are dotted with woodlands of blue oak (and the occasional live oak). Reach the junction at the start of the loop; you can travel in either direction, but the route is described here traveling clockwise. A guided tour, taken in late 2011 when this book was researched, involved taking a singletrack option through the woodlands on a cattle path that roughly paralleled the main trail, but staying on the ranch road and following the trail signs will get you to the pond in about the same distance.

While you're hiking scan the skies, treetops, and wetlands for some of the more spectacular birds that frequent the preserve, including golden eagles, tricolored blackbirds, and kestrels. Interesting geologic formations include low vertical rocks that jut from the grasses, looking almost like stone fences. These standing stones can be found all along the edge of the foothills uplift. And in late fall watch where you put your feet or your hiking poles: Tarantulas, big, hairy, and harmless, reside on the preserve.

North Pond sits in a small basin. Ringed in cattails and reeds, amenities are minimal—there's a salt lick for the cattle that run on the property in winter—but it makes a great place for a snack or a picnic. One day there may be a picnic table at the pond, but only if that fits with the rustic, undeveloped nature of the preserve.

From the pond hike up onto a wooded hill, then down through a gentle swale to Crevis Creek, which has carved a mini-canyon into the soft soils of its bed. The creek is dry in late season, but can be wet in winter.

Climb up and around a low, oak-shaded ridge, then along the well-defined trail next to the creek. The trail continues around a shallow basin—a natural pond or vernal pool that holds water into July and is dry until the rain returns in late October or November. From the pond the trail climbs gently through grasslands to hitch up with the ranch road. Turn left on the road, and retrace your steps back to the trailhead.

Deer Creek Hills Preserve contains 170 species of birds, 105 mammal species, 58 species of amphibians and reptiles, and an estimated 5,000 kinds of insects, according to the park's Sacramento County website.

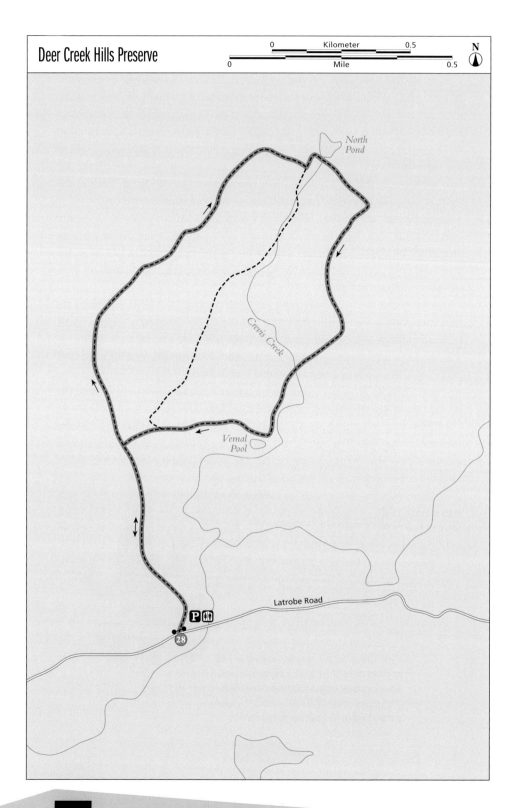

Deer Creek Hills Preserve

0   Kilometer   0.5

0   Mile   0.5

N

North
Pond

Crevis Creek

Vernal
Pool

Latrobe Road

P

28

MILES AND DIRECTIONS

0.0 Start by hiking up the ranch road to the north.

0.4 Reach the signed trail junction at the start of the loop portion of the hike. Stay on the ranch road, heading toward the North Pond. The ranch road eventually splits, with the trail heading right (east) to the pond.

1.3 Reach the North Pond. Cross the dam, then climb the singletrack path up into an oak-lined swale.

1.5 At the trail marker go right on the cattle path.

2.0 Reach and cross Crevis Creek.

2.2 At the trail marker go right, then right again, passing along the edge of a natural pond.

2.7 Close the loop on the ranch road. Turn left and retrace your steps to the trailhead.

3.1 Arrive back at the trailhead.

HIKE INFORMATION

Hike tours: To participate in docent-led hikes on the eastern portion of the property, which resembles the Scottish Highlands when it greens up in winter, visit the Sacramento Valley Conservancy website at www.sacramentovalley conservancy.org.

Restaurants: Get a good cup of coffee and a snack at MarShaTes, in Rancho Murieta's only shopping center, 7238 Murieta Dr., Rancho Murieta; (916) 354-3992.

Other resources: Sacramento County's regional parks page, www.msa2.sac county.net/parks/Pages/default.aspx, also includes information on Deer Creek Hills Preserve. Contact the regional parks through the Sacramento County Municipal Services Agency, 700 H St., Sacramento 95814; (916) 875-6961.

Carry your cell phone with you, but set it on vibrate or airplane mode. Deer Creek Hills, like many other parks and preserves in the Sacramento area, has full cellular coverage.

Meander through riparian thickets that border the Cosumnes River, the largest dam-free river in northern California. The broad, slow waterway nourishes habitat for birds in remarkable number and variety.

Start: Adjacent to the visitor center at the signed River Walk trailhead

Distance: 3.3 miles of interlocking loops

Hiking time: 2 hours

Difficulty: Easy

Trail surface: Boardwalk, dirt singletrack, dirt road

Best season: Spring for wildflowers; spring and fall for color and bird migrations

Other trail users: None

Trailhead amenities: Parking, restrooms, water, information kiosks

Canine compatibility: Dogs not permitted

Fees and permits: None, but donations welcome

Schedule: Open daily, sunrise to sunset, year-round

Maps: USGS Bruceville CA; trail maps available at Cosumnes River Preserve Visitor Center and at www.cosumnes.org

Trail contact: Cosumnes River Preserve, 13501 Franklin Blvd., Galt 95632; (916) 684-2816; www.cosumnes.org

Other: The visitor center is open weekends from 9 a.m. to 5 p.m. year-round; in July and Aug, as well as some other times of the year; it is also open weekdays from 8 a.m. to noon (call for the schedule). Inside you'll find interpretive displays that describe the Cosumnes River ecosystem and the resident and migratory birds you might spot in the preserve. Interpretive publications and trail maps are also available.

Finding the trailhead: Travel south from Sacramento to the preserve via either I-5 or CA 99. If traveling down I-5, take the Twin Cities Road exit and head east. Follow Twin Cities Road for 1 mile to Franklin Boulevard. Turn right (south) on Franklin Boulevard and continue for 2 miles to the visitor center parking area on the left (east).

Alternatively, take CA 99 south to the Twin Cities Road/CA 104 exit. Go west on Twin Cities Road for 7.4 miles to the stop sign at Franklin Boulevard and turn left (south). Follow Franklin Boulevard south to the preserve. GPS: N38 15.933'/W121 26.430'

THE HIKE

The Cosumnes River, unobstructed from its headwaters in the Sierra Nevada to where it empties into the Mokelumne River (and ultimately the Sacramento–San Joaquin River delta), is the only river in the state that looks and acts much as it has for millennia. No dams slow its flow, and no giant levees corral its floods, at least within the Cosumnes River Preserve.

This remarkable waterway supports a wide variety of wildlife, including both resident and migratory birds. It, like many of the wetland sanctuaries in the Central Valley, lies on the Pacific Flyway. Seasonal visitors include sandhill cranes, ancient birds with a 7-foot wingspan that stop here in winter, along with tundra swans and Canada geese. Resident birds are equally impressive, ranging from Swainson's hawks to black-crowned night-herons and kites. The riparian thickets and stands of valley oaks that crowd the riverbanks provide cover for a range of songbirds, as well as mammals such as raccoons, mule deer, and mink. In the water itself, hikers may spy river otters and beavers.

The Cosumnes River Preserve, established by The Nature Conservancy in 1987, protects a portion of the lower reaches of the river and its surrounding flood-plain. This natural area includes freshwater wetlands; riparian zones crowded with

A bridge spans Willow Slough at the outset of the Cosumnes River Walk.

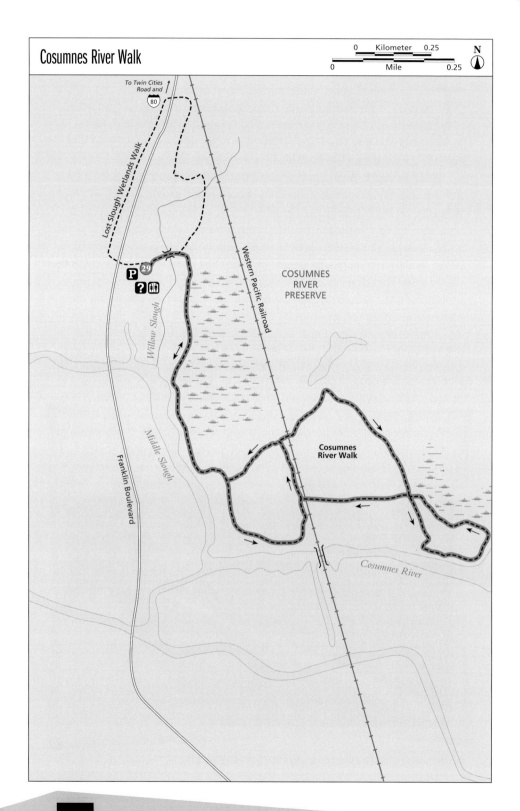

Cosumnes River Walk

0   Kilometer   0.25

0   Mile   0.25

N

To Twin Cities Road and 80

Lost Slough Wetlands Walk

P 29 ? ♿

Willow Slough

Middle Slough

Franklin Boulevard

Western Pacific Railroad

COSUMNES RIVER PRESERVE

Cosumnes River Walk

Cosumnes River

cottonwoods, willows, and oaks; and meadowlands that bloom with wildflowers in season. The Cosumnes River Walk leads you through each of these ecosystems.

Like all rivers, the 80-mile-long Cosumnes rises and subsides with the seasons, occasionally spilling out of its channel when swollen with snowmelt and rainfall. The flooding, typical of all Central Valley rivers before dams and levees contained them, deposited rich, fertile soil in the valley bottom. Outside the preserve the bottomlands support one of the nation's breadbaskets, with wildly productive farms and ranches serving as the foundation of central California's agricultural powerhouse.

Within the preserve the rich soils, as well as the wetlands, support a diverse habitat that attracts large numbers of birds . . . which in turn attract large numbers of bird watchers. But you don't have to be a birder to enjoy hiking in the preserve—there are other critters to spy, wildflowers to see and smell, and benches along a lazy river to rest and relax upon.

The Cosumnes may not harbor a dam, but it is not untouched by development. The railroad tracks and the scenic railroad bridge at the south end of the trail are one example; the hum of traffic from the nearby interstate, pervasive background noise to the birdcall, is another.

The Cosumnes River Walk begins on a boardwalk and bridge that leads across the birdsong-filled Willow Slough, which, despite being more than 100 miles from the Golden Gate, is influenced by the tides. Beyond the bridge the trail splits, with the Wetlands Walk (a nice addition if the Cosumnes walk is not enough) headed left (north) and the River Walk headed right (south).

Lined with interpretive markers keyed to a guide available at the visitor center and online, the dirt River Walk travels through a bower of tangled willow, cottonwood, wild rose, and berry brambles, tracing the little levee containing Middle Slough. Circling around the south end of the route, side trails drop right to the riverside, and a scenic railroad bridge spans the wide, calm river.

Pass under the elevated Western Pacific railroad tracks, and follow the trail as it winds through savanna and past the marsh to the signed nature trail. Circle through the trees, following the blue trail markers. A series of benches overlooks

🍂 **Green Tip:**
Even if it says it's biodegradable, don't put soap into streams or lakes. If you need to use soap, take water from the source and carry it 200 yards away.

the broad, calm river. Heading back toward the savanna, birdcall from the tule marsh to the right (north) can completely drown out any car noise you may hear.

Beyond the riverside loop the trail leads through shady stands of oak into savanna, where wildflowers flourish and the occasional valley oak provides shade. Walk north through the meadow to yet another marsh, then head back under the railroad tracks, crossing yet another stretch of meadow to hitch back up with the levee-top path next to Middle Slough. Turn right and retrace your steps back to the trailhead and visitor center.

Though the Cosumnes River Walk is adequately signed and lined with interpretive posts, there are a number of options that may shorten or lengthen your tour. These options may be confusing, but there's no danger of getting lost: With the river as one landmark and the railroad tracks as another, you won't lose your way.

MILES AND DIRECTIONS

0.0   Start on the boardwalk north of the visitor center, which leads down and across the bridge over Willow Slough.

0.1   The River Walk and the Wetlands Walk split. Go right (south) on the signed River Walk.

0.3   Reach a trail intersection. Continue straight (south) at this junction.

0.7   Reach a three-way trail intersection. Stay straight (south), ignoring the trail that leads left (east) into the savanna and toward the elevated railroad tracks (you'll visit these later). Pass marker 8 and continue alongside Middle Slough.

1.0   The trail curves east along the riverbank, passing interpretive markers 9 and 10, and side trails leading to the river. Pass the railroad bridge.

1.2   The trail breaks out of the woodlands at a trail sign that describes invasive plants and animals. Head north on the broad roadway that parallels the elevated tracks, passing the first trail that leads right (east) into the savanna. You will return to this junction via this trail after completing a short loop.

1.3   Go right (east), passing under the tracks.

1.5   Pass marker 14 and a bench overlooking the marsh, then swing southeast through a meadow.

1.6   Cross a roadway and continue straight on the signed nature trail.

1.7 At the next intersection go right (south) on the signed nature trail.

1.8 At the four-way trail junction, go straight (south) toward the river.

1.9 A nature trail sign points you right on the riverside path.

2.0 Pass marker 13 as the loop swings back to the west, passing a marsh.

2.2 The trail hops onto a levee and skims northwest through brambles toward the savanna.

2.3 Arrive at a four-way trail junction. Go straight (west) toward the railroad tracks, passing marker 11.

2.5 Cross a road and pass under the tracks to the junction with the first trail loop. Turn right (north), and walk the path again parallel to the railroad tracks.

2.7 At the junction turn left (west), crossing the meadow to link up with the trail alongside Middle Slough. Go right (north) back toward the visitor center.

3.3 Arrive back at the trailhead and parking area.

HIKE INFORMATION

Hike tours: The paved Lost Slough Wetlands Walk is a 1-mile trek through the wetlands on the west side of Franklin Boulevard, offering the opportunity for further exploration of this lovely sanctuary. In addition, occasional guided tours are offered; visit the preserve website at www.cosumnes.org.

🌿 Green Tip:
Keep to established trails as much as possible.
If there aren't any, stay on surfaces that will be least affected,
like rock, gravel, dry grasses, or snow.

Howard Ranch Trail

This sprawling tour of the Rancho Seco Lake shoreline and a working cattle ranch offers a sampling of big-sky country in the Central Valley, with views stretching across the prairie to the Sierra Nevada. Vernal pools along the route bloom with wildflowers in season.

Start: At the signed Howard Ranch trailhead in Rancho Seco Recreation Area

Distance: 6.9-mile lollipop

Hiking time: 4 to 5 hours

Difficulty: Challenging due to length

Trail surface: Dirt singletrack, dirt ranch roads

Best season: Spring for vernal pools; late fall for moderate temperatures and color along the lakeshore

Other trail users: None

Trailhead amenities: Parking, restroom, trash cans, information board with trail map

Canine compatibility: No dogs permitted

Fees and permits: Day-use fee

Schedule: Open daily at 7 a.m., year-round. Closing hours change seasonally, but generally correspond with sunset.

Maps: USGS Goose Creek CA; map and fact sheet can be downloaded from www.cosumnes.org/recreation/howard%20Trail.pdf. Trail maps also available at the Cosumnes River Preserve Visitor Center, located about 17 miles east of Rancho Seco at 13501 Franklin Blvd. near Galt.

Trail contact: Sacramento Municipal Utility District, 6301 S St., Sacramento 95817 (mailing address: PO Box 15830, Sacramento 95852-1830); (888) 742-SMUD (7683); www.smud.org. The recreation area phone number is (209) 748-2318.

Special considerations: You'll travel through a working cattle ranch on this hike. The cows you may encounter are gentle creatures that most likely will scatter as you approach. Please don't chase them. Be sure to stay on trails and close all gates behind you.

Finding the trailhead: From Sacramento head south on CA 99. Take the Twin Cities Road/CA 104 exit and head east toward Jackson and Ione. Drive 13.9 miles, through Herald and into Clay, staying left when the road splits at Clay East Road (which leads to the decommissioned Rancho Seco nuclear facility). The signed park entrance is on the right (south). Follow the access road for 0.3 mile to a left (east) turn into the park proper. Pass the entry kiosk and continue for 0.6 mile to a gravel road on the left signed for the Howard Ranch Trail. Follow the gravel road for 0.3 mile to the dirt parking lot. The trailhead is in the northeast corner of the lot at the information board. GPS: N38 20.425'/W121 05.800'

THE HIKE

Canyon walls, levees, and barriers of trees and shrubs hem in many trails in the Sacramento Valley, but at Howard Ranch, boundaries fall away. Open range rolls in all directions, spotted with cattle and the occasional lonely oak or sycamore, and seasonally abloom with wildflowers reflected in the still waters of vernal pools. The only visible obstacle is the distant rampart of the Sierra Nevada, hovering on the eastern skyline.

But if you seek cottonwoods, willows, and water, never fear: This hike is not all big sky and big prairie. The trail begins as a sinuous meander along the tree-shrouded shoreline of Rancho Seco Lake. Gently curving, beautifully constructed boardwalks span seasonal streams feeding into the lake. In summer the lake and its campgrounds bustle with visitors, creating an engaging, active scene. When the weather cools and the days shorten, the lake grows as quiet and calm as the grass-lands that surround it.

The Howard Ranch once belonged to Charles Howard, owner of the legendary racehorse Seabiscuit. Still a working ranch, it operates under a conservation ease-ment that protects its rare ecosystems, including vernal pools. The vernal pools are a huge attraction, the subject of guided hikes and solitary explorations in win-ter, when they fill, and in spring, when they bloom. Rare and threatened species associated with the ephemeral ponds include fairy shrimp and the California tiger salamander; wildflowers include vibrant spreads of goldfields and meadowfoam.

A significant, provocative tableau looms over the ranch and lake, the highlight of the western viewscape. Rancho Seco's neighbor is a decommissioned nuclear power plant, its two huge cooling towers rising from the flats adjacent to the park. For the most part the towers are out of sight, behind you as you walk east across the ranch and hidden by grassy rises as you curve south and west—which is pretty amazing given their height and bulk. Arguably the towers do not detract from the attractiveness of this long hike—they aren't unlovely, just unlikely, and add depth and complexity to the journey. No matter how you feel about nuclear power as a political or environmental issue, the towers spark the imagination and present the opportunity to consider the issues posed by any interface of wildland and human development.

The route is well marked and easy to follow, even if trail markers have toppled out of their rock cairn bases, likely pushed over by cattle using them to rub up against. It begins as a singletrack along the lakeshore, linked by boardwalks and small bridges spanning seasonal inlet streams. Pass through a gate, and the views grow Montana-big across the grasslands, stretching eastward to the distant Sierra. As you approach the 1.5-mile mark, you enter vernal pool territory, where depressions in the landscape hold water after the rains have stopped, blooming brilliantly as the water evaporates. When dry, rocks litter pockets in the fields.

The trail widens to ranch road beyond the second gate, where odd, orderly hummocks pop from the otherwise rolling landscape. You can't see what's on the other side, but the presence of trees indicates the existence of a pond. Where the trail splits at the start of the loop, go left, heading toward the mountains.

Boardwalks have been artfully placed along the shore of the Rancho Seco Lake. In addition to helping hikers keep their feet dry, the walkways protect fragile wetland plants and habitat.

The trail narrows to singletrack again as it weaves through the grasslands at the southeastern reach of the loop. More rugged now, the track and the landscape show little sign of human handiwork.

Swing westward, and what you forgot about as you headed east—the nuclear plant's cooling towers—now pop in and out of view. You are on high ground: The prairie drops to the southeast, dotted with cattle, fences, and ponds. The track swoops through several broad swales overlooking the pastoral scene as it proceeds south and west.

The final stretch of the loop follows a ranch road along a ruler-straight fence line to the start of the loop. From there, retrace your steps to the trailhead.

MILES AND DIRECTIONS

0.0 Start in the northeast corner of the trailhead parking lot by the information signboard.

0.2 The trail winds along the lakeshore, crossing the second of many boardwalks that curve over seasonal streams.

0.7 Cross a wooden bridge.

1.0 Cross a set of twin bridges.

1.1 Reach a ranch road and gate. Pass through the gate (be sure to close it behind you) onto the obvious singletrack trail.

1.4 Cross a bridge over a gentle depression in the range, an area where vernal pools form.

1.8 Pass through the second gate, closing it behind you, and turn right (south) on the ranch road. Hummocks rise on your left (east).

2.0 Arrive at the start of the loop. You can go in either direction, but it is described clockwise. Turn left (east) on the singletrack trail.

2.1 Cross the first of a series of small bridges spanning seasonal streams that feed man-made ponds on the left (north).

2.5 The trail swings south at a fence line.

2.8 The trail curves west through a huge swale.

3.9 Reach a fence line and trail marker at a ranch road, and turn right (north).

4.3 Veer away from the fence on the roadway, still headed north, and pass a trail marker.

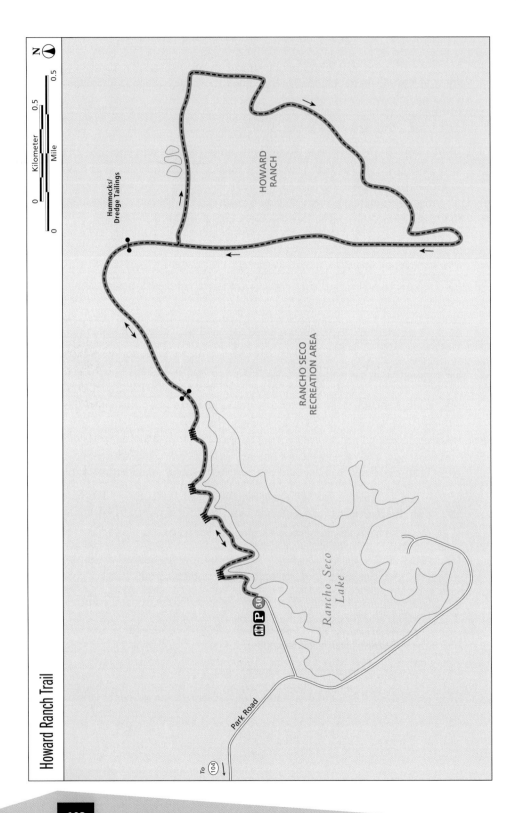

Howard Ranch Trail

HOWARD RANCH

Hummocks/
Dredge Tailings

RANCHO SECO
RECREATION AREA

Rancho Seco
Lake

Park Road

To 104

N

0   0.5   Kilometer
0   0.5   Mile

4.5 Pass through an area that may be mucky when wet, then the road returns to the fence line.

4.9 Reach the trail junction at the start of the loop. Stay straight (north) on the ranch road, retracing your steps to the trailhead.

6.9 Arrive back at the trailhead and parking area.

HIKE INFORMATION

Local information: Information about Galt, located just west of the Rancho Seco Recreation Area, is available from the city of Galt, 380 Civic Dr., Galt 95632; (209) 366-7130; www.ci.galt.ca.us.

Local events/attractions: Rancho Seco Recreation Area offers a bounty of outdoor activities, including boating, camping, fishing, swimming, and picnicking. For more information contact SMUD by calling (916) 732-4913, or visit the Rancho Seco website at www.smud.org; enter Rancho Seco into the search box and you'll be directed to the recreation area's page.

The Amanda Blake Memorial Wildlife Area, named for the actress who played Miss Kitty on TV's *Gunsmoke* (1955–1975), is part of SMUD's Rancho Seco complex. The preserve is a refuge for exotic animals born in captivity, including emus, ostriches, and African antelope. The refuge is open from 9 a.m. to 3 p.m. Mon through Thurs. Call (916) 732-4913 for more information.

Hike tours: Tours of the vernal pools at Howard Ranch are offered through the Cosumnes River Preserve. For more information and a schedule, call (916) 684-2816 or visit the website at www.cosumnes.org/recreation/vernal_pool_walks .html.

Camping: Tent, RV, and group camping is available at Rancho Seco Recreation Area. To make a reservation, call (916) 723-4913.

Many species of shrimp occupy Sacramento's vernal pools, thriving only in this ephemeral environment. They include the fairy shrimp (a threatened species), the seed shrimp, the vernal pool tadpole shrimp, and the clam shrimp.

Follow the North Trail through a mixed evergreen forest containing vibrant stands of fragrant incense cedar and maroon-barked manzanita to a reconstructed Sierra Miwok village where the focal point is the largest chaw'se, or grinding rock, in North America.

Start: At the signed trailhead in front of the Chaw'se Regional Indian Museum
Distance: 1.6-mile loop
Hiking time: About 1 hour
Difficulty: Easy
Trail surface: Dirt singletrack, pavement
Best season: Spring, summer, and fall
Other trail users: None
Trailhead amenities: Parking at trailhead; restrooms, information, water, and other amenities in the museum
Canine compatibility: Dogs not permitted on trails, but may be on leash in the parking area
Fees and permits: Day-use fee
Schedule: Open daily, sunrise to sunset, year-round
Maps: USGS Pine Grove CA; online at www.parks.ca.gov/?page_id=25307
Trail contact: California State Parks, Indian Grinding Rock State Historic Park, Chaw'se Regional Indian Museum, 14881 Pine Grove–Volcano Rd., Pine Grove 96556; (209) 296-7488; www.parks.ca.gov/igr

Finding the trailhead: From Sacramento take CA 99 south to the Twin Cities Road / CA 104 exit. Go east on Twin Cities Road for about 23 miles to Ione, then another 2.2 miles beyond Ione to the junction with CA 88. Turn left on CA 88 and go 17.9 miles, through the foothills town of Jackson, to Pine Grove. Turn left on Pine Grove–Volcano Road (with a sign for Volcano) and drive 1.6 miles to the park entrance on the left. GPS: N38 25.505'/W120 38.465'

For generations the Sierra Miwok gathered in a lovely foothills meadow that is now part of Indian Grinding Rock State Historic Park to prepare meals and share stories. A huge flat rock lies at the heart of the meadow and there the women worked, in one of the most glorious kitchens nature could provide, surrounded by a woodland scented with incense cedar and thick with the oaks from which the Miwok harvested their staple crop, acorns.

On the rock, outfitted with pestles and good company, the women prepared the acorns. The nuts were cracked, then the meats removed and ground into meal or flour between the pestle (a handheld stone) and what, over time and with repeated use, became mortars—circular depressions in the bedrock itself. Once the acorns were ground, they were taken to the creek and soaked, so the tannins that cause bitterness could be leached away. When the process was complete, the acorn meal could be prepared as desired: cooked in a basket with hot stones into a soup, or baked into cakes or bread, served with whatever game or fish the hunters brought to the table, and with whatever berries or greens had been gathered from the woods and meadows.

This bedrock mortar, or chaw'se, is the largest grinding rock in North America and a primary draw for visitors to Indian Grinding Rock State Historic Park.

Native Californians left bedrock mortars all over the state—indeed, two other examples lie along hikes in this guide, at Miners Ravine and Rush Ranch—but this chaw'se trumps the rest. It's massive, and the number of individual mortars ground into the limestone is staggering—more than 1,100 of them. And there are more than 360 petroglyphs carved into the stone as well, though these are harder to discern. This was no simple kitchen—it was a place where feasts were made, where births and deaths and harvests were celebrated, where women laughed and cried and fought and gossiped and comforted one another.

The park has done a wonderful job of showcasing the chaw'se and the lost way of life it represents. Surrounding the bedrock mortar are re-creations of the native structures that were destined to return to the earth over time, including bark houses typical of those found in Sierra Miwok villages and a roundhouse that is still used for ceremonial and social events. Finely crafted interpretive signs describe native beliefs and practices. Native plants that have medicinal uses are nurtured in a small garden. And the Chaw'se Regional Indian Museum is a must-see: Its exhibits encompass the gamut of the native Californian experience, from life before the arrival of the Spaniards to the present day.

Begin exploring the park in the woods, following the North Trail away from the village and museum. The path is wedged between the park road and Volcano Road for a stretch, then crosses the park road near a historic farmhouse that, in the late nineteenth century, was part of the ranching and farming operation of Serafino Scapuccino. An interpretive sign at the site suggests that Scapuccino allowed the Sierra Miwok to use the chaw'se even after he laid claim to the land.

The trail switchbacks up into a more secluded section of the park, passing the first junction with the signed Loop Trail. Thick stands of manzanita, with its distinctive burgundy-colored bark and bell-shaped flowers, crowd the edge of the trail, as do baby incense cedars, their distinctive featherlike needles vibrantly green. Oaks are also present, dropping their leaves thickly in fall, which is when the acorns can be gathered as well.

More than sixty different tribes, speaking sixty different languages, occupied California before the arrival of the Spanish in 1769. Four of the tribes are generally considered to be Miwok, being related through linguistics. They include the Sierra Miwok (living on the western slope of the Sierra Nevada in the foothills); the Coast Miwok (living north of San Francisco Bay); the Plains Miwok (living in the northern delta area around the confluence of the Cosumnes, Mokelumne, and Sacramento Rivers); and the Lake Miwok (living near Clear Lake).

Climb over a low ridge, then drop past the second junction with the Loop Trail. Quick switchbacks deposit you in a drainage that holds water in the rainy season and then dries out; cross the creeklet a couple of times before reaching the edge of the meadow (take note of the mature cedar with spreading boughs on the right).

After a quick jog across the gravel park road, then across the creek, then past the reconstructed bark huts, the North Trail meets up with the interpretive South Nature Trail. A second bridge crosses the stream just above a confluence, then the trail climbs to the property line. Interpretive signs mark your passage: Pick up a guide near the trailhead at the museum.

The steepest climb on the route follows the property line, then dips into and out of a drainage to a bench near a big dead-standing (fire-blackened) madrone. Ignore the social trails, staying left on the main track. Off in the woods to your right is another massive madrone, a virtual twin of the first but alive.

The trail leads down past the campground into the interpretive area, ending on the broad path near the sloping bark roof of the roundhouse. Go right on the trail, which leads past the roundhouse entrance and the game field. (Park literature explains that ball games were played girl versus boy: To even things out, boys could only kick the ball, but girls could kick, throw, and run with it . . . however, if a girl with the ball didn't unload it quickly enough, a boy could pick her up and carry her to the goal.) The platform overlooking the chaw'se is on the left, along with a cluster of bark houses. Interpretive signs notable for their colorful art and insightful stories line the path leading back to the museum and trailhead.

Reconstructed bark houses are clustered near a section of the South Nature Trail at Indian Grinding Rock State Historic Park.

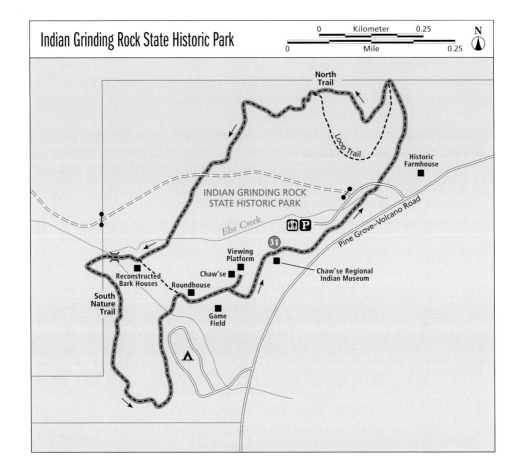

0   Kilometer   0.25   **N**

0   Mile   0.25

North Trail

Loop Trail

INDIAN GRINDING ROCK
STATE HISTORIC PARK

Else Creek

Historic Farmhouse

Pine Grove–Volcano Road

Viewing Platform

Chaw'se

Chaw'se Regional
Indian Museum

Reconstructed Bark Houses

Roundhouse

South Nature Trail

Game Field

MILES AND DIRECTIONS

0.0   Start on the signed North Trail next to the Chaw'se Regional Indian Museum. The trail climbs a flight of steps into the woods.

0.1   Cross a little stream via a small bridge, then cross the park road. Pick up the signed trail on the other side, walking past the historic farmhouse.

0.3   At the signed junction with the Loop Trail, stay right and uphill on the North Trail.

0.4   At the second junction with the Loop Trail, again go right on the North Trail.

0.6   Go sharply left on the North Trail at the signpost.

0.7   Reach the meadow. Go right on the service road, then quickly left onto the signed trail leading to the South Nature trailhead and to the interpretive area.

0.8 Cross a bridge over the stream, then stay right where the path splits at the bark houses on the South Nature Trail.

0.9 A trail sign directs you up along the property line.

1.1 Climb to a bench near a huge dead madrone. Stay left on the South Nature Trail.

1.25 Skirt the campground by staying left on the gravel path.

1.3 Enter the interpretive area near the roundhouse and go right, past the roundhouse.

1.4 Check out the platform overlooking the chaw'se, then return to the main path and continue toward the museum.

1.6 Arrive back at the trailhead.

HIKE INFORMATION

Local information: Pine Grove Civic Improvement Club; (209) 296-7626; www .pinegroveca.com/index.html. The website is a clearinghouse of things to see and do in the historic mining town, as well as in surrounding towns.

Local events/attractions: The Big Time, an annual Native American ceremony celebrating the acorn harvest, is held in Sept. Spectators are invited. Contact the park for more information.

The Chaw'se Regional Indian Museum—well worth a visit before or after your hike—is open Fri through Mon from 11 a.m. to 2:30 p.m.

Black Chasm Cavern National Natural Landmark, 15701 Pioneer Volcano Rd., Volcano; (866) 762-2837; www.caverntours.com/BlackRt.htm. Guided tours of the cavern are conducted year-round.

Camping: A 22-site campground in the park is open from mid-March through September, the camp operates on a first-come, first-served basis. See the park website for more information and to confirm months of operation, as they are subject to change due to budget constraints.

Organizations: Chaw'se Association, PO Box 1458, Pine Grove 95665; (209) 296-8045. This nonprofit organization provides support for the park.

🌱 **Green Tip:**
Don't take souvenirs home with you. This includes both natural materials, such as plants, rocks, shells, and driftwood, and historic artifacts such as fossils and arrowheads.

China Gulch Trail

The wide, gentle trail leading to China Gulch and beyond is popular with equestrians and hikers alike. It follows old ranch roads through rolling meadows still grazed by big-eyed bovines. The loop winds through a pastoral setting, open to sun and wind with only scattered stands of oaks providing shade, but with expansive views extending out across Camanche Reservoir.

Start: China Gulch staging area

Distance: 3.2-mile lollipop

Hiking time: About 2 hours

Difficulty: Easy

Trail surface: Dirt ranch road, dirt path

Best season: Spring for wildflowers; late fall for cool weather

Other trail users: Equestrians

Trailhead amenities: Dirt parking area, restrooms, trash cans

Canine compatibility: Leashed dogs permitted

Fees and permits: A trail permit is required and may be purchased at the entry station or online at www.ebmud.com/recreation/trail-use-permits.

Schedule: Open daily, sunrise to sunset, year-round

Maps: USGS Wallace CA; online at www.ebmud.com/sites/default/files/pdfs/Sierra%20Trail%20Map.pdf; available at the Camanche Reservoir entrance station

Trail contact: East Bay Municipal Utility District, PO Box 24055, Oakland 94623; (866) 40-EBMUD (403-2683); www.ebmud.com/recreation/camanche-recreation-area

Special considerations: This trail bakes in the summer sun, with little shade and no access to water. Bring plenty of drinking water, use sunscreen, and wear a hat if you decide to hike on a hot day.

Finding the trailhead: From Sacramento head south on CA 99 for 24.7 miles to the Liberty Road exit. Go left on Liberty Road for 19.9 miles (crossing CA 88 at the stop sign) to Camanche Road. Turn right on Camanche Road and go 0.8 mile to the entrance station. Follow the park road for 0.1 mile; at the junction, stay left toward China Gulch. Continue 0.4 mile to the China Gulch staging area parking lot and trailhead. GPS: N38 14.218'/W120 56.512'

THE HIKE

Hiking at Camanche Reservoir is perfect in the off-season, when the lake is quiet and still, glinting under a winter sun hanging low in the sky. The houseboats are moored, and only the occasional sound of motors drifts up onto the China Gulch Trail. The grasses will start greening up after the first rain (though the setting is still lovely, if a little more crunchy, when the sun has dried them gold). Wildflowers begin to bloom even in winter, though they may be tiny and hard to find, and increase in abundance, size, and color into and through the spring—showy California poppies and bright blue lupine among the most vibrant.

Besides, it can be screaming hot here in the summer: You'll want to be on the water then, not on the sun-baked trail.

Camanche Reservoir and its adjacent recreation area and trails are operated by the East Bay Municipal Utility District (EBMUD), which provides water and other utility services to communities in San Francisco's East Bay. The lake covers more than 12 square miles, and recreational activities—other than hiking on extensive trail systems on both the north and south shores of the lake—include boating and water sports such as swimming, windsurfing, and waterskiing, as well as camping,

The former ranch road that serves as the treadway for the China Gulch Trail at Camanche Reservoir makes it easy for hikers and equestrians to pass.

China Gulch Trail

0 Kilometer 0.25
0 Mile 0.25

N

China Gulch Trail

To Entry
Station and
Camanche Road

32

China Gulch
Staging Area

Loop Trail

Camanche Reservoir

tennis, and fishing. Trails that begin on the south shore of Camanche Reservoir link with EBMUD's Mokelumne-area trails, including the lengthy Mokelumne Coast to Crest Trail, which climbs along the shoreline of neighboring Pardee reservoir and up the Mokelumne River into the Sierra foothills.

The China Gulch Trail is on the north shore of Camanche Reservoir and follows fire roads for 5.1 miles, taking in the sites of former mining towns at China Gulch and Lancha Plana. The Loop Trail takes in a portion of the longer route, but leaves the China Gulch route to traverse above the reservoir, incorporating the path of an old water canal along the way.

Be prepared to share the trail with two large ungulates. Cows graze along the route to China Gulch. In addition to providing themselves with sustenance, the cattle's consumption of the grasses helps control the spread of noxious weeds and also reduces fire danger by removing some of the fuel load. Bovines are timid and will likely run away when you approach, but in the event they don't, slow your pace and say a quiet hello, and they will passively watch you walk by. The other hoofed trail users are horses; their riders generally ensure that encounters are friendly and risk-free. Again, quiet hellos are encouraged.

To begin, pass through the cattle gate and sign in on the register. Low signposts identify the trail; you'll pass these periodically. A broad gravel ranch road, the China Gulch route climbs gently at first, then drops through a grassy swale. The reservoir is behind you, and shielded by widely spaced stands of oaks.

Top another small crest then drop into another swale, with a strip of gray riprap laid in the bed of the seasonal stream that runs through it. Pass a faded China Gulch signpost, then the junction with the Loop Trail, which is where you'll close the loop on the return. Like a long, lazy roller coaster, the trail/road rises out of the swale into a mixed oak woodland, with a few buckeyes thrown in. The first trees to leaf out in spring and the first to lose their leaves in midsummer, buckeyes are distinctive for their fruits: orbs with fuzzy coats that hang like Christmas ornaments from the bare branches. Shuck the fruit to expose the smooth, rusty orange nut. The tree also produces fragrant flowers in late spring.

When the deciduous oaks have lost their leaves, usually by early December, check the bare branches for balls of mistletoe, which look like big, round, messy birds' nests. It's also easy to spot woodpeckers in the trees in the winter months: The acorn woodpecker, black with white wing patches and a flashy red patch on the top of its head, can often be seen flitting from tree to tree. Though you may think the bird is stockpiling the nuts in a variety of trees, in fact the acorn woodpecker typically has only one storehouse, called a granary tree, and acorns are stored in various cavities in this single tree.

After rounding a switchback, the trail winds through another fold in the hills. The fence line of the reservoir property is on the left. Pass another trail marker, then head downhill past a trail post and a cattle trail that branches right, leading across the broad swale. Stay straight (left) on the China Gulch route, which drops into the bottom of the swale and to the second junction with the Loop Trail.

Turning right onto the Loop Trail, you'll hike through the base of the drainage, which can be boggy (and may even boast a vernal pool) in spring. The stream, dry in late season, runs to the trail's left. Cattle can be found in this basin as well. Cross the rocky streambed twice before the trail narrows to singletrack and climbs onto a hillside overlooking Camanche Reservoir.

The long traverse across open slopes overlooking the lake can be hot in summer, but affords beautiful views year-round. The springtime wildflower bloom is lovely, and lone trailside oaks lend drama to the vista. The trail bends into an arm of the reservoir and loops through a triad of gullies, wet in winter and bone dry in late season, which offer the only shade you'll experience along this leg of the loop. Look for a stand of digger pines on the hillside to the right of the third gully.

Cross the riprap swale to close the loop on the China Gulch road. Turn left and retrace your steps to the trailhead.

MILES AND DIRECTIONS

0.0 Start by walking down the gravel road and through the gate. Sign in, then proceed up the ranch road.

0.5 Pass a China Gulch Trail post and an unmarked cattle track.

0.6 The Loop Trail takes off to the right (this is the return route). Stay straight (left) on the China Gulch Trail.

0.8 Pass a trail post.

1.0 Pass another trail post at a cattle trail that breaks right. Stay left on the China Gulch Trail.

1.2 Reach the second junction with the Loop Trail. Turn right on the Loop Trail, dropping down toward the lake through the bottom of the swale.

1.3 Cross a rocky streamlet and pass a trail post.

1.4 Cross another rocky creek bed and pass another trail post. The route then narrows to singletrack and climbs onto a hillside overlooking the lake.

2.0 Curve north, away from the lake proper, and traverse above an inlet.

2.1 Bend through the first gully.

2.3 Round the second gully. Ignore the horse trail that takes off to the right, uphill.

2.6 Switchback through the third gully. Close the loop on the China Gulch trail/road less than 0.1 mile beyond. Turn left to retrace your steps.

3.2 Arrive back at the trailhead.

HIKE INFORMATION

Local information: Lake Camanche Recreation; (209) 763-5121; www.camanche recreation.com. Recreation area concessions, including boating, camping, fishing, and cabins, are offered by the Camanche Recreation Company.

Camping: Camping is available on the north and south shores of the reservoir. Camps with complete amenities, as well as a primitive campsite, are available on the north shore. For information and reservations contact Lake Camanche Recreation; (209) 763-5121; www.camancherecreation.com; camping@camanchere creation.com.

Foothills

The trail atop Monroe Ridge in Marshall Gold Discovery State Historic Park looks down on Coloma and the site of Sutter's Mill, where California's famed gold rush began (Hike 40).

Sacramento is the gateway to the Sierra Nevada. The main attraction within an hour's drive of the metro area is the Auburn State Recreation Area, a large tract encompassing fine foothills landscapes such as the confluence of the north and middle forks of the American River. Given the scenic value of the recreation area, as well as its proximity to the Sacramento metropolitan area, the bulk of trails in this section lie within its boundaries.

An abandoned railroad grade, a dam, a secluded falls, gold rush mementoes, and snow-capped peaks...

Routes in Auburn SRA include a trail that follows an abandoned railroad grade, a trail that climbs to the dam at Lake Clementine, a trail that follows a tributary of the American River to a secluded falls, and a long trail circling through the upper reaches of the recreation area. These selections are just a few of the options available in the region; feel free to explore above and beyond.

Trail gems in the foothills aren't limited to the recreation area, however. Regional parks offer great opportunities for outings, including routes through Cronan Ranch and down to Hidden Falls. Venture back in time, to the days of California's gold rush, at the Marshall Gold Discovery State Historic Park outside Placerville. And the long tour around Jenkinson Lake provides a taste of what you'd enjoy if you ventured higher into the Sierra Nevada, with dense forest crowding the path and views of snow-capped peaks.

Trails in the foothills are accessed via I-80 and US 50, both of which connect Sacramento with the Lake Tahoe basin. Scenic CA 49 runs north—south between the interstate and US 50, linking two mountain towns with mining heritages, Auburn and Placerville (as well as Grass Valley and other Gold Country hamlets).

The Knickerbocker Creek crossing is both the low point and the high point of the Olmstead Loop. Located in a cool and shady draw, it's a great place to rest before the long climb back to the trailhead at Cool (Hike 36).

Hidden Falls Regional Park

Waterfalls and cataracts on two streams that run through Hidden Falls Regional Park are the focal points of this double-loop hike. Hidden Falls drops 75 feet or so over stair-step cliffs, with an overlook platform offering easy access to the view. The Seven Pools can be seen from a high rock outcrop, water spilling from basin to basin within a rock-walled hollow.

Start: On the signed Poppy Trail to the right (east) of the restrooms

Distance: 5.2-mile double loop

Hiking time: 3 to 4 hours

Difficulty: Moderate due to distance and the climbs into and out of Deadman Canyon

Trail surface: Dirt singletrack, gravel roadway

Best season: Spring, when the wildflowers are in bloom and flows in the falls and cataracts are high

Other trail users: Lots of equestrians; the more occasional mountain biker

Trailhead amenities: Parking, restrooms, trash cans, picnic sites, information signboard with park map

Canine compatibility: Leashed dogs permitted

Fees and permits: None

Schedule: Open daily, sunrise to a half hour after sunset, year-round

Maps: USGS Gold Hill CA: online at www.placer.ca.gov/Departments/Facility/parks/hiddenfalls.aspx. Maps are also posted at numbered trail junctions, along with mileages.

Trail contact: Placer County Facilities Services, 11476 C Ave., Auburn 95603; (530) 886-4900; www.placer.ca.gov/Departments/Facility/parks/hiddenfalls.aspx

Other: The Hidden Gate Trail offers a short, paved, wheelchair-accessible option to Hidden Falls park visitors.

Special considerations: This park is extremely popular with all trail users. All trail traffic yields to equestrians; step to the downhill side of the trail to allow horses to pass. Expanding opportunities at the park are also in the works, including the addition of nearly 1,000 acres and the designation of a natural interpretive area.

Finding the trailhead: From Sacramento head east on I-80 for about 25 miles to the exit for CA 49 to Grass Valley and Placerville in Auburn. Go north on CA 49 toward Grass Valley. Drive 2.5 miles to the junction with Atwood Road and turn right onto Atwood. Follow Atwood Road for about 1.7 miles to where it becomes Mount Vernon Road, then follow Mount Vernon Road another 0.5 mile (2.2 miles total) to a T junction with Joeger Road. Go left, continuing on Mount Vernon Road for another 2 miles to the intersection with Mears Road on the right. Turn right on Mears Road and drive 0.5 mile to Mears Place. Turn right on Mears Place and go 0.2 mile to the signed park entrance. GPS: N38 57.516'/W121 09.830'

THE HIKE

Hidden Falls spills through Deadman Canyon with enough force and noise to wake the dead. A gem of an overlook deck offers visitors a perfect platform from which to enjoy the waterfall, which remains vigorous year-round. This platform is a social gathering place along the trail, where couples come to picnic, dog walkers allow their furred friends to meet, and hikers share tales of the trail with their comrades.

Where Hidden Falls is gregarious, the Seven Pools are reclusive. It would take a feat of bushwhacking through tick- and snake-infested brush to reach them from the rocky overlook perched high above on the Seven Pools Vista Trail. The pools lie along Coon Creek, which spills through a steep-walled canyon and overflows basin after basin in short bursts of whitewater.

The trails that link these two park highlights cruise into and out of the canyons that hold the streams, traversing slopes shaded by a variety of oaks and the occasional digger pine, bay laurel, and manzanita, with bracken fern, blackberry, toyon, poison oak, and wildflowers enlivening the understory.

The route begins by dropping away from the parking area on the Poppy Trail, a well-maintained path broad enough to allow hikers—or horses—traveling in opposite directions to pass without having to step off the track. The trail drops into Deadman Canyon via a few switchbacks, then runs alongside the creek down to a convergence of trails at a bridge spanning the waterway. The main track is obvious, though several use trails break right toward the creek, which is bordered in blackberries and other riparian brush.

Continue down from the bridge on the trail signed Falls Overlook, which traces the creek downstream. A signed hikers-only trail breaks left, dropping down a short flight of stone steps. Stay right where a social path leads down to the creek through purple-flowering vinca, which competes with blackberry as the ground cover in a grove of spindly oaks.

Views of the creek below, flowing through rock-lined pools that form perfect swimming holes for dogs and people alike, open as the trail switchbacks. Pass a stone staircase on the right that leads down to the swimming holes before reaching the wooden deck overlooking the falls. The deck offers a great vantage of the stepped spill, which remains vigorous year-round but is most spectacular (and loudest) in spring when the creek is flush with meltwater from the Sierra. The platform is also a gathering place for park visitors and their dogs: Acquaintances are made, lunches are shared, and dogs are allowed to meet and greet each other and the humans that accompany them.

From the platform you can retrace your steps to the trailhead for an easy 3-mile out-and-back hike. But the rest of the park invites exploration. To continue the double-loop route, head back to the start of the hikers-only trail and turn left, climbing up to a shaded picnic site. Continue uphill on Turkey Ridge Trail, a gravel access road, toward the crest of the ridge.

One of the Seven Pools along Coon Creek is spied from on high on the long loop through Hidden Falls Regional Park outside Auburn.

Just before topping out near a restroom, take the trail that breaks left, the Quail Run Trail. Quail Run meets up with the Seven Pools Loop, which in turn drops around switchbacks into the Coon Creek canyon, passing through thickets of manzanita, poison oak, and scrub oak along the way. The route parallels the stream for a distance, passing a junction with the Pond Turtle Trail (an option back to the trailhead), then begins to climb away from the waterway. As you ascend, the trail is bordered by toyon, with its bright red fruits glowing in the autumn sunlight. Below, the creek tightens into cataracts.

When you arrive at the next trail junction, take the signed SEVEN POOLS VISTA TRAIL. This leads up to a rock outcrop that offers a bird's-eye view of the Seven Pools, spilling through the rocky, brush-choked canyon. The pools are all but inaccessible, with nary even a social trail ferreting down through the tangle of brush and rocks.

From the overlook the vista trail climbs back onto the ridge separating the Deadman and Coon Creek drainages. Pick up the Blue Oak Trail on the other side of Turkey Ridge Trail, and descend via sweeping traverses and a switchback into Deadman Canyon. The Blue Oak Trail ends at the bridge and the junction with the Pond Turtle, Poppy, Turkey Ridge, and Falls Overlook trails. Climb the broad Pond Turtle Trail—actually a gravel road, wide enough for horses to travel side by side and still leave plenty of room for a hiker to pass. Look for bracken fern and wild grape on the hillside above and below the roadway as you climb; this gives way to grassland at the end of the route. Pass the junctions with the paved Hidden Gate Trail and the Poppy Trail, then arrive back at the trailhead.

MILES AND DIRECTIONS

0.0 Start by passing the restrooms and information signs. Where the Pond Turtle Trail, the paved Hidden Gate Trail, and the singletrack Poppy Trail meet, take the Poppy Trail to the right.

0.1 At the second trail junction (with a map board), stay right on the Poppy Trail.

0.6 After the third switchback, the trail follows Deadman Creek downstream.

0.8 The Poppy Trail ends at the bridge, where it meets the Pond Turtle Trail. Cross the bridge to the trail junction on the other side, and go left on the signed trail to the Falls Overlook.

1.1 Pass a cattle gate, being sure to close it behind you.

1.3 Reach the junction with the hikers-only trail down to the falls. Go left on the path signed FALLS TRAIL, staying right where a social trail breaks left toward the creek.

Snakebit

Encountering wildlife on the trails is to be expected. And treating that wildlife with respect is a necessity for anyone who travels on trails frequently.

I would qualify myself as one of those people. I've startled bears, nearly stepped on tarantulas, had stare-downs with coyotes and raccoons, and run across bobcats on my journeys. The only time I've seen a mountain lion was from the safety of my car, and the hiking gods permitting, that's as close as I ever want to get.

But close encounters with snakes? Well, that's a different story.

I've been snakebit. Not by a rattlesnake, thankfully. This was a gopher snake, and it was on a little path that led from a paved trail alongside a creek to a soccer complex in the middle of suburbia. My dog stepped over the snake, and startled it. My husband stepped over the snake, and pissed it off. I stepped over the snake, and it sunk its little fangs right into my shin.

I launched myself skyward and launched the snake outward, into the brush. My husband pursued the poor terrorized creature, quickly determining it was not a rattler. But not quite quick enough, because in the meantime I stood, also terrorized, waiting for the poison to start coursing through my veins. Nothing happened, of course. Nothing, that is, except that I now see snakes wherever I go.

Which is not a bad thing. Because, hiking down into the Coon Creek drainage in Hidden Falls Regional Park on a cool November afternoon, I saw the rattlesnake before it saw me. It had just poked its distinctive triangle-shaped head out of the grass alongside the trail. I stopped . . . and no, I did not run screaming. Instead I watched from a safe distance, even took a picture. I didn't bother it, and it didn't bother me. It wasn't until some equestrians came by that the reptile slithered across the track and into the shelter of the grass. We continued on our separate ways, mutually respectful and, I assume, mutually hopeful that our paths wouldn't cross again.

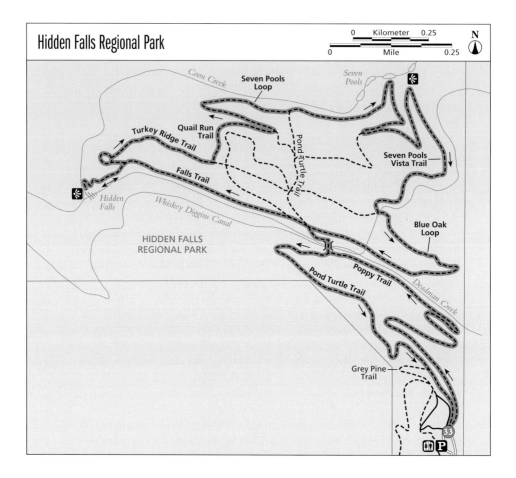

Hidden Falls Regional Park

0   Kilometer   0.25

0   Mile   0.25

N

Coon Creek

Seven Pools Loop

Seven Pools

Quail Run Trail

Turkey Ridge Trail

Pond Turtle Trail

Seven Pools Vista Trail

Falls Trail

Hidden Falls

Whiskey Diggins Canal

Blue Oak Loop

HIDDEN FALLS REGIONAL PARK

Pond Turtle Trail

Poppy Trail

Deadman Creek

Grey Pine Trail

33

P

1.5   Arrive at the observation deck overlooking Hidden Falls. Enjoy the views and visit the swimming holes, then retrace your steps to the beginning of the hikers-only trail.

1.7   At the junction of the Hidden Falls access route and the hikers-only path, turn left and climb to a shaded picnic area. Go left on the Turkey Ridge Trail, a gravel road.

1.9   Stay right on the Turkey Ridge Trail where an unsigned dirt road breaks to the left.

2.1   Pass through a cattle gate (close it behind you) and climb to a trail junction just below the restroom on the ridgetop. Go left on the singletrack Quail Run Trail.

2.2   Arrive at the signed junction on the Quail Run Trail. Go left on Quail Run, which loops back toward the cattle gate, then arcs sharply right into the woods.

2.4 At the signed junction (with a trail map board; this is junction 14), go left on the Seven Pools Loop.

2.9 At the signed junction with the Pond Turtle Trail, stay straight on the Seven Pools Loop.

3.1 Round a switchback with a trail sign, then cross a little bridge over a seasonal stream.

3.25 At the signed trail intersection, go left on the Seven Pools Vista Trail.

3.5 Arrive at the rock outcrop that serves as the Seven Pools overlook. Check out the views, then continue up the Seven Pools Vista Trail.

3.8 The Seven Pools Vista Trail ends on the Turkey Ridge Trail. Cross the road to the Blue Oak Trail, and descend via the Blue Oak into Deadman Canyon.

4.25 A small bridge spans a seasonal stream.

4.4 Reach the bridge and junction with the Falls Trail. Go left, across the bridge, then right on the broad Pond Turtle Trail.

5.0 The Grey Pine Trail merges with the Pond Turtle track. Beyond, pass a trail map board and a junction with the Poppy Trail.

5.2 Arrive back at the trailhead.

HIKE INFORMATION

Local information: The City of Auburn, 1225 Lincoln Way, Auburn 95603; (530) 823-4211; www.auburn.ca.gov. The city site offers information for residents as well as visitors.

Further information about Auburn and its environs can be found at the Auburn Visitor Center and through the Old Town Auburn Business Association. Call (530) 823-3836 or visit www.oldtownauburnca.com.

Local events/attractions: Both the Western States Endurance Run/UltraMarathon and the Western States Endurance Ride/Tevis Cup (an equestrian event) are staged in the foothills surrounding Auburn each year. For more information on the run, visit the website at http://ws100.com. For information about the ride, go to www.teviscup.org.

Restaurants: Awful Annie's Restaurant, 160 Sacramento St., Auburn; (530) 888-9857; www.awfulannies.com. Offering some of the best breakfast scrambles in the region, Awful Annie's is also known for its Sandwitchery, where you can order up scrumptious meals between two slices of bread.

The abandoned bed of the Mountain Quarry Railroad rolls across the historic No Hands Bridge below the confluence of the middle and north forks of the American River, then follows the river downstream through a lovely stretch of canyon.

Start: At the gate (#150) on the east side of the highway just past the CA 49 bridge over the confluence of the north and middle forks of the American River

Distance: 4.2 miles out and back

Hiking time: About 2 hours

Difficulty: Moderate due only to trail length

Trail surface: Dirt and ballast on a former railroad bed

Best season: Spring and fall. Summer may be very hot, but you can cool off in the water. Winter rains or snow may render the track muddy, but it generally dries out within a couple of days.

Other trail users: Trail runners and equestrians. Mountain bikers are not permitted on the trail, but tracks in the dirt indicate they poach the route.

Trailhead amenities: Limited roadside parking, trash can. Restrooms are at the Stagecoach trailhead on the west side of the Old Foresthill Bridge, about 0.5 mile north of the CA 49 trailhead for the Mountain Quarry Railroad Trail. No water is available; bring all that you need.

Canine compatibility: Leashed dogs permitted

Fees and permits: None

Schedule: Open daily 6 a.m. to 9 p.m. in summer; 7 a.m. to 7 p.m. in winter

Maps: USGS Auburn CA; Auburn State Recreation Area brochure available at recreation headquarters on CA 49 and online at www.parks.ca.gov. Note that in some resources the trail is known as the Railroad Bed Section of the Western States Trail.

Trail contact: Auburn State Recreation Area, 501 El Dorado St., Auburn 95603-4949; (530) 885-4527; www.parks.ca.gov

Finding the trailhead: From I-80 head east to the CA 49 exit in Auburn. Take CA 49 south through Auburn (toward Placerville), following the signs for 0.5 mile through the downtown area to where the highway plunges down into the American River canyon. CA 49 meets Old Foresthill Road at the base of the hill at 2.5 miles. Turn right (southeast), cross the bridge, and park alongside the road. The trailhead is at the gate (#150) immediately on the southeast side of the bridge. GPS: N38 54.894'/W121 2.404'

THE HIKE

Abundant riches typical of California's gold country surround this easy route. Not riches that can be mined from mountainsides or sifted from river bottoms, mind you, but the wealth of a self-propelled journey down the steep-walled American River canyon.

The Mountain Quarry Railroad Trail lies on the bed of a historic rail line that linked the limestone quarry on the Middle Fork American River with the town of Auburn and Southern Pacific tracks that continued from the foothills town down into Sacramento. The rail-trail includes passage over the No Hands Bridge, so named, according to local trail guides, because for many years it didn't have guardrails (now it does). Once the longest bridge of its kind in the world, the scenic bridge survived the collapse of the Hell Hole dam in 1964, as well as subsequent floods, and now provides hikers with a tangible encounter with history.

Enjoyably straightforward, the trail deviates from the original rail line only where trestles have been removed. Their concrete abutments, overgrown with shrubs and inscribed with the dates they were poured—1915, 1921—overlook the gullies that they spanned. Unable to negotiate the steep curves in the river

Located just below the confluence of the north fork and middle fork of the American River, the No Hands Bridge offers a scenic start and end to a hike on the Mountain Quarry trail.

canyon's walls, trestles straightened the rail line so trains could pass. Hikers don't need straight lines, and swinging through folds in the terrain poses no hardship to those on foot.

Along the track you'll encounter numerous signs of the defunct rail line, including sections where cut-and-fill construction techniques left grass-covered berms on either side of the trail. Railroads, even in the mountains, had to follow gentle grades, and the Mountain Quarry line was no exception. You'll encounter only one steep set of pitches along the route, where the trail dips into a gully washed by a small waterfall dubbed the "Black Hole of Calcutta." The year-round cascade offers a dark, cooling respite along the track.

The rest of the route is flat, sunny, and pleasant, offering great views down to the river. The exposed section of trail at the base of Eagle Rock, a steep, flaking monolith with debris spilling downslope, is particularly striking. Side trails lead both uphill and down to the riverside, but stay straight and flat, and you'll never lose your way.

If there's a downside to this route, it's only that road noise from nearby CA 49 echoes in the canyon. The scenic and historic attributes of the route mitigate this potential distraction.

The Mountain Quarry Railroad Trail is a portion of the Western States Trail, 100 miles long and the venue for endurance races for runners and equestrians. No need for endurance on this trek, however. A water bottle, a granola bar, and a camera are all you'll need. The interpretive guide put together by the Auburn State Recreation Area Canyon Keepers is also a helpful resource. Keyed to posts along the trail, it provides information about the natural and human history of the route.

Interpreting the Confluence

You can link a hike on the Mountain Quarry rail-trail with the first 0.5 mile of the Lake Clementine Trail in an interpretive loop that focuses on historic bridges in the American River canyons. The Confluence Interpretive Trail is marked with numbered posts along both stretches of the trails that are keyed to an interpretive guide included in the *American River Canyon Hikes* booklet put together by the Auburn SRA Canyon Keepers. A short stretch of roadside hiking separates the Mountain Quarry Railroad Trail from the Lake Clementine trailhead. Follow CA 49 back across the bridge, then follow Old Foresthill Road right (north), across the Old Foresthill Road Bridge to the Lake Clementine trailhead, and hike upstream toward the towering Foresthill Bridge.

MILES AND DIRECTIONS

0.0   Start by passing the gate at the trailhead.

0.2   Pass the junction with the steep Pointed Rocks Trail (which leads up toward Cool) on the left (south). Go right (west) across the No Hands Bridge.

0.3   Reach marker 3 on the west side of the No Hands Bridge and continue on the obvious rail-trail. An interpretive sign at the end of the bridge offers information about its historic significance.

0.6   Pass a Western States Trail sign and a pair of side trails. Remain on the obvious rail-trail.

0.8   Reach the first trestle abutment. The trail departs from the railroad grade, narrows to singletrack, and scoops through a gully.

1.0   Pass a trestle foundation dated 1915.

1.1   Reach the only steep drop and climb of the route, through the "Black Hole of Calcutta." Once back on the railroad grade, you'll pass another Western States Trail marker.

1.3   Pass another trestle abutment.

1.4   At the unmarked trail intersection, stay left (straight/west) on the obvious railroad grade.

1.7   Skirt Eagle Rock, a giant, flaking rock face.

2.1   Pass a mile marker and another Western States Pioneer Express Trail marker at the end of the railroad grade. This is the turnaround point. Retrace your steps to the trailhead.

4.2   Arrive back at the trailhead.

HIKE INFORMATION

Local information: The City of Auburn, 1225 Lincoln Way, Auburn 95603; (530) 823-4211; www.auburn.ca.gov. The city site offers information for residents as well as visitors.

Information about Auburn and its environs can be found at the Auburn Visitor Center and through the Old Town Auburn Business Association. Call (530) 823-3836 or visit www.oldtownauburnca.com.

Local events/attractions: Both the annual Western States Endurance Run/Ultra-Marathon and the Western States Endurance Ride/Tevis Cup, an equestrian

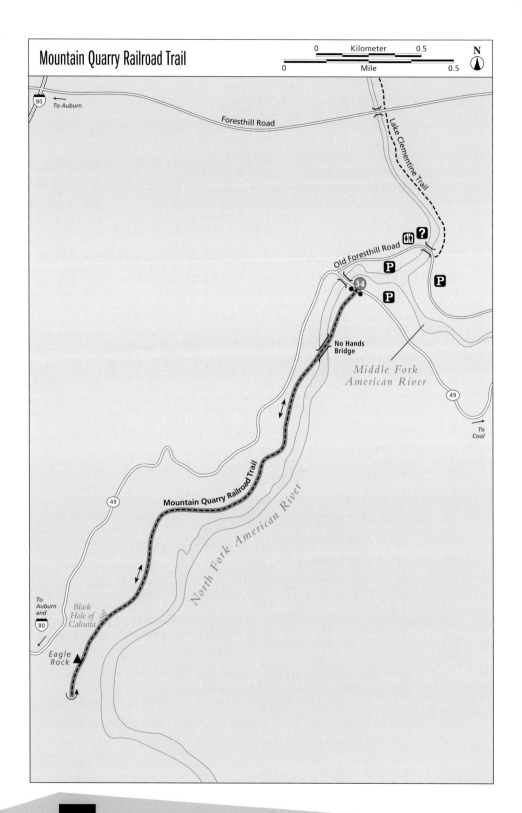

Kilometer
0 0.5

Mile
0 0.5

N

To Auburn

Foresthill Road

Lake Clementine Trail

Old Foresthill Road

34

No Hands
Bridge

*Middle Fork
American River*

To
Cool

Mountain Quarry Railroad Trail

North Fork American River

To
Auburn
and

*Black
Hole of
Calcutta*

*Eagle
Rock*

event, pass through Auburn. For more information on the run, visit the website at http://ws100.com. For information about the ride, go to www.teviscup.org.

Hike tours: Docent-led interpretive hikes are conducted throughout the recreation area. Visit the Auburn State Recreation Area Canyon Keepers website at www.canyonkeepers.org for more information.

Restaurants: Awful Annie's Restaurant, 160 Sacramento St., Auburn; (530) 888-9857; www.awfulannies.com. Offering some of the best breakfast scrambles in the region, Awful Annie's is also known for its Sandwitchery, where you can order up scrumptious meals between two slices of bread.

Organizations: Auburn State Recreation Area Canyon Keepers are volunteers that help with a variety of programs in the recreation area, from leading hikes to supporting the ranger staff. Visit the website at http://members.psyber.com/asra for more information, or contact the Auburn SRA ranger station.

Other resources: *American River Canyon Hikes,* a guide to trails along the middle and north forks of the American River, is a wonderful compendium of hiking options in the Auburn State Recreation Area. Compiled by members of the Auburn SRA Canyon Keepers, it is available locally and from online retailers.

Begin your hike down this former railbed by passing over the American River via the historic No Hands Bridge.

Lake Clementine Trail

This scenic stretch traces the north fork of the American River, passes one of the impressive towers of the Foresthill Bridge, offers access to a cool swimming hole, and culminates at an overlook of Lake Clementine's waterfall spillway.

Start: At the gate signed #139 on the east side of Old Foresthill Road Bridge

Distance: 4.6 miles out and back

Hiking time: 2 to 3 hours

Difficulty: Moderate due to trail length

Trail surface: Dirt roadway, short stretches of paved road, dirt singletrack

Best season: Spring and fall

Other trail users: Mountain bikers, trail runners

Trailhead amenities: None. Restrooms, information boards, and additional parking are at the Stagecoach trailhead on the west side of the Old Foresthill Bridge. There is also a restroom across the road from the trailhead in the roadside parking area. Bring plenty of drinking water.

Canine compatibility: Leashed dogs permitted

Fees and permits: None

Schedule: Open daily 6 a.m. to 9 p.m. in summer; 7 a.m. to 7 p.m. in winter

Maps: USGS Auburn CA; Auburn State Recreation Area brochure available at recreation headquarters on CA 49 and online at www.parks.ca.gov

Trail contact: Auburn State Recreation Area, 501 El Dorado St., Auburn 95603-4949; (530) 885-4527; www.parks.ca.gov

Finding the trailhead: From I-80 in Auburn take the CA 49/Placerville exit. Follow CA 49 through downtown Auburn (signs point the way) for about 0.5 mile to where the highway dives into the American River canyon. Proceed another 2.5 miles to the floor of the canyon and the junction of CA 49 and Old Foresthill Road. Continue straight for about 0.5 mile on Old Foresthill Road to the trailhead on the left, on the east side of the Old Foresthill Bridge. Parking is alongside the roadway just beyond the bridge. The trail begins behind the gate (#139, signed for Lake Clementine). GPS: N38 54.978'/W121 2.129'

THE HIKE

The confluence of the north and middle forks of the American River, in the bottom of a steep, spectacular canyon, draws thousands of visitors to the Auburn State Recreation Area (SRA) each year. The river valleys—and the historic sites within them—have long been slated for submersion beneath a huge and controversial reservoir. But the proposed Auburn Dam, which has been besieged by seismic, environmental, and economic concerns since construction began in the mid-1960s, was brought to an apparently permanent halt in late 2008 when water rights held by the US Bureau of Reclamation were revoked. If completed, the dam would drown the river behind a 690-foot wall, and the popular trails that explore the forks would drown along with it. Now (hopefully) they can be enjoyed in perpetuity.

The trail to Lake Clementine showcases the lovely natural setting of the canyon, but man-made structures along the route also demand attention. The green lattice arches and massive concrete support columns of the Foresthill Bridge frame the trail's outset, the boom and clank of cars passing overhead echoing into the canyon. The high-flying bridge, reportedly the tallest in California, was built to span a reservoir that has never materialized; the water would reach as high as 22 feet

The overlook of Lake Clementine's dam and spillway highlight the turnaround point for this relaxing out-and-back trek.

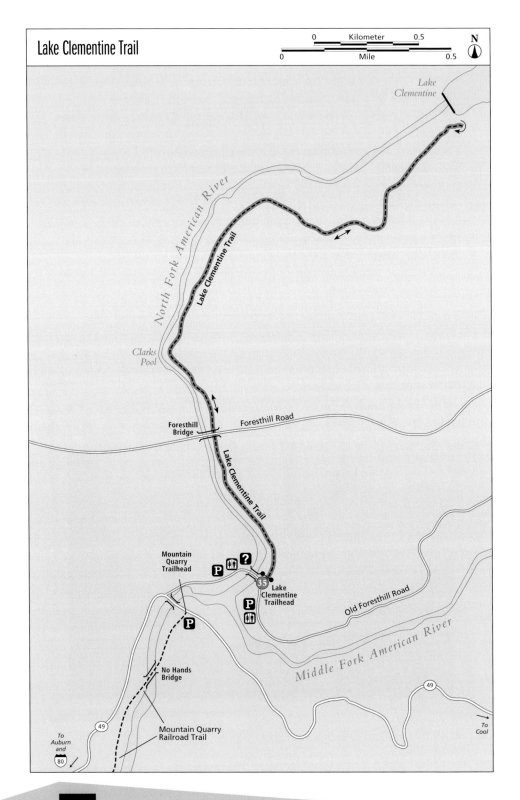

Lake Clementine Trail

Lake Clementine

North Fork American River

Lake Clementine Trail

Clarks Pool

Foresthill Bridge

Foresthill Road

Lake Clementine Trail

Mountain Quarry Trailhead

Lake Clementine Trailhead

Old Foresthill Road

No Hands Bridge

Mountain Quarry Railroad Trail

Middle Fork American River

To Auburn and 80

49

To Cool

49

Kilometer

Mile

N

below the deck if the lake was filled. More information on this bridge, and others along the route, is provided in an interpretive guide produced by the Auburn SRA Canyon Keepers.

Below the structure the wide dirt road to Lake Clementine follows the river's curves, with anglers' trails dropping off to the left to the rocky banks. The foundations of smaller historic bridges jut from forested hillsides, which are also scarred by minor slides and small fires. Islands and rocky shoals in the midst of the river harbor stands of willow that blush yellow in fall.

A little less than a mile upstream from the confluence, the river widens and deepens into Clarks Hole, a popular swimming spot formed by an "underwater dam" built by placer miners more than one hundred years ago. This is a popular destination in and of itself, and makes a great turnaround spot for those seeking a shorter hike.

Beyond Clarks Hole the trail begins an easy, steady climb through a mixed evergreen forest, heavy on the oaks and light on the pines. It eventually reaches the paved Lake Clementine Road; a short trek down the pavement and along a singletrack trail on the left leads to an up-close and personal view of the waterfall spillway of the North Fork Dam, with Lake Clementine pooling behind. The dam overlook is a perfect place to snack, rest, and watch boats ply the smooth waters of a reservoir that filled behind a dam built to capture mining debris.

From the dam, retrace your steps to the trailhead.

MILES AND DIRECTIONS

0.0 Start by passing the gate (#139) at the signed trailhead.

0.1 Stay left (riverside) at the unmarked trail fork.

0.2 Pass interpretive marker 7 at the concrete bridge abutment.

0.5 The trail narrows to singletrack as it passes beneath the massive support tower of the Foresthill Bridge.

0.8 Reach the southernmost edge of Clarks Hole. Social trails drop left to the riverside for the length of the pond-smooth pool. This is a good turnaround point for families and those seeking a shorter hike.

1.0 The abutment for a historic (now defunct) covered bridge juts from the opposite bank. The trail begins to climb.

1.2 Pass a social trail leading down to the riverside. The trail continues to climb through oaks and scrub, with limited views opening of the North Fork Dam and Lake Clementine.

1.8 Arrive at the end of the dirt road/trail at a gate. Go left (north, then northeast) on the paved roadway.

2.2 A singletrack path leads left (north) toward the dam overlook.

2.3 Reach the overlook, take in the views, then retrace your steps to the trailhead.

4.6 Arrive back at the trailhead.

HIKE INFORMATION

Local information: The City of Auburn, 1225 Lincoln Way, Auburn 95603; (530) 823-4211; www.auburn.ca.gov. The city site offers information for residents as well as visitors.

Information about Auburn and its environs can be found at the Auburn Visitor Center and through the Old Town Auburn Business Association. Call (530) 823-3836 or visit www.oldtownauburnca.com.

Local events/attractions: Both the 100-mile Western States Endurance Run/UltraMarathon and the 100-mile Western States Endurance Ride/Tevis Cup (an equestrian event) are staged in the foothills surrounding Auburn each year. For more information on the run, visit the website at http://ws100.com. For information about the ride, go to www.teviscup.org.

Hike tours: Docent-led interpretive hikes are conducted throughout the Auburn SRA. Contact the Auburn State Recreation Area Canyon Keepers at www.canyonkeepers.org for more information.

Restaurants: Ikedas, 13500 Lincoln Way, Auburn; (530) 885-4243; http://restaurant-bakery-auburn-ca.com/gourmet-food-produce. Ikedas features fresh produce grown locally, homemade canned goods such as dipping sauces and salsas, incredible homemade pies, and diner-style fare, including the best BLT you'll ever taste.

Organizations: Auburn State Recreation Area Canyon Keepers help with a variety of programs in the recreation area, from leading hikes to supporting the ranger staff. Visit the website at www.canyonkeepers.org for more information, or contact the Auburn SRA ranger station.

Other resources: *American River Canyon Hikes,* a guide to trails along the middle and north forks of the American River, is a wonderful compendium of hiking options. Compiled by members of the Auburn SRA Canyon Keepers, it is available locally and from online retailers.

To cross the Foresthill Covered Bridge, built in 1875 and located upstream from Clarks Hole on the North Fork American River, the Auburn SRA Canyon Keepers report folks were charged tolls of 6 cents per cow, 50 cents for a horseman, and $1 for a wagon pulled by two horses.

Olmstead Loop

The terrain covered on this long foothills loop encompasses oak woodlands, ranch-lands, and hollows, including a verdant drainage where Knickerbocker Creek waters bay laurels, maples, and other stalwarts of riparian zones. Plan to be out in the back-country all day.

Start: At the Olmstead/Knicker-bocker trailhead behind the fire station in Cool

Distance: 8.6-mile loop

Hiking time: 4 to 5 hours

Difficulty: Challenging due to trail length and elevation changes

Trail surface: Dirt singletrack, dirt and gravel roadways

Best season: Spring, for wildflower blooms and cool temperatures

Other trail users: Mountain bik-ers, equestrians

Trailhead amenities: A pair of large gravel parking areas (one for equestrian use), picnic sites, rest-rooms, information kiosk. Other amenities, including gas stations and cafes, are just up CA 49 in Cool.

Canine compatibility: Leashed dogs permitted

Fees and permits: Day-use fee

Schedule: Open daily 6 a.m. to 9 p.m. in summer, 7 a.m. to 7 p.m. in winter

Maps: USGS Auburn CA and Pilot Hill CA; Auburn State Recreation Area brochure available at the recreation headquarters on CA 49 and online at www.parks.ca.gov

Trail contact: Auburn State Rec-reation Area, 501 El Dorado St., Auburn 95603-4949; (530) 885-4527; www.parks.ca.gov

Finding the trailhead: From Sacramento follow I-80 west for about 24 miles to the CA 49 exit (for Placerville / Grass Valley) in Auburn. Exit and head right on CA 49, toward Placerville, following the signs that lead through down-town Auburn to where CA 49 dives into the American River Canyon. Drop a steep and scenic 2.5 miles to the junction of Old Foresthill Road and CA 49. Turn right on CA 49, heading south toward Cool. Climb out of the canyon to St. Florian Court, at the fire station just before you arrive in the little town of Cool, a total of 3.4 miles from the junction with Old Foresthill Road and the bridge over the American River. Turn right on St. Florian Court and go about 0.1 mile to the signed Knickerbocker Area parking lot and fee station. The trailhead is in the southeast corner of the larger parking lot (used by eques-trians for their trailers). GPS: N38 53.346'/W121 01.044'

THE HIKE

The Olmstead Loop mirrors the scenic drive you must make to reach it from Auburn. The trail begins amid the mixed evergreen forest and rolling grasslands that characterize the foothills at Auburn's elevation (about 1,500 feet). It then drops into a canyon cradling a waterway (in this case Knickerbocker Creek, not the American River), then climbs back into oaks and meadows. Toss in some wonderful vistas looking west toward the Sacramento Valley, a couple of relatively steep descents and climbs, and seclusion, and Olmstead supplies just about everything a hardy hiker seeks.

Once known as the Knickerbocker Loop (as evidenced on some signs), the trail was renamed for hiker and mountain biker Dan Olmstead, who championed the trail's construction and promoted cooperative trail use among equestrians, mountain bikers, and hikers. He died in 1993 of cancer, but his legacy continues to not only accommodate, but also delight, adventurers on wheels, heels, and hooves.

That said, unless cyclists on a group ride have chosen the Olmstead route for a day's outing, you're more likely to see equestrians on the trail than mountain bikers. And once you are a mile or two down the trail, it's a good bet you won't encounter another user at all, as the route's length and the variety of terrain virtually guarantee plenty of space between you and anyone else.

You can travel the loop in either direction; it's described here circling clockwise. Pass through the fence at the trailhead, and the dirt path immediately splits. No sign identified the Olmstead route at this point in 2011—and indeed, signage was sketchy at intersections with spur trails along the beginning of the route. You will encounter plenty of signs farther along, however, including mileage markers that, for the most part, appeared to be right on. Olmstead trail markers are generally pale green. While they may not identify junctions, the markers are a nice reassurance that you're on the right track. Still, keep a map and/or directions handy as you hike.

Go left at that initial split, on the wide dirt track that roughly parallels CA 49 for a couple of miles or so. The trail rolls through grassy former ranchland studded with spreading oaks, passing country homes and sometimes within sight of the highway itself. It swings away from civilization for a brief stretch, devolving into narrow singletrack overgrown with blackberry as it crosses the marshy upper reach of Knickerbocker Creek. A small footbridge enables you to cross the creek without getting your shoes too wet, though the path through this section can be boggy.

> ### Green Tip:
> *Never let your dog chase wildlife.*

At the unsigned junction above the footbridge, go right; the trail widens and the surroundings dry out as it leaves the creek behind.

Reach a trail access point at the Cave Valley Gate behind Northside Elementary School. Stay straight on the Olmstead trail, which continues to roll through scenic oak woodland. Though climbing and falling in fits and starts as you proceed, at one point trail posts line up like beacons ahead, straight and sure amid the waving grasses.

Cross another stream, wet even in the dry season, via a footbridge. Wind past a last home on the left, and the trail bends southwest into former ranchland. Barbed wire fences split the hillsides into pastures, and an old watering trough rests beside the route. Views open out across the foothills to the Sacramento Valley, and the trail itself is an open red-dirt roadway—clear, unshaded, and unobstructed. The last signs of civilization you'll see for a while are on the left, in the form of cell towers that clearly were placed here for the same reasons the views are so good.

The views disappear as you enter a woodland. Now descending, the trail intersects a couple of old ranch roads, but the signage is good and it's easy to stay on track. Slip through a gentle hollow watered by a seasonal stream, then drop into the cool, densely shaded drainage that cradles Knickerbocker Creek.

The long and winding Olmstead Loop, shared by mountain bikers, equestrians, and hikers, features sections of singletrack augmented by bridges and boardwalks where needed, as well as dirt roadbeds.

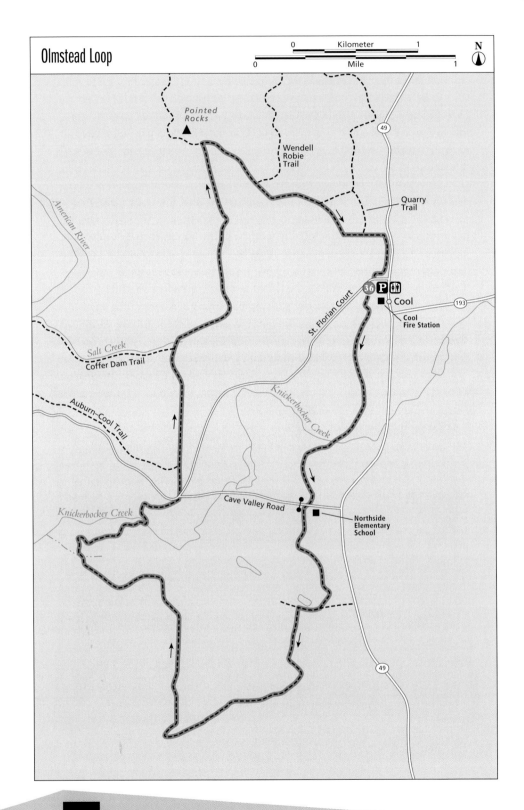

Olmstead Loop

0 | Kilometer | 1
0 | Mile | 1

N

Pointed Rocks ▲

Wendell Robie Trail

Quarry Trail

49

American River

193

36 **P** 🚻
■ ○ Cool
Cool Fire Station

St. Florian Court

Salt Creek
Coffer Dam Trail

Knickerbocker Creek

Auburn–Cool Trail

Knickerbocker Creek

Cave Valley Road
■ — Northside Elementary School

49

Water is a powerful force in the Sierra foothills, evidenced spectacularly by the American River's canyons. But water's power can also be quiet, as shown at Knickerbocker Creek. The drainage is deep, but it's softened by the lush greenery thriving on moisture it draws from the waterway. Bay laurel, maples, madrone, manzanita, and oaks comingle, with an understory of blackberries (not native but producing tasty fruits in August), ferns, poison oak, and coffeeberry tangled below. It's lovely and cooling, features to be savored considering the climb that is to come.

A stonework dam/walkway assists passage across the creek when the water is high; when it's low in late summer and autumn, you can walk across without getting the topsides of your shoes wet. A steep climb leads to a traverse across a grassy slope to the junction with the paved road. An extension of St. Florian Court, the roadway begins behind the gate at the trailhead in Cool and descends down toward the canyon rim of the American River. This is an optional return route if you want to carve a few miles off the loop. Otherwise, signs direct you straight onto a dirt track, then through an intersection with the Auburn-Cool Trail.

A rather steep descent takes you past the junction with the Coffer Dam / Salt Creek Loop Trail and then down into the Salt Creek drainage. You'll follow the stream, which pools in its rocky bed to the right of the trail, for a short distance, then climb through more oak woodland. At the top of the climb, the path reenters the grasslands of ranch country and commences a rolling run through a pastoral landscape that is lush with wildflowers in spring.

Take a sharp right at the junction with the Training Hill Trail/Pointed Rocks Trail, which drops steeply to the left, down to the Western States Trail and other routes in the Auburn State Recreation Area. The Olmstead route is well defined and signed from this point on. As you complete the hike, you'll pass junctions with the Wendell T. Robie Trail and the Quarry Trail, then drop down to a short section that borders busy CA 49. The roadside stretch ends at St. Florian Court, then curves back to the trailhead.

MILES AND DIRECTIONS

0.0 Start by passing through the break in the fence. The trail splits immediately; stay left on the unsigned trail. You'll encounter the first trail post as you come out of a swale a bit farther on.

0.5 Pass a second trail marker. Country homes border the route on the left.

0.8 Cross the footbridge over upper Knickerbocker Creek. At the unsigned trail junction above the bridge, go right.

0.9 A trail merges in from the right, as the main route widens into a rough dirt road. Stay left.

1.0 Climb past a trail marker.

1.25 Reach the Cave Valley Gate (#156) at a trail access point behind a school-yard. Stay straight on the Olmstead Loop (a trail post partially hidden in the brush points the way). Do not go right on the Cave Valley roadway.

1.4 At the top of a hill, the trail splits. Stay left (straight) on the main unsigned path.

1.5 At the unsigned junction at the base of the hill, stay left (straight) again.

1.75 Cross a footbridge over a little stream.

2.0 Pass two trail markers as the treadway narrows. Go left past a sign that defines which trail user must yield to which, then pass the 2-mile marker.

2.25 Several trail markers direct you through a stand of oaks at the top of a climb. Descend past a roadway leading up to a ranch house on the left.

2.5 Pass the 2.5-mile mark and a cement water basin for livestock.

2.6 Unsigned trails merge; stay on the nice red-dirt main track, with a fence running alongside.

3.0 Pass the 3-mile marker.

3.1 Look for the Loop Trail sign, which keeps you on the Olmstead trail.

3.5 Pass the 3.5-mile marker.

3.6 Reach a junction and stay straight on the signed trail (there's a No Motorized Vehicles on Trail sign here, too). Beyond, you'll pass through a broken gate.

4.0 At the 4-mile marker, the track splits. Stay left, as the arrow on the trail marker indicates.

4.5 Descend past the 4.5-mile marker then through a hollow watered by a tributary of Knickerbocker Creek.

5.25 A steep drop lands you beside Knickerbocker Creek. Cross the creek via stones or by wading, then climb out of the drainage.

5.3 Cross the paved road.

5.4 At the junction with the Auburn-Cool Trail, stay straight on the signed Olmstead trail.

6.0 Reach the 6-mile marker and the signed junction with the Coffer Dam / Salt Creek Loop Trail to Auburn. Turn sharply right on the Olmstead trail and drop into the Salt Creek drainage.

6.4 At the junction with a side trail, stay left on the rocky roadway, passing a trail marker.

7.0 Pass the 7-mile marker.

7.25 At the signed junction, the Training Hill Trail / Pointed Rocks Trail drops to the left. Go right; a sign indicates it is 1.7 miles to Cool.

7.5 Pass a junction; stay right on the Olmstead Loop.

7.7 Trails merge at a fence line. Go left and uphill on the Olmstead trail.

7.8 At the junction with the Wendell T. Robie Trail, stay straight (right) on the Olmstead Loop.

7.9 At the junction, stay right on the Olmstead trail.

8.1 Drop through a meadow to an unsigned junction. Go left on the well-used roadway along the fence line.

8.4 Pass the Quarry Trail junction as you climb the hill. The trail drops from here to CA 49.

8.5 Take a sharp right to follow the trail as it runs parallel to the highway.

8.6 Arrive back at the trailhead.

HIKE INFORMATION

Local information: Historic Hwy 49.com is an online resource for all the gold country hamlets located along CA 49, from Cool to Coloma. Visit the website at www.historichwy49.com.

Local events/attractions: The annual Way Too Cool 50K Endurance Run begins and ends in tiny Cool. As if hiking more than 8 miles wasn't enough. For more information visit www.wtc50k.com.

> *Endurance seems to be the name of the game in the foothills surrounding Cool. In addition to the Way Too Cool 50K Endurance Run, parts of the Olmstead Loop have also been incorporated into the American River Classic, an equestrian endurance ride that dates back to 1972 and typically spans the distance between Folsom Lake and the foothills town.*

Codfish Falls

The trail to Codfish Falls has the flavor of an alpine adventure, skimming through a secluded portion of the North Fork American River canyon to a pretty cascade tucked away in a narrow gorge.

Start: At the metal guardrails at the north abutment of the bridge over the American River (at the bottom of Ponderosa Way)
Distance: 3.2 miles out and back
Hiking time: About 2 hours
Difficulty: Moderate due to length and uneven trail surface
Trail surface: Dirt singletrack
Best season: Spring and fall. The summer sun can be blistering (though you can cool off in the river), and winter rain and snow may render the trail inhospitable.
Other trail users: None
Trailhead amenities: Roadside parking for about 10 cars. No restrooms. Bring drinking water.
Canine compatibility: Leashed dogs permitted

Fees and permits: None
Schedule: Open daily 6 a.m. to 9 p.m. in summer, 7 a.m. to 7 p.m. in winter
Maps: USGS Colfax CA and Greenwood CA; Auburn State Recreation Area brochure available at recreation headquarters on CA 49 and online at www.parks.ca.gov
Trail contact: Auburn State Recreation Area, 501 El Dorado St., Auburn 95603-4949; (530) 885-4527; www.parks.ca.gov
Special considerations: The trailhead is remote, reached via a steep, winding country road. The final 2.4 miles of the road are unpaved, and a high-clearance vehicle is recommended.

Finding the trailhead: Follow I-80 east to the town of Weimar in the Sierra foothills (about 11 miles east of Auburn). Take the Weimar Cross Road exit. Turn right (west, then southwest) on Ponderosa Way. Follow Ponderosa Way to a gate at the end of the pavement at 3.2 miles, then drive down the steep, rutted dirt  road into the canyon. The dirt road leads 2.4 miles to the bridge over the North Fork American River (5.6 miles total). Park along the wide stretch of road just northeast of the bridge. The trail is beyond the metal guardrails at the bridge's north abutment. GPS: N39 00.028'/W120 56.391'

THE HIKE

Summertime in the foothills of the Sierra Nevada most often means blue skies and unrelenting sun. Where better to beat the heat than along the American River and in the narrow canyon cooled by Codfish Falls?

The trail leading to these secluded falls follows the North Fork American River, skirting cool pools that invite side trips to sandbars and rocky beaches along the riverbank. The falls flow down a jumble of dark rocks in a shady enclave just north of the river valley. They run year-round and water a pocket of verdant mosses, oaks, and grasses in an otherwise parched environment.

Ponderosa Way, which dives into the American River canyon from Weimar, offers a huge hint at how out-of-bounds this stretch of trail in the Auburn State Recreation Area is. The dirt road falls steeply into the gorge, requiring a driver's

In late season, Codfish Falls narrows to a thin trickle over mossy rock in a shady canyon. It's a different story in winter—fuller and whiter—and worth visiting year-round.

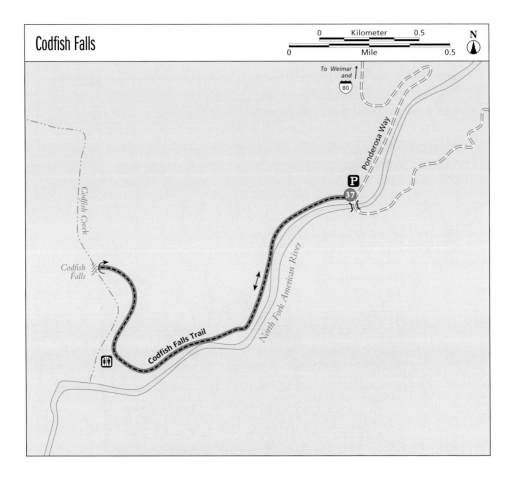

To Weimar and

80

Ponderosa Way

P

37

Codfish Creek

Codfish Falls

North Fork American River

Codfish Falls Trail

full concentration and heightening anticipation as the terrain grows more rugged and remote.

The narrow trail departs from the north abutment of the sturdy but rustic metal-trussed Ponderosa Way bridge, which spans the north fork at the bottom of the canyon. A beach spreads below the trailhead, offering access to the cooling waters of the river—the first of several such opportunities to take a break and dip your toes.

The dirt path traces the watercourse for about 1 mile before curving north into the Codfish Creek canyon. River views dominate, a lovely and classic tableau of water and rock walls. The trail is sometimes uneven and sometimes exposed, but always easy to negotiate. Markers along the way are keyed to an interpretive guide that may be stocked in the box at the trail sign 0.25 mile downstream from the bridge . . . and maybe not. Just to be sure, you can download and print a copy from the website at www.parc-auburn.org/codfish_creek.pdf. Compiled by a local high school student as a senior project, the guide describes the plant and animal life you'll see along the trail.

Straddling the interface between the oak woodlands that dominate at lower elevations and evergreen forests that flourish higher up, the mixed forest that insulates the trail includes live and black oaks, red-barked mountain manzanita, bay laurel, redbud (gorgeous in spring), the occasional madrone, and ponderosa pines. Pause at the golden-barked pines to sniff their vanilla scent—hugging a tree has never smelled so sweet.

Though the river is placid and clear in late season, it swells with snowmelt in spring and early summer. Wait for the flow to mellow before you dip your toes into the water. Fishing and rafting are also popular riverine pastimes.

Pass an outhouse as you curve away from the river and into the Codfish Creek canyon. The falls themselves are about 25 feet high, vigorous when fed by winter rains and thinning to a trickle in the summer season. Still, they provide enough moisture to support a healthy coat of moss for the dark rocks on either side of the waterfall.

After your visit, retrace your steps to the trailhead.

MILES AND DIRECTIONS

0.0   Start on the north side of the Ponderosa Way bridge, climbing over the guardrail onto the singletrack trail.

0.25   Pass a Codfish Falls / Discovery Trail sign and the box that may hold interpretive guides.

0.4   Flat sheets of shale pave a patch of trail. Pass markers 3 and 4.

0.6   Pass marker 6; the trail is about 30 feet above the river, separated from the water by a relatively steep, rocky slope.

0.8   The trail narrows in a gully, showing signs of erosion.

1.0   A narrow social trail breaks left (southeast) to the river. Stay straight on the obvious Codfish Falls trail.

1.1   The trail curls northwest, away from the river.

1.2   Pass a little outhouse. The trail splits just beyond, with a couple of social tracks leading left (southeast) back toward the river. Stay right (northwest), heading up the side canyon toward the falls.

1.4   Cross a seasonal stream, dry in the late season. The trail gently climbs through the mixed evergreen forest.

1.6   Reach Codfish Falls and the final interpretive marker (14). Enjoy the falls, then return as you came.

3.2   Arrive back at the trailhead.

Local information: The city of Colfax, located about 5 miles east of Weimar on I-80, offers a variety of services, restaurants, and community events. The municipal website, at www.ci.colfax.ca.us, includes links to visitor information and recreational and historical resources.

Organizations: Protect American River Canyons (PARC) is an organization "dedicated to the protection and conservation of the recreational, cultural, and historical resources" of the North and Middle Fork American River canyons. Visit www.parc-auburn.org for more information; you'll also find links to the Codfish Falls interpretive guide and a nice map of the trails around the confluence on the website.

> **Green Tip:**
> *Observe wildlife from a distance. Don't interfere in their lives—both you and they will be better for it.*

The trail to Codfish Falls begins along the American River and offers several opportunities to drop off the path to swimming holes in summer and fall (after runoff).

Cronan Ranch Regional Trails Park Loop

Winding ranch roads sweep through meadows thick with wildflowers in spring, then drop to beaches along a rumbling stretch of the South Fork American River. Pass a cluster of old ranch buildings as you climb away from the river and back into the ranchlands.

Start: At the signed trailhead on the east side of Cronan Ranch Regional Trails Park's parking area
Distance: 4.4-mile lollipop
Hiking time: 2 to 3 hours
Difficulty: More challenging due to distance and steep pitches on the descent to riverside
Trail surface: Dirt ranch roads
Best season: Spring for wildflowers; fall for cool weather and great color
Other trail users: Equestrians, mountain bikers, trail runners
Trailhead amenities: Parking for passenger cars and horse trailers, restrooms, trash cans, information board with maps
Canine compatibility: Leashed dogs permitted; however, dogs commonly run off-leash. If you allow your dog to run off-leash, keep him/her under voice control to avoid conflicts with equestrians. Unleashed dogs also risk encountering unfriendly wildlife, including rattlesnakes.
Fees and permits: None
Schedule: Open daily, sunrise to sunset, year-round
Maps: USGS Coloma CA; trail map and brochure available at www.ca .blm.gov/folsom
Trail contact: Bureau of Land Management, Folsom Field Office, 63 Natoma St., Folsom 95630; (916) 985-4474; www.ca.blm.gov/ folsom; www.blm.gov/ca/st/en/fo/ folsom/cronan.html

Finding the trailhead: From I-80 in Auburn take the CA 49/Placerville exit and head south toward Placerville. Follow CA 49 for 11.5 miles, through Auburn, into the American River canyon, then up through the hamlets of Cool and Pilot Hill, to Pedro Hill Road on the right (west). Follow Pedro Hill Road south for 0.1 mile to the signed parking area on the left (south) side of the road.

Alternatively, you can take US 50 east out of Sacramento to the junction with CA 49 in Placerville. Turn left (north) on CA 49 and follow it for 14.2 miles, through Marshall Gold Discovery State Historic Park, to Pedro Hill Road on the left (west). GPS: N38 48.242'/W120 53.687'

THE HIKE

On cool autumn afternoons, with the sun low in the sky, the hills of Cronan Ranch Regional Trails Park take on smoky hues, darker where the forests grow thick on north slopes and lighter where the sun catches the golden annual grasses. The scene is arresting.

A wonderful network consisting of about 12 miles of trails laces through Cronan Ranch, spreading equestrians, mountain bikers, and hikers along ridges and tucking them into long valleys. All roads eventually lead down to the South Fork American River, which defines portions of the property's southern and eastern boundaries. The river, even when the flow is low, rumbles swiftly over its bed, more inviting to rafters and anglers than to swimmers and waders. Still, spread a picnic on a blanket on the rocky shore, with the relentless music of the water rushing by, and you'll enjoy a restful and invigorating break. It was a steep climb down to the riverside; it's worth taking a break before making the steep climb back up to the trailhead.

The grasses coating the hills of Cronan Ranch—and most of California, for that matter—are nonnative annuals, inadvertently brought to the New World by Spanish conquistadors and missionaries in the late 1700s. The grasses grow green in the rainy season and are painted with a succession of native wildflowers—fiddlenecks, lupines, poppies, yarrow, asters, Indian paintbrush—as spring passes into summer. By the time the dog days roll around, in late August, the wildflower blush has faded, and the grasses have been fried golden by the summer sun. The grasses

The loop through Cronan Ranch Regional Trails park traverses foothills meadowlands that blush green in winter and dry to gold in summer.

have long supported grazing animals, including the cattle that the Cronan family raised after purchasing the property from the Central Pacific Railroad in 1891. A cluster of ramshackle ranch buildings at the junction of the Long Valley Trail and Cronan Ranch Road hearken back to what must have been a monastic occupation for the Cronans and the ranching families that followed them.

Today the property is part of a plan to create a South Fork American River trail corridor that would stretch from Greenwood Creek to Salmon Falls, according to Bureau of Land Management (BLM) literature. Equestrians, mountain bikers, and hikers easily share the trails already in place on Cronan Ranch . . . and they also share with paragliders, who climb to high launching points, then ride the thermals with the hawks and vultures.

This route descends into the river canyon via the Down and Up and East Ridge Trails, easy-to-follow ranch roads that drop steeply in sections. Once beside the river, you'll walk downstream past rocky bars and picnic sites, any of which makes a perfect place to stop, rest, and enjoy.

The climb back to the trailhead follows the more gently inclined Long Valley Trail, which leads past the ranch buildings and up along a seasonal stream that blushes green even when the surrounding landscape is brown and dry. You can do the loop in the opposite direction, but the climb up the East Ridge Trail is punishing.

The forested north-facing slope of the river canyon, on the opposite side of the south fork, hosts dirt tracks used by off-road vehicles; the whine of motorcycle engines sometimes rips through the otherwise quiet canyon. No motorized vehicles are allowed in the regional park itself.

MILES AND DIRECTIONS

0.0 Start by leaving the parking area on Cronan Ranch Road, heading uphill through the grassland.

0.1 At the junction with the West Ridge Trail, stay straight (south) on Cronan Ranch Road.

0.2 Arrive at an information board and the junction with the Down and Up Trail. Go left (east) on the Down and Up Trail, also a former ranch road.

0.6 Pass the wind sock used by paragliders launching off the hilltop to the left (north) of the trail.

0.8 At the intersection of the Down and Up Trail and the East Ridge Trail, go right (southwest) on the East Ridge Trail. Views open down toward the river valley.

1.0 Pass the junction with the Hidden Valley Cutoff, staying left (south) on the East Ridge Trail. The route is open, with only scattered shade, and saturated with views of the cushioning hills and glinting river.

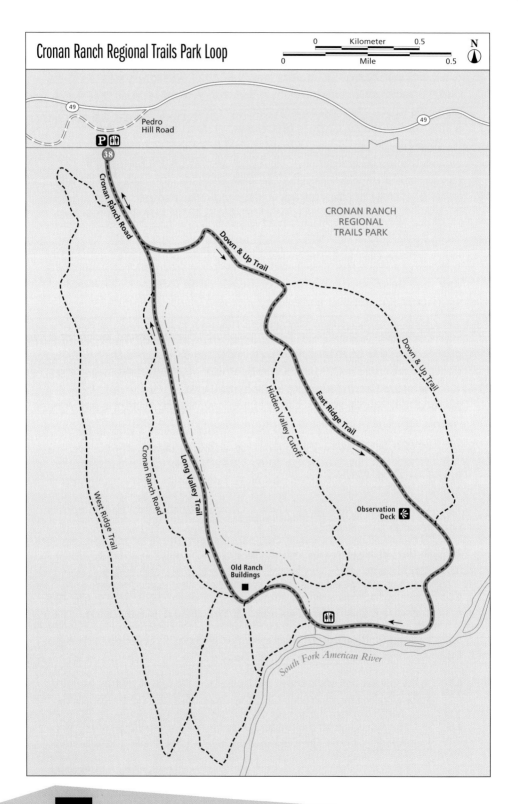

Cronan Ranch Regional Trails Park Loop

0   Kilometer   0.5

0   Mile   0.5

N

49

Pedro
Hill Road

P

49

38

Cronan Ranch Road

CRONAN RANCH
REGIONAL
TRAILS PARK

Down & Up Trail

Down & Up Trail

Hidden Valley Cutoff

East Ridge Trail

West Ridge Trail

Cronan Ranch Road

Long Valley Trail

Observation
Deck

Old Ranch
Buildings

South Fork American River

1.5 A side trail leads to a rickety observation platform. The vistas are great whether you take them in from the platform or not. The trail steepens as you continue.

1.8 Arrive at the lower junction of the Down and Up and East Ridge Trails. Go right (southwest) on the Down and Up Trail, passing through a fence line.

2.1 At the next junction, marked by a trail sign bearing only an arrow, stay left (south/downhill) into the riverside bottomlands.

2.3 Ignore side trails that lead left as you reach the river. Continue right (down-river/west) until you find the perfect spot to soak your feet, eat your lunch, and let the dog go for a swim. The riverfront is dotted with portable toilets, but no potable water is available.

2.6 Pass the first road/trail that climbs right (north/uphill) out of the river valley. The trail is unsigned. Stay straight (west) on the riverside track.

2.7 Pass a restroom with an unsigned trail leading uphill behind it, cross a seasonal stream, then take the second trail leading uphill (north). This is Cronan Ranch Road.

2.9 Climb past a signed intersection with the Down and Up Trail. Stay left (up/west) on Cronan Ranch Road.

3.1 Bear right on the ranch road through a cluster of old ranch buildings to a three-way trail intersection. An unsigned trail departs to the left (south), Cronan Ranch Road is the middle track, and the Long Valley Trail departs to the right (north). You can follow either Cronan Ranch Road or Long Valley to the trailhead: The Long Valley Trail is described, traveling up the valley floor alongside the seasonal stream.

3.7 Cross a culvert that channels an intermittent stream.

4.0 The Long Valley Trail ends on Cronan Ranch Road. Turn right (north) on Cronan Ranch Road.

4.2 Reach the end of the loop at the junction with the Down and Up Trail. From here, retrace your steps to the trailhead.

4.4 Arrive back at the trailhead and parking area.

HIKE INFORMATION

Local information: Historic Hwy 49.com is an online resource for all the gold country hamlets located along CA 49, from Cool to Coloma. Visit the website at www.historichwy49.com.

Dave Moore Nature Trail

This sweet little route meanders through oak woodlands down to a rocky beach on the South Fork American River, offering the wheelchair-bound, the stroller-bound, and the able-bodied easy access to a backcountry experience.

Start: Behind the restroom at the north end of the parking lot
Distance: 1.1-mile loop
Hiking time: 1 hour
Difficulty: Easy
Trail surface: Wheelchair-accessible decomposed granite path, dirt singletrack
Best season: Spring, summer, and fall
Other trail users: None
Trailhead amenities: Gravel parking lot, vault toilet, picnic tables. Bring drinking water.
Canine compatibility: Leashed dogs permitted

Fees and permits: None
Schedule: Open daily, 8 a.m. to sunset, year-round
Maps: USGS Coloma CA. The trail is straightforward enough that no map is needed.
Trail contact: Bureau of Land Management, Folsom Field Office, 63 Natoma St., Folsom 95630; (916) 985-4474; www.blm.gov/ca/st/en/fo/folsom/dmna.html
Other: The first 0.5 mile of the trail is wheelchair and stroller accessible. For those traveling on wheels, the trail must be taken out and back.

Finding the trailhead: From I-80 in Auburn take the CA 49 / Placerville exit and head south. Follow CA 49 for about 15.7 miles, through Auburn, down through the American River canyon, then up through the hamlets of Cool and Pilot Hill, to the nature area's entrance on the right (west). The entry is well signed and bordered by large cobblestone walls. Follow the dirt access road west for 0.1 mile to the parking area.

Alternatively, you can take US 50 east out of Sacramento to the junction with CA 49 in Placerville. Turn left (north) on CA 49 and follow it for about 10 miles, through Marshall Gold Discovery State Historic Park, to the trailhead access road on the left (west). GPS: N38 48.923'/W120 55.246'

THE HIKE

ollowing the sweeping curves of the Dave Moore Nature Trail is reminiscent of walking a labyrinth. The first half-mile curls thoughtfully through oak woodlands, offering travelers ample chance to contemplate what draws them outdoors—how the sun filters through a forest canopy, the unique shapes of rocks and boulders, how fleeting glimpses of a nearby river quickens the senses.

Surfaced in decomposed granite, the wheelchair-accessible portion of the route spans seasonal streams via sturdy bridges and handles grades via gentle switchbacks that sweep past, among other things, a huge old madrone ring, a boulder that pops from the forest floor like a button mushroom, and the handi-work of Chinese laborers who, during the gold rush, carved ditches and built rock walls to aid miners in their quest to recover precious nuggets.

The trail is dedicated to the memory of a Bureau of Land Management (BLM) conservation ranger who was stricken with multiple sclerosis at a young age. David Moore was an avid outdoorsman, and his disability heightened awareness among his BLM colleagues of the challenges faced by the wheelchair-bound on trails. This trail route was designed with his needs—and the needs of other physically impaired individuals—foremost.

A mushroom-shaped boulder lies just off the handicapped-accessible portion of the Dave Moore Nature Trail.

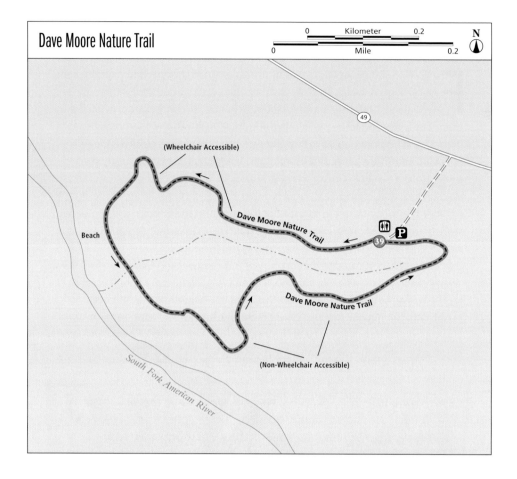

The wheelchair-accessible stretch ends on a rocky little riverside beach. The South Fork American River is shallow here in summer and fall, skipping over a pebbly bed. Willows and oaks shade the spot, which is perfect for picnicking and wading. The river is higher in spring, when snowmelt descends from the high country, and may push recreationalists back into the woodland for their rest and snack.

The second half of the loop is decidedly not wheelchair accessible. Wildflowers, willows, and reeds encroach on the path, which narrows and becomes rocky as it skirts trees and rock outcrops parallel to the river. Signs designate this stretch a habitat restoration area.

The path bends back through the woodlands toward the trailhead. You'll find seclusion on this segment, as many visitors return down the gravel path. But the woodlands are serene, and worth the walk-through, especially a parklike grove of oaks that line the trail like an avenue. A final bridge crossing, and you arrive back at the trailhead.

MILES AND DIRECTIONS

0.0 Start at the trailhead on the north side of the parking area, just behind the restroom.

0.1 At the trail fork stay left on the rock-lined path toward a picnic table, then switchback down to where the paths merge and cross the bridge.

0.2 Cross another bridge amid blackberry brambles, then pass the button mushroom rock and a picnic table on the left. The path narrows through a gully where the trail is softened by pine needles. A broad switchback leads down to and across another bridge, and rambles alongside a rock wall built by Chinese workers who created channels and earthworks to aid gold miners.

0.4 Switchback around two bridges, then arrive on the rocky little beach on the South Fork American River. The wheelchair-accessible portion of the trail ends here. Picnic and play, then return to the trail and, if you are able, go right (southeast) on the dirt path. Otherwise, return as you came.

0.5 Continuing on the non-wheelchair-accessible portion of the trail, cross a bridge spanning a seasonal stream.

0.7 Swing left (north), away from the river, into a cut in the bank. A split-log bridge spans a seasonal stream. Stay on the maintained trail along the streambed, avoiding social paths that are blocked by water bars.

0.9 Climb into a parklike grove of oaks, then circle northeast toward the parking lot, passing a restoration sign.

1.1 Cross a bridge over a seasonal stream, pass a trail that leads right (east) to a picnic spot, and arrive back at the trailhead parking area.

HIKE INFORMATION

Local information: Historic Hwy 49.com is an online resource for all the gold country hamlets located along CA 49, from Cool to Coloma. Visit the website at www.historichwy49.com.

Rafting is popular on all three forks of the American River. A number of rafting outfits, which can be recommended by local management agencies including the Bureau of Land Management and the Auburn State Recreation Area, offer guide services on the river.

Monroe Ridge / Marshall Monument Trail Loop

Climb through oak woodlands to viewpoints above the snaking American River, then tour a historic gold rush town, including the site where the precious metal was first discovered in 1848.

Start: North Beach parking area of Marshall Gold Discovery State Historic Park

Distance: 3.8-mile loop

Hiking time: 2 to 3 hours

Difficulty: More challenging due to trail length and generous changes in elevation

Trail surface: Dirt singletrack, some paved roadways and rustic sidewalks, gravel paths

Best season: Year-round, though winter storms and cold may render the trail inhospitable

Other trail users: None

Trailhead amenities: Parking, restrooms, water, and picnic facilities at the North Beach trailhead. There is no water along the trail, but a drinking fountain is located at the Marshall Monument site.

Canine compatibility: Leashed dogs permitted

Fees and permits: Day-use fee, payable at visitor center

Schedule: Park open daily, 8 a.m. to sunset, year-round

Maps: USGS Coloma CA; state historic park map available at the visitor center / museum and online at www.parks.ca.gov

Trail contact: California State Parks, PO Box 942896, Sacramento 94296; (800) 777-0369; www.parks .ca.gov. The park address is PO Box 265, Coloma 95613; (530) 622-3470.

Finding the trailhead: From downtown Sacramento head east on US 50 to Placerville and the junction with CA 49. Turn left (north) on CA 49 and follow the scenic road for 9 miles, through the town of Coloma and past the Marshall SHP visitor center, to the North Beach picnic and parking area on the right (east). Park in the southernmost part of the parking lot; the trailhead is across CA 49, at a break in the split-rail fence near the old mining cabin. GPS: N38 48.245′/W120 53.698′

THE HIKE

You can still pan for gold along the South Fork American River in Marshall Gold Discovery State Historic Park, but arguably that's not the most valuable thing that can be gleaned from these hills in modern times. The canyon walls hovering over historic Sutter's Mill offer spectacular views up and down the river valley, and the state park that commemorates the discovery of gold is a treasure chest of historic sites and information.

The story is familiar to most Californians, but here's a recap: In 1848 James Marshall, who ran a Coloma lumber mill in partnership with John Sutter, was checking the mill's tailrace and discovered gold flakes in the detritus that had backed up there. One of the largest gold rushes in history followed, with thousands of fortune seekers racing to the Sierra Nevada from all over the world. The rush itself was short-lived, but in its aftermath California, acquired from Mexico in the same year Marshall made his discovery, became America's "Golden State." That legacy, of bold action, invention, and the search for quick riches, still informs the psyche of the state today.

Re-creations of historic structures such as Sutter's Mill, as well as a museum and the chance to pan for gold yourself, are among the highlights of an exploration of the Monroe Ridge / Marshall Monument Trail Loop.

The town of Coloma and the state historic park are pretty much one and the same. Some old miners' cabins, including that of James Marshall, are preserved intact; other historic homes have been transformed into bed-and-breakfasts and private residences. Storefronts that date back to the gold rush now house historic exhibits, restaurants, and gift shops. Along the Gold Discovery Loop Trail, which meanders down by the river, a reproduction of Sutter's Mill overlooks picnic grounds, and a striking river rock monument marks the original mill site. A bronze statue of James Marshall himself stands on a pedestal on the southwest side of the canyon, overlooking the entire scene.

This route, while saturated in history, also rises above it. It begins and ends at the Monroe homesite: The matriarch of the Monroe family was a former slave who purchased her son's freedom with money earned working for miners. The family remained in Coloma for more than a century before selling their property to the state.

The trail climbs the steep canyon wall via a number of switchbacks, winding through stands of red-barked mountain manzanita, oaks, and, in its upper reaches, ponderosa pines. Road noise from CA 49 filters up through the trees, but fades as you gain altitude and distance.

The route tops out on a forested ridge, where a picnic table overlooking the river valley offers a comfortable place to rest. Pass remnants of mining operations as you continue across the ridge. Beyond a second picnic table and overlook, the trail begins its descent, dropping around more switchbacks through the mixed woodland toward the town below. Pass a cistern then meet up with a paved park road, which leads down to the Marshall Monument, where you can enjoy the same views

The Gold Discovery Museum

Located in the heart of Coloma, every hike in the state historic park must begin at the Gold Discovery Museum and Visitor Center. It's not just a matter of paying the day-use fee; it's also about the exhibits inside, which offer insights into the discovery that turned a sleepy Mexican frontier into the Golden State.

The museum houses dioramas depicting the lifestyles of native tribes that hunted and gathered in the area before the arrival of the forty-niners, as well as the area's natural history. But it's the artifacts of the gold rush that mesmerize: reproductions of gold nuggets; collections of old bottles, assay instruments, household items . . . even an old stagecoach.

The museum is open Tues through Sun from 10 a.m. to 4 p.m. Apr through Oct, and from 10 a.m. to 3 p.m. Nov through Mar. It is closed Mon and Thanksgiving, Christmas Day, and New Year's Day. The address is 310 Back St., Coloma 95613; the phone number is (530) 622-3470.

that the bronzed man will enjoy for eternity. Take in the views, read the interpretive signs, drink the sweet water from the fountain, then continue down into town.

The path back to the Monroe homesite meanders along peaceful roads lined with historic buildings, including Marshall's cabin, a tiny Catholic church, and the old jailhouse. An interpretive trail winds through an exhibit of mining equipment outside the park's museum.

Cross the highway, and head toward the banks of the American River. Here the Gold Discovery Loop Trail leads past the original mill and discovery site. The discovery site is simple and provocative: a pond of still water where even the most skeptical visitor can't help but hope she'll spot a precious nugget . . .

Back at North Beach you can rest on the riverbank and mull the possibilities: A pan, a red flannel union suit under your dungarees, a little elbow grease, and you too could be a placer miner.

MILES AND DIRECTIONS

0.0 Start on the Monroe Ridge Trail, climbing past a mining cabin and through the remnants of the Monroe family orchards.

0.1 Stay right (up/southwest) on the singletrack Monroe Ridge Trail, avoiding the fire road on the left.

0.2 Switchbacks lead to a staircase and bridge across a flume that was used for mining and irrigation.

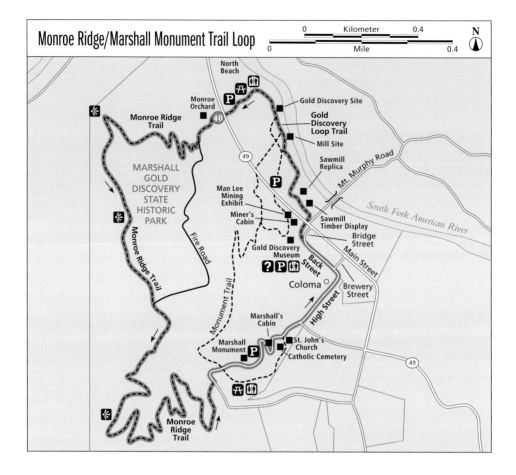

Monroe Ridge/Marshall Monument Trail Loop

0.6 Pass a twisted manzanita that reaches north to valley views at a switchback. Keep up!

0.8 A long ascending traverse attains the ridgetop, then follows its spine south to a picnic table in a stand of oaks. Spectacular views drop hundreds of feet to the river and Coloma.

1.1 Pass a side trail to a fenced-off pit on the left (south). Stay right (southwest) on the Monroe Ridge Trail.

1.2 Reach a saddle with low-slung power lines overhead.

1.5 Arrive at a second picnic bench and overlook. Enjoy a rest, then continue on the now-descending Monroe Ridge Trail. Switchbacks drop across sunny south-facing slopes that bloom with wildflowers in season; pass a trail sign and a short path to a vista point.

2.1 More than a half-dozen switchbacks lead down to a trail marker at a clearing in the woodland. A covered cistern sits uphill to the right (south). Stay left (east), heading toward the Marshall Monument.

2.2 The path meets the paved park road at a picnic area. Walk left (uphill) on the road toward a park residence, then go right (east) on the signed Marshall Monument path (also paved). Stairs lead up to the monument site, where Marshall's bronzed likeness stands atop a marble and granite pedestal. Descend the steps to the paved roadway and go left (east), heading down into the historic district.

2.8 Reach Marshall's Cabin and St. John's Catholic Church and cemetery. Continue northeast on High Street.

3.0 At the corner of Back and Brewery Streets, turn left (north), passing the ruins of the El Dorado County Jail.

3.1 Back Street leads to Bridge Street and the visitor center/museum. Follow the interpretive trail through the mining equipment exhibit. Cross CA 49 and turn left (north), passing the Gold Trail Grange building, to the Gold Discovery Loop Trail.

3.3 Visit the Sutter's Mill replica, then follow the crushed granite riverside path left (north).

3.5 Pass the original site of Sutter's Mill and the gold discovery site in quick succession.

3.8 Arrive back at the North Beach trailhead and parking lot.

HIKE INFORMATION

Local information: Coloma-Lotus Chamber of Commerce; (530) 295-3488; www.colomalotus.com. The chamber offers information on local businesses and events.
Organizations: The Gold Discovery Park Association is a nonprofit group that works to promote and support educational and historical programs at the state historic park, including gold-panning demonstrations. The association also runs annual events at the park, such as Christmas in Coloma. For more information call (530) 622-6198 or visit the website at http://marshallgold.org.

Jenkinson Lake Loop

Circumambulating Jenkinson Lake, in the Sierra foothills east of Placerville, you'll meander through a restored meadowland at the mouth of Hazel Creek, visit a waterfall near the outlet of Park Creek, and enjoy long roller-coaster stretches of easy woodland walking with great lake views.

Start: At the Stonebraker boat launch parking area
Distance: 8.9-mile loop
Hiking time: 5 to 6 hours
Difficulty: Challenging due to trail length
Trail surface: Dirt singletrack, with short sections of paved roadway, dirt roadway, and boardwalk
Best season: Early summer for wildflowers; late fall and winter for serenity
Other trail users: Mountain bikers, equestrians on some sections
Trailhead amenities: Large paved parking area, restrooms, picnic sites, trash cans, boat launch
Canine compatibility: Leashed dogs permitted
Fees and permits: Day-use fee
Schedule: The Sly Park Recreation Area is open daily, sunrise to sunset, year-round. If you are camping at the lake and enjoy hiking in the dark, the trail is accessible 24 hours a day.
Maps: USGS Sly Park CA; available at the park entrance station
Trail contact: Sly Park Recreation Area / Jenkinson Lake, 4771 Sly Park Rd., Pollock Pines 95726; (530) 644-2545; http://168.143.6.148/recreation/recreation.htm
Other: Jenkinson Lake offers a variety of recreational opportunities, including camping, boating, and fishing. Visit the website at www.webreserv.com/eldorado irrigationdistrictca for details.

Finding the trailhead: From Sacramento head east on US 50 for about 50 miles, traveling through Placerville, to Pollock Pines. Take the Sly Park Road exit and go right (south) on Sly Park Road. Drive 4.2 miles to the Sly Park Recreation Area entrance on the left. GPS: N38 43.857'/W121 32.589'

THE HIKE

n a very nice way, Jenkinson Lake is two-faced. The north shore, you might say, is the prom queen, all gussied up with campgrounds and boat launches and picnic areas—a little flashy, a little loud, outfitted for a party, and a load of fun. The south shore is the lake's tomboy side: rugged and challenging, dressed down but very pretty, and just as much fun. That's the one thing the two shorelines have in common—they both will show you a good time.

You can pick up the trail almost anywhere along the north shore. The challenge, on busy summer days, will be finding a place to park and get on the trail. Regardless of where you start, or which direction you travel (the route is described here in a clockwise direction), you'll hike a good distance on well-maintained footpaths, with a few sections of gravel road, some campground road, and a sliver of boardwalk in the mix.

Beginning at the Stonebraker boat launch and picnic area, toward the northeast corner of the reservoir, descend a flight of steps to the Sierra-Chimney Trail, which is unsigned but obvious. Head left (east) on the singletrack, enjoying great lake views. Here, and for most of the loop, you'll pass plenty of places where you can drop off the trail to the lakeshore for a rest, a snack, or a swim.

A pair of stone chimneys, one little more than a heap of rock, stand sentinel at the Chimney Camp on the shores of Jenkinson Lake.

The Sierra-Chimney Trail segment of the loop empties onto the paved lake service road at the Chimney campground. Aptly named, there are two stone chimneys on the beach, one still upright, the other little more than a heap of broken rock.

Follow the paved road east to Hazel Meadow, where you'll drop onto a boardwalk lined with interpretive signs describing the flora and fauna of the restored wetland surrounding one of Jenkinson Lake's inlet streams. The viewing platform affords great views down the length of the lake to one of its distant dams. Interpretive signs describe the importance of water conservation, the different species of bats in the park, and the annual ladybug migration in spring, when the bright red, lucky bugs swarm on the trunks of the evergreens that line the meadow.

Hazel Creek camp is behind the meadow, with picnic areas and restrooms. For a shorter hike of about 2.2 miles, you can turn around here and retrace your steps to the trailhead.

The loop resumes on the signed South Shore Trail, at the bridge over Hazel Creek. On this side of the lake the path will fork repeatedly, with horses directed onto one path and hikers and bikers onto another (and sometimes bikers onto a separate trail of their own). Follow the signs, and don't worry if you make a "wrong turn"; the trails always merge again.

At about the 2-mile mark, the path leads into the Park Creek drainage. Take a detour before you cross the bridge over Park Creek to visit the waterfall. There is no sign here but the side trail is obvious, leading straight back along the creek (around a fallen log) for less than 0.1 mile to the falls. The whitewater spill of about 25 feet lands in a clear pool, where you can wet your feet (or more), depending on the season. The pool is surrounded by a smooth rock outcrop, which is perfect for sunning and picnicking. Again, this is a great turnaround point if you don't want to make the full loop (about 4 miles out and back).

From Park Creek the trail begins a roller-coaster ramble through mixed evergreen forest, with occasional side trails leading down to the lakeshore. It's an easy walk despite the ups and downs, with good lake views through the trees. Circle into another drainage, passing some excellent lakefront picnic beaches. Different use trails merge and diverge, but signs keep you on track, mostly to the right, near the water. You'll pass through another drainage about 1 mile on, where side trails again will merge, and again you'll stay lakeside.

The resident bats in Sly Park are capable of consuming 1,000 insects each per night. Bad news for pesky mosquitoes, but visitors should still be sure to bring along insect repellent.

As you near the first dam, the trail widens. A brief ascent, then descent, drops you to the paved Mormon Emigrant Trail (not a trail, but a two-lane roadway). Go right, across the dam, to the signed trail on the far side.

And welcome back to civilization. The well-signed trail parallels the road for a stretch, then crosses it again and switchbacks down to the spillway below the second dam. Follow the steep horse trail up to the roadway and cross again to regain the lakeside path, which is now back on the north side of the lake. Be sure to take advantage of the views from the boat launch parking area: Looking east across Jenkinson Lake, the Sierra crest, snowbound much of the year, is visible. Beyond the boat launch the wide path passes through a stately evergreen forest, with the trees lined up in columns on either side.

The last few miles of the loop pass through the developed areas of the Sly Park Recreation Area, with campgrounds and picnic areas bordering the route. Occasionally the trail follows a stretch of paved campground road; sometimes it grows rugged again, circling through drainages and crossing bridges and boardwalks that span seasonal inlet streams. The final leg, back on the signed Sierra-Chimney Trail, echoes the wild feel of the south shore, passing close to the water at the lake's narrow point, before cruising back into the Stonebraker boat launch area. Climb the stairs back to the trailhead and parking area.

MILES AND DIRECTIONS

0.0 Start by dropping from the Stonebraker parking area via a staircase to the unsigned Sierra-Chimney Trail. Go left on the dirt footpath.

0.25 Cross a little bridge in a wooded drainage.

0.6 Arrive at the paved road at the Chimney campground. Go right on the road, following Trail signs painted on the pavement.

1.1 Reach Hazel Meadow and the Hazel Creek campground. Cross the boardwalk and the bridge over Hazel Creek, now on the signed South Shore Trail.

1.3 The trail splits. Stay right on the signed hiking trail (cyclists and equestrians are directed onto the left path). Social trails break right to the lakeshore; if you stay to the left, you'll stay on the loop trail.

1.75 The horse/bike and hiking trail merge. Stay right on the path.

2.0 Arrive at the bridge over Park Creek. Go straight on the path around the fallen log to reach the waterfall, then return to the bridge and go left, continuing the loop.

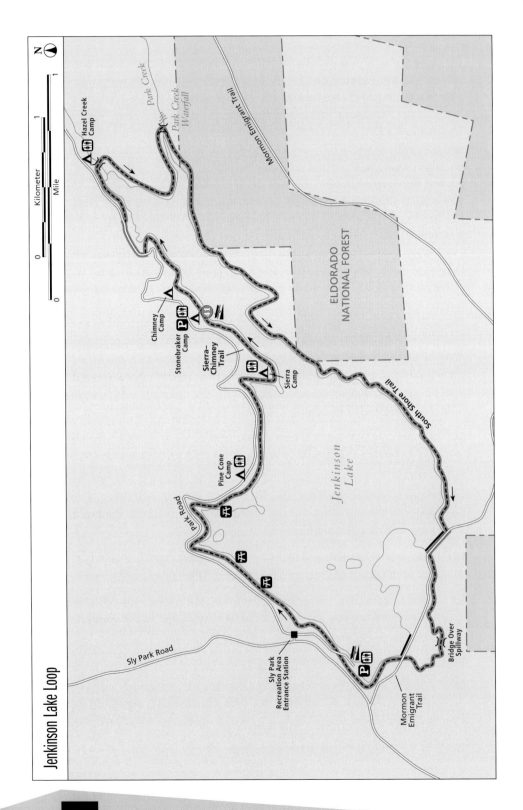

Jenkinson Lake Loop

Park Creek

Park Creek Waterfall

Hazel Creek Camp

Chimney Camp

Stonebraker Camp

Sierra–Chimney Trail

Sierra Camp

ELDORADO NATIONAL FOREST

Pine Cone Camp

Park Road

Jenkinson Lake

South Shore Trail

Sly Park Road

Sly Park Recreation Area Entrance Station

Mormon Emigrant Trail

Bridge Over Spillway

Mormon Emigrant Trail

N

Kilometer

Mile

2.3 The horse trail splits to the left, followed by a second split with mountain bikers directed left. The hiking trail stays right, then climbs a flight of stone steps to rejoin the bike trail.

3.0 Different use trails merge as the main path curves through another creek drainage. Stay right along the lakeshore, following the signs.

4.0 Reach another stream drainage, where use trails merge again. Go right on the signed hike/bike trail.

4.6 The horse trail meets the hike/bike trail. Stay right on the main path, which widens to roadway width.

4.75 Drop to the paved Mormon Emigrant Trail roadway and the first dam. Turn right, cross the dam, and pick up the trail signed Mtn. Bike / Hike Trail on the other side.

5.0 At the paved park road, head left for about 25 yards to pick up the signed hiking/biking trail. Do not continue on the gated road. At the second park road crossing, go straight on the trail.

5.2 The trail empties onto the two-lane Mormon Emigrant Trail roadway again, just above the main dam. Cross the road to the trail signed Mt. Bike / Hiking Trail to Bridge and descend switchbacks.

5.4 Cross the bridge over the dam spillway. Continue straight on the signed horse trail for about 100 yards to a trail Y. Go right and steeply uphill on the rugged horse trail.

5.6 Arrive at a junction with the Mormon Emigrant Trail again. Drop onto the road, cross it, and pick up the dirt anglers' trail on the other side, heading left. The lakeshore is on your right.

5.8 The anglers' trail merges into the formal hiking/biking trail at a stone staircase and trail sign, which are on the left. Continue straight on the trail.

6.0 Arrive at the boat launch parking area. Admire the views of the Sierra crest across the lake. Cross the lot to pick up the signed trail near the restroom. The path is bounded by a stone retaining wall on the left and the lake on the right.

6.8 Enter a picnic area that stretches for about 0.2 mile along the lakeshore. The tables (and trail) have wonderful views and access to the water.

7.0 Go right on the obvious path; the left track leads up to the park road.

7.3 The trail narrows to singletrack as it approaches the park road; the Miwok Nature Trail is across the road. Go left, across the bridge.

7.5 Enter Pine Cone camp. Go right on the paved camp road / bike trail, along the lakeshore.

8.0 The camp road ends on the park road. A sign for the Sierra camp marks the resumption of the dirt singletrack on the right. Pick this up and continue the loop.

8.2 A fence line marks the boundary with the Sierra camp. Climb up along the fence to the camp road and go right on the paved campground road.

8.4 Pick up the signed Sierra-Chimney Trail on the right. Follow the dirt track toward the Chimney camp (1 mile ahead).

8.9 Arrive back at the Stonebraker trailhead.

HIKE INFORMATION

Local information: Placerville City Hall, 3101 Center St., Placerville 95667; (530) 621-CITY (2489); http://ci.placerville.ca.us. The city website includes information about recreational and cultural opportunities in the region, as well as local restaurants and businesses.

Camping: Campgrounds line the north shore of the lake, including Pine Cone, Sierra, Jenkinson, Stonebraker, Chimney, and Hazel Creek. To make reservations call the Sly Park Recreation Area reservations line at (530) 644-2792.

> 🍃 **Green Tip:**
> *Jenkinson Lake is a water supply. Please don't let your pet swim, and young children should wear swim diapers if they go in the water.*

Honorable Mention

The canyons of the three forks of the American River are chock-full of hiking opportunities. Many of the trails lie within the Auburn State Recreation Area (SRA). Some other trails to consider include the Foresthill Divide Loop Trail, the Stevens Trail, and the Windy Point Trail. To learn more about hiking in the Auburn SRA, visit the park's website at www.parks.ca.gov or call the park office at (530) 885-4527. To learn more about specific hikes in the canyons of the Auburn SRA, visit the Auburn State Recreation Area Canyon Keepers website at http://members.psyber.com/asra. The site includes links to individual hiking pages produced by the state parks department, which have route descriptions and directions to the various trailheads.

Be Prepared

Hiking in the Sacramento Valley and surrounding mountainous areas is generally safe. Still, hikers should be prepared, whether they are out for a short stroll along the Sacramento River waterfront or venturing into the secluded American River canyon. Some specific advice:

Know the basics of first aid, including how to treat bleeding, bites and stings, and fractures, strains, or sprains. Pack a first-aid kit on each excursion.

Familiarize yourself with the symptoms of heat exhaustion and heat stroke. Heat exhaustion symptoms include heavy sweating, muscle cramps, headache, dizziness, and fainting. Should you or any of your hiking party exhibit any of these symptoms, cool the victim down immediately by rehydrating and getting him or her to an air-conditioned location. Cold showers also help reduce body temperature. Heat stroke is much more serious: The victim may lose consciousness, and the skin is hot and dry to the touch. In this event, call 911 immediately.

Regardless of the weather, your body needs a lot of water while hiking. Consuming a full 32-ounce bottle is advisable for hikes less than 5 miles long. Add more for longer distances. Bring water with you, regardless of whether water is available at the trailhead or along the route.

Don't drink from streams, rivers, creeks, or lakes without treating or filtering the water first. Water from these sources may host a variety of contaminants, including giardia, which can cause serious intestinal unrest.

Carry a backpack in which you can store extra clothing, ample drinking water and food, and whatever goodies, like guidebooks, cameras, and binoculars, you might want.

Many area trails have cell phone coverage. Bring your device, but make sure you've turned it off or got it on the vibrate setting while hiking.

Keep children under careful watch. The bigger rivers have dangerous currents, and are not safe for swimming. Hazards along some of the trails include poison oak, uneven footing, and steep drop-offs. Make sure children don't stray from the designated route. Children (really, all hikers) should carry a plastic whistle: If they become lost, they should stay in one place and blow the whistle to summon help.

Hike with a partner. There is safety in numbers, even if that number is only two.

Organizations, Hiking Clubs, and Other Associations

LAND MANAGEMENT ORGANIZATIONS

The following government and private organizations manage public lands described in this guide, and can provide further information on these hikes and other trails in their service areas.

California State Parks, Department of Parks and Recreation, 416 9th St., Sacramento 95814; PO Box 942896, Sacramento 94296; (800) 777-0369 or (916) 653-6995; www.parks.ca.gov; info@parks.ca.gov. A complete listing of state parks is available on the website, along with park brochures and maps.

Sacramento County Regional Parks Department, 3711 Branch Center Rd., Sacramento 95827; (916) 875-6961; www.msa2.saccounty.net/parks; parksinfo@ saccounty.net. The park office is open from 8 a.m. to 5 p.m. daily.

Bureau of Land Management, Folsom Field Office, 63 Natoma St., Folsom 95630; (916) 985-4474; www.blm.gov; www.ca.blm.gov/folsom.

Cosumnes River Preserve, 13501 Franklin Blvd., Galt 95632; (916) 684-2816; www.cosumnes.org. This organization provides information about both the Cosumnes River Preserve and the Howard Ranch Trail outside Galt.

Sacramento Audubon Society, PO Box 160694, Sacramento 95816; www .sacramentoaudubon.org.

Sacramento Valley Conservancy, PO Box 163351, Sacramento 95816; www .sacramentovalleyconservancy.org.

HIKING CLUBS AND TRAIL GROUPS

Auburn State Recreation Area Canyon Keepers; http://members.psyber.com/ asra. A clearinghouse for all things recreational in the Auburn State Recreation Area, this group publishes a wonderful guide to hiking trails in the north and middle forks of the American River, and leads guided hikes in area.

Sacramento Hiking Meetup Group; www.meetup.com/sachikinggroup. The group has more than 3,000 members and organizes hikes throughout the region, from the coastal region to the Sierra Nevada.

Sacramento Hikers with Kids; www.meetup.com/Sac-Hikers-With-Kids. Join other families on kid-friendly trails that typically involve a lake or picnic site.

REGIONAL TRAILS

Regional trails in the area include the Jedediah Smith National Recreation Trail and the Western States Pioneer Express Trail. Portions of these regional trails are described in this guide. More information on the Jedediah Smith National Recreation Trail can be found at www.msa2.saccounty.net/parks. For the Western States trail, visit the Western States Trail Foundation at www.teviscup.org.

Further Reading

Alden, Peter, and Fred Heath. *National Audubon Society Field Guide to California*. New York: Alfred A. Knopf, Inc. (Chanticleer Press), 1998.

Avella, Steven M. *Sacramento: Indomitable City*. Charleston, SC: Arcadia Publishing, 2003.

Evans, Steven L. *Top Trails Sacramento: Exploring Valley, Foothills, and Mountains in the Sacramento Region*. Berkeley, CA: Wilderness Press, 2008.

Ferris, Jim, Michael Lynch, and Sheila Toner. *American River Canyon Hikes: Practical Guides to Trails in the Canyons of the North and Middle Forks American River*. Audubon State Recreation Area Canyon Keepers, 2005.

Summers, Jordan. *60 Hikes Within 60 Miles: Sacramento*. Birmingham, AL: Menasha Ridge Press, 2008.

Index

About the Author

Tracy Salcedo-Chourré has written guidebooks to a number of destinations in California and Colorado, including *Hiking Lassen Volcanic National Park, Exploring California's Missions and Presidios, Exploring Point Reyes National Seashore and the Golden Gate National Recreation Area, Best Rail-Trails California,* and Best Easy Day Hikes guides to San Francisco's Peninsula, San Francisco's North Bay, San Francisco's East Bay, San Jose, Lake Tahoe, Reno, Sacramento, Fresno, Boulder, Denver, and Aspen.

She is also an editor, teacher, and gardener. She lives with her family and a small menagerie of pets in California's Wine Country. You can learn more by visiting her website at www.laughingwaterink.com.

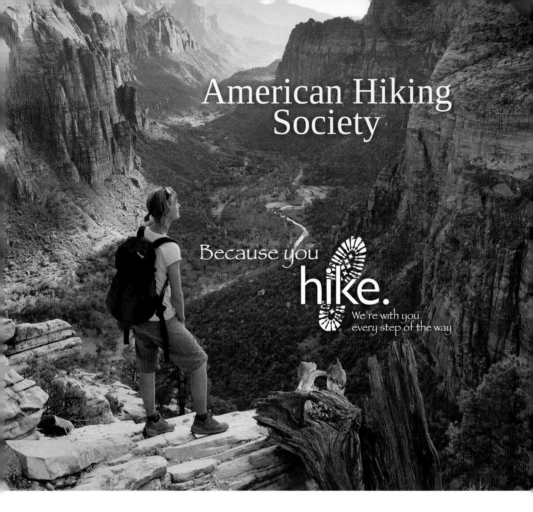

American Hiking Society

Because you hike.

We're with you every step of the way

As a national voice for hikers, **American Hiking Society** works every day:

- Building and maintaining hiking trails
- Educating and supporting hikers by providing information and resources
- Supporting hiking and trail organizations nationwide
- Speaking for hikers in the halls of Congress and with federal land managers

Whether you're a casual hiker or a seasoned backpacker, become a member of American Hiking Society and join the national hiking community! You'll enjoy great member benefits and help preserve the nation's hiking trails, so tomorrow's hike is even better than today's. We invite you to join us now!

American Hiking Society